STATE COLLEGE 101

STATE COLLEGE 101

A Freshman Writing Class

Alan Feldman

Library of Congress Number:		2001116890
ISBN #:	Hardcover	1-4010-0000-2
	Softcover	1-4010-0001-0

This book was printed in the United States of America.

To order additional copies of this book, contact:

Xlibris Corporation

1-888-795-4274

www.Xlibris.com

Orders@Xlibris.com

For Paul LeBlanc, Desmond McCarthy, and Edward Nobles—
among many who made me glad to teach

CONTENTS

INTRODUCTION

Phillip Lopate

THIS INVALUABLE BOOK, among the truest and most subtly observed studies of the educational process to have appeared in years, dares to look steadily at one of the most crucial, prevalent yet unsung activities: a freshman writing class. Millions of young Americans undergo such classes every year; tens of millions of hours are spent, by them and their teachers, trying to shape a requirement into a learning adventure, or at least something finer than mere duty. Freshman comp courses represent an important crossroads in the future maturation of these students, and it could be equally said of their challenge what Tolstoy said of grade school, that when he entered a classroom of laughing, chattering children, he saw a room full of drowning men.

The students at Framingham State are, as the author notes, "the ignored middle": neither the Ivy Leaguers and rough-diamond math geniuses of *Good Will Hunting,* nor the dramatically (and therefore more media-worthy) under-privileged strivers from minority ghettoes, these are your white working-class suburban kids, who continue to hold down jobs of thirty or more hours while in college, and who graduate, on average, at twenty-four instead of twenty-one. Their modest goals are to get a job, rather than presume to be the future leaders of America. Their efforts to secure a good college education are complicated often by focus problems (exhaustion), family problems (divorce, alcoholism), car problems (lemons and gas guzzlers), love problems (loutish boyfriends), roommate problems (one student gets turned in by hers for breaking a dormitory regulation), and alienation from hostile or mediocre instructors. Then again, there are the teachers who give their all.

The heroine of this educational romance is Professor Elaine Beilin, who has taken it upon herself to stretch each of her enrolled students' thinking and writing abilities, both by taking them seriously enough to expect that they can do better, and by creating a learning environment open enough to encourage them to reach that goal.

As one who has done similar kinds of teaching, I read this account in a state of continuous suspense: How will Beilin handle the latest student question or lack of effort? Will she rise to the occasion? By and large, she does, with remarkable eloquence, persistence, love. She is uniquely resourceful and communicative, but she is also Everyteacher, trying to respond humanly, as we all do, and failing at times. There are the students who don't get reached.

And there behind Professor Beilin is our author, Alan Feldman, observing all like a fly on the wall—a rather large fly, I might add, though he never pretends that his presence has no effect, that he can evade Heisenberg's Law. He is typing away on his laptop for all to see. Feldman began as a poet and still is a poet, as can be appreciated in many passages in the text. Poets are known to have very large egos. But what is even more impressive than his lyrical economy and fine ear and psychological sensitivity is his selflessness, a sympathetic quality he shares with Beilin. Nothing could be more alien to our present culture or more unfashionable than this selflessness: it helps to account for the strange, disquieting dignity underlying the text.

In the end, Beilin asks, having read Feldman's powerful account of the students in her freshman writing course, "But I wonder if anyone else will be as interested in them as we are." You want to say, Of course readers will be, everywhere! They must! But her doubts are realistic. Indeed, it is hard to imagine any topic of daily reality that has less "buzz" about it, that would be harder to pitch to a jaded magazine editor, than freshman comp in a suburban second-tier college. The very fact that so beautifully-executed a study had to be printed outside the protective confines of commercial publishing suggests that the powers that be really don't care about these kids. What ought our response to be to such a stunning indifference? Anger, perhaps? Disgust, maybe? Outrage? All appropriate reactions, in their separate ways; yet after we have shuddered through these emotions, let us put them aside and go back to Alan Feldman's own tone of stoical wisdom and open curiosity. The high road is to read, re-read and ponder this book.

PREFACE

I WALKED UP to a group of students in the library. "What's it like here?"

"What are you?" they wanted to know.

My dress in those days left my status ambiguous: a rumpled corduroy jacket with a turtleneck. I had a beard, but it was dark blond then. I was twenty-seven.

"I'm thinking of teaching here," I told them. They were seated in low, block-shaped purple upholstered chairs in a lounge area of the sunny Bauhaus-style building. Through the floor-to-ceiling windows, to the east beyond the pale green spring trees, I could see the top of the Prudential Center in Boston on the horizon.

I could see them trying to assess me. I wasn't much older than they (though at the time I felt I was), but I had the impression that they were not comfortable speaking to professors.

I didn't have the luxury of considering whether I'd be comfortable with them. It was 1972 and the job market for new Ph.D.'s had narrowed to a trickle. Coming from Columbia, and then a large state university, I knew nothing about a small state college such as this one. At an interview with the academic vice president (who looked to me like Melvin Laird, Nixon's Secretary of Defense), when asked why I wanted to come to Framingham, I found myself terrified that I might not answer. I couldn't very well say I wanted to come here simply because I needed a job. I looked

5517-FELD

out the window and saw the apple trees blooming and made up something about the beauty of the New England landscape.

The vice president saw, even before I started teaching at Framingham, that I'd have trouble fitting in. It turned out that the small sample of students I'd encountered in the library was representative. When I began as a new professor the following fall, I had classes where students seemed obstinately silent. Having taught in New York City public schools, where it was difficult at any time to keep students from talking, I regarded this population as a mystery. What made them so quiet? What did they care about?

When poet and activist June Jordan visited Framingham State in 1996 (she had just been speaking at Harvard), she said to the students, "You are the future leaders of America." The students countered that they did not think of themselves that way. They were at college, they explained, in the hope of becoming better employed.

An annual survey we use to compare our students to national norms reveals that most college students are unrealistically self-confident about their academic ability: fully half believe they are in the top 10% academically.[1] Framingham's 3,000 undergraduate day students are more realistic. Indeed, it's not overconfidence but lack of self-confidence that is more often the problem at Framingham.

These students tend to be from the top half, but not the top 10% of their high school classes—not the behavior problems, the truants, or those with obvious special learning difficulties, but also not typically enrollees in honors or advanced placement classes. Over 40% of this group—the ignored middle, of whom not enough has been expected—report doing less than two hours of homework per week in high school. Few seem intellectually self-motivated: over half report spending less than one hour per week reading for pleasure.

Moreover, they come from families for whom success in school and graduation from college are new goals in response to a changing economy. The General Motors plant in downtown Framingham has been converted to a wholesale car auction where high-paying manufacturing jobs have been replaced by low-paying jobs driving used cars around. Working class and lower middle class parents are urging their children to complete college, though few are able to give them enough financial help—or to coach them. For many of these families, the whole world of college learning is new. More than three-quarters of the parents of Framingham students have not graduated from college.[2]

Professors at Framingham understand that these students may be less likely than the sons and daughters of college graduates to read the college's catalog, seek out a professor for advice, understand how the college does its billing, be willing to go to the Counseling Center, or understand that there's no shame in seeking help at the Center for Academic Support. They may be less likely than other college students to live on campus, have their closest friendships on campus, or have jobs on campus, and thus their worlds may be centered elsewhere. Most troubling, many of these students average over twenty hours a week of work at paid jobs, and do not set aside enough time for studying, or for the other college activities from which students also learn—running for class office, editing the college newspaper, singing in the chorus, or playing a sport.

Still, what makes working with these students challenging and satisfying is that, against these odds, they sometimes do, quite impressively, succeed. Professors at Framingham can cite many examples: the child of a factory worker goes on to law school, the daughter of a nurse's aide becomes a published poet, or, as in the case of my former student, Paul LeBlanc, a stonemason's son becomes a college president. (Paul was made President of Marlboro College at the age of thirty-nine.)

In 1995, after I'd been chairman of the English Department for three years, our college was told to find out why our retention rate was so low. Approximately 40% of our entering students do not return for their second year. We soon learned that Framingham was about average for colleges across the country, and a host of reasons that contribute to students dropping out. The key factor seemed to be a lack of attachment to the college community, both socially and academically. I wondered whether the freshman writing course—the one course all our students have to take—could help students feel more committed to staying in college.

I decided to learn more about the students by stepping outside the role of being their professor. Instead of teaching a freshman class that semester, I would become an observer interested in how they felt about what they were studying. I would pick out a freshman writing course to observe for the entire fall semester of 1996. During that semester I would also interview the students several times—at least those who were willing to be interviewed—and conduct weekly interviews with the instructor as well. I would even attend some office hours, sitting in on conferences with individual students. Of course, I needed to find an instructor with a strong interest in examining her own teaching. She would also have to be self-confident enough to share her thoughts, both positive and glum. Most important, she would need to become inured to my constant presence in the classroom. I thought Professor Elaine Beilin, whom I had known as a friend and colleague for almost twenty years, and who had done faculty development work to help others with their teaching, might be a good candidate, and I was fortunate to be able to talk her into the project.

I'm sure that I never quite blended into the classroom like the furniture. However used to my presence the students grew, it must have made it more difficult for them to feel comfortable, though they never explicitly told me so. Transcribing everything using a laptop, I could only hope that the tap-tapping of my keyboard would begin to seem like one of the ambient noises in the room, akin to the clicking of the radiator. I was also afraid that having a colleague in the room might distract Elaine from focusing on the students. It didn't seem to, but, as with most of us who teach, there were many times when Elaine was feeling that the class could have gone better. Yet only once—during the final, fatiguing, (or, to use her term) "low compliance" part of the semester—did she reach the verge of demanding that I leave temporarily to give her and the class a break. (Somehow I managed to talk her out of it.) Perhaps it's unbearable for a professor to be observed for so long, not only in class, but even in conferences with students?

When I began to think about writing a book telling the story of one state college class, from start to finish, I was surprised to learn that nothing like this had ever been done—not for a class in any subject at any college.[3] Part of the difficulty of doing such a project may be an ingrained individualism among American professors. Few get to team teach, and even fewer would be willing to allow another professor to observe long-term. Elaine deserves credit for opening her classroom to a colleague who could be critical. She told me that the only other time in her life she felt so exposed was when she was delivering a baby, and the obstetrician called over some male residents to have a look.

Still, she and I, and, I think, many of the students felt that the project was too important to drop.

As someone who received an education as if by birthright, much of what I have done in the past twenty-five years at Framingham, I realize now, has been to pass along, to students who cannot take their education for granted, what my parents gave to me. My parents were both teachers and enjoyed teaching their children. They had inherited some money and could afford to pay our expenses at Ivy League colleges. My father taught college math. My mother, who taught Latin and English, who was herself the daughter of a teacher, prided herself on being able to teach us anything, even skating (although she couldn't skate).

In my family, love was expressed via teaching. In April, a month after my seventh birthday, my parents took me out of second grade so our family could travel in Europe for three months. My sister, who was eight, and I were constantly quizzed on what we'd seen and heard. That summer we had to complete our schoolwork by home schooling. I remember Dad telling me it would be adequate to do every *other* subtraction problem on the crowded workbook page. And he made everything clear, of course. But he also sat patiently next to me, something that didn't happen with any other activity. To teach me, he had to be close—physically close.

My mother worked with me on my writing, including my handwriting and spelling. Even when I was in high school, if I wanted to do well on a piece of writing or a speech, my mother sat with me, praised what she liked, and tactfully tried to persuade me to drop the things that weren't good or relevant.

So teaching and love have always been connected in my life—a connection my students at Framingham haven't always been fortunate enough to make. I can still hear my mother talking to me about my writing. "Pretend your topic sentence is your target," she would say. "You have to aim every sentence at your target." Though this was many years ago, and my mother has been dead for twenty years, I can remember sitting next to her going over a piece of writing. Her criticisms could be irritating, yet they brought us closer. And there are times when I'm working with my own students that I feel this closeness. In a way I don't understand, in a physics that seems to have no law of entropy, a teacher's love, like a parent's, is never used up, its current is never weakened. And even now, having written that sentence, I can hear my mother questioning whether it isn't excessive.

When I graduated from college, hailed as one of the better student writers, though not one of the academic stars, my parents were disappointed. (My father had been tenth in his class at Harvard, my mother salutatorian at Adelphi at the age of eighteen.) They ignored the fact (and so did I) that I had spent much of my undergraduate energy on writing and had won the *Saturday Review* prize for the best short story of the year in a college literary magazine. The fiction and poetry I had written on my own, outside of class, turned out to form the basis for my desire for further study.

I loved literature as a writer does—because it put me in conversation with other writers. My father told me not to bother to go on for a literature Ph.D., since there were no college jobs, but if I decided to, I should at least finish the degree quickly, he advised. I received a fellowship. He sent me money anyway. I finished in twenty-six months, the first in my family to get a doctorate. I suppose that, like my students, I was a kind of pioneer.

My students at Framingham are struggling to become educated with much less help, both financial and psychological, than I received. From my vantage point, as the son of two teachers—or Elaine's, as the mother of two girls who are growing up in an educated, culturally enriched household—many of the students at Framingham have not had the best family, schooling, or community environment to help them succeed in academic life. Their disadvantage seems small compared with that of billions of others in the world—but it's impossible to overlook if you get to know the lives of these students.

So, for me, Elaine's story is of someone who attempts, through her daily work, to decrease the world's injustice. In writing this book I wanted to look hard and long at the microcosm of one kind of work—work I know particularly well—to see if I could observe (like a person trying to see a leaf unfolding) the way a better, more just world is being made.

As I recently found myself explaining to my own students, I don't believe that world will appear soon. We were reading Antonio Skármeta's novel, *Burning Patience*, and they wanted to know why a book that could be so sexy ends by being so bitter. The covers of their books were all stamped with "The Postman," the title of the successful movie version. But the true title comes from a sentence of Rimbaud's: "At dawn, armed with burning patience, we shall enter the splendid cities." By watching Elaine and some of her students—by watching the ardent patience shown in their day-to-day labor—we get a glimpse of how we might get closer to those shining cities.

In the fall of 1996, one of Elaine's venues for fixing the world was the freshman writing classroom—an all-too-familiar site of struggle for those who teach college English. (That year 1.67 million students enrolled full-time in college for the first time, most to take a semester or a full year of freshman English.[4]) Unfortunately, the relatively new field of composition studies—which grew out of the quest to find theories and methodologies useful in such courses—still behaves like an embattled discipline. Compositionists still perceive themselves as an underclass in English departments controlled by literature scholars.[5] Particularly in four-year colleges like Framingham, professors trained in literature still teach most of the freshman writing courses. In an academic form of circling the wagons, compositionists don't welcome accounts of teaching by literature scholars in the pages of *CCC*, their field's premiere journal. Debates over whether writing comes out of the self (as "expressivists" contend) or whether it is socially constructed (as "social constructivists" believe) make little difference to most writing teachers who tend to hold both truths in mind at once—or by turns. Nothing can inoculate this book against criticism by specialists who will want to know where Elaine and I stand on issues that loom large in the narrow confines of critical debate among them but don't come into play in the mind of a typical teacher entering a first-year writing classroom.

More than any other, however, the field of composition studies can be credited with bringing pedagogical issues to the forefront in college English departments. In faculty development work with new professors in many fields, I try to convey the news—both comforting and disquieting—that other people's classrooms don't run smoothly on rails either. Many narratives of teaching are written to advocate one method or another, and, as a by-product, convey an impression that experts know at all times exactly how to conduct their classes—as though once they devise their methods all of their students will actually cooperate! I try to encourage newer college teachers to ask continually, "Is this really working?" Perhaps this questioning is particularly important in teaching first-year, first-generation students.

So many events influence how these students will learn, and whether they will successfully complete their courses. If the students could be depended on to be in class, to turn in work on time, to keep in contact with their professors—then, perhaps, the professors could afford to be complacent. But, as this narrative makes clear, this is not at all the case.

In observing Elaine's class I was struck by the relationship between students' difficulties in the course and the characteristics of their outside lives—the dorms, their jobs, or their home environment. They also told me stories of courses they were taking—courses no student should have had to take—with professors who were arbitrary and incoherent, the ones savvy upperclassmen stayed away from and who therefore still had plenty of space in their classrooms when the freshmen got their turn to register. I came to believe that for students like these a more coordinated curriculum—a cluster of courses helping to establish interdisciplinary connections and working on writing across the curriculum—would encourage better attendance and commitment. A goal of each of these courses should be to connect academic work to the world of dorm living, to the communities students come from, and, especially, to the "real world" of professional activity these students hope someday to enter. Crucial to the success of this idea, however, would be staffing freshman classes with some of the best teaching professors.

Though I think we should keep seeking better ways to teach composition, and better ways to organize our colleges, for me the key element in education will always be the individual teacher. Feeling as I do, it seems natural that I found myself writing this account like a novel (though it was based on more than a thousand pages of transcripts and notes). Just as a novel has a protagonist, so my narrative places the teacher—or, for brief stretches, a student—at the center, assuming that person's point of view based on what I was told in interviews. Like a heroine in a novel, Elaine is driven by desire—in this case, the desire to have her students succeed. Unlike the students in articles and books about method—the students who always succeed—Elaine's students sometimes don't, at least not in ways the registrar might record.

Still, in her classes, students who may never have thought of themselves as scholars are offered a model for what a scholar is, and can dream about entering an academic world that they may not have been born into. Attention must be paid when such things happen—though a mere handful of elite schools form the public's image of higher education in America.

State colleges enroll over 3.4 million students nationwide, nearly a million more than public research universities. Yet students in state colleges often feel—or are made to feel—that they didn't graduate from a real college. In Pennsylvania, as well as here in Massachusetts, public officials have attacked the credibility of these colleges. Just as in the early 1960s, when state teachers' colleges evolved into general purpose B.A. granting institutions, state colleges once again find themselves in the midst of an identity crisis. Considered lesser versions of the flagship state universities, they are thought of as "the undistinguished middle child of public higher education," according to *The Chronicle of Higher Education*[6]—not ignored, like the students, but certainly not well-understood.

Community colleges should be available for anyone who has completed high school—they are "democracy in action."[7] And the role of the research universities, both in graduate education and in educating masses of qualified undergraduates at relatively low cost, is also clear. But what about the state colleges? State colleges primarily serve their locality, offering the possibility of earning a degree near to home. Especially if state colleges are small-scale, they also offer the possibility of long-term personal contact between professors and students—a selling point for private colleges.[8] All the students I describe in this book—whether shaky or successful—have the chance to be guided by faculty for a full four years or even beyond.

Recent thinking calls upon the universities to put undergraduate students in closer contact with professors, and to get them involved in research.[9] At Framingham, notably in the sciences, students participate closely in research related to their professors' interests, sometimes gaining access to equipment they'd hardly get to glimpse at a university, where it would be reserved for graduate students and post-docs. In the humanities, students can take senior seminars with professors who taught them during their first year, professors who have published in the specialized area the seminar is studying.

However, as this book makes clear, for many students at Framingham, this ideal isn't realized. Some plan to transfer, even as freshmen. Others can't keep up with their courses. (A higher admissions standard, the same B average required by the university, was supposed to fix that problem, but hasn't.) The success rate of the more seasoned transfer students who will replace them is higher—and a more encouraging book could be written called *State College 404*. But when I teach freshmen these days I think of myself as a venture capitalist.

Recently I got into a conversation about parking with a man who works at Framingham State's counseling center. "Where do *you* park?" I asked him. (At our college, this is like talking about the weather, since the small, hilltop campus is always short of space.)

"Well, I'm assigned to the State Street lot," he grinned, "but I sneak into O'Connor."

"Oh," I said. "I've been working here so long I'm entitled to park right in front of May Hall—if I can ever find a spot."

He looked at me, surprised. "How long *have* you been here?"

"More than twenty-five years," I told him.

"I've only been here eleven years," he said, musing. "Listen, maybe you can tell me something," he said. "Why does this college get so little respect?"

That question, I thought. "Maybe it's New England provinciality," I said. "You know—the famous private schools?"

"I came here from Tufts," he said. "Everything I've observed about this place is first-rate. The students work so hard—many of them hold down two jobs. They don't expect *anyone* to do anything for them, so if you help them they really appreciate it. They say thank you! That's what keeps me here—these students. Why is it that no one seems to value what's going on here?"

"I don't know, but I'm trying to understand that, too. I've been writing a book," I offered. "About a freshman writing class here."

He nodded. He had simply fallen in love with these students, something that can happen. But he wanted the college to be appreciated too. Like many of us, he thinks of it as a place where people—most people, at least—try to do their best for students who, before college, haven't been taught well enough, helped intelligently enough, or even noticed enough.

The class I observed in the fall of 1996 was one of about twenty sections of Essentials of Writing. Though it was a section set aside for English majors—and though these students might enjoy reading and writing more than others—I knew that their test scores and levels of skill would not be much different from those of our typical students: about average for the country. What might be more unusual would be a senior professor with Elaine's research background teaching a freshman course. But at Framingham, as at most four-year colleges, such assignments do occur.

Before I begin the story of Professor Beilin and her class, I would like to thank Arthur Doyle, vice president for academic affairs, for giving me extra time (by allowing me to skip teaching a course) to observe this class and repeatedly to interview Professor Beilin and her students (whose names and towns of origin have been changed here). Tracy Kidder took time from his Fourth of July weekend to advise me about how to start the project. Betsey Houghton and Jean Scionti helped with research. Elliot Krieger, Carl Dennis, Terri Payne Butler, Judy Ferrara, and Helen Heineman read the entire manuscript at its various stages and made valuable suggestions, and Nan White, who copy-edited the near-to-final version, made some important suggestions about its substance as well. My wife, Nanette Hass Feldman, produced four beautiful cover drawings, making it hard to choose. Mostly, I want to thank the students in the class, and Elaine herself, for being willing to share so much of the private exchange that real teaching and learning can be. That I wasn't a total "outsider" could only have made having me constantly there more difficult for them. To repay them, I want to try to capture with my writing the labor they shared.

1. VOICES

THE BLINDS ARE pulled halfway down in Professor Elaine Beilin's classroom, May Hall 213, to shield it from the strong early-morning sun. It's only 8:25, five minutes before the new school year is scheduled to begin, but already around the large table that just about fills the room nearly every seat is taken.

"I'm a morning person," Elaine says, striding through the doorway and finding one of the few remaining chairs by the far wall, in front of the windows. What she sees in front of her is a group of freshman students: a young man growing a reddish brown goatee, a woman wearing a white cotton sweater decorated with Mickey Mouse and Goofy, another woman with a pony tail held in place by a black "scrunchy." She reads a message on a T-shirt that says "Rage" in ragged letters, and below that, "We determine that your whole system sucks."

That slogan seems incongruous here, since the students don't look surly or resistant to her. In fact, they look respectful and neat. Some of the women have carefully combed hair still wet from showering. The group seems impassive, mildly curious.

"I predict that you may develop the same despair my family has," Elaine tells them in a somewhat thin, quavery, tentative voice, as if she is having to persuade herself to speak. She likes rising early, the only one in her family who does, and she tells them she's afraid she may seem annoyingly cheerful. These students, she knows, prefer early morning classes (so they can hold down jobs in the afternoons and evenings) but, whether because of working, studying, or parties, they often arrive tired in the morning, hard to rouse to any enthusiasm, like her own family. Elaine, though, enjoys rising early, she explains. By the time she gets to school, even for an early morning class like this one, she's made tea, gone for a long walk.

She appears to be in her middle or late forties, her hair a mixture of dark brown and gray cut in a page boy, her skin still smooth around the neck. Her eyes are pale green. Sweet, youthful, enthusiastic and ironic by turns, something about her small, aquiline nose, the rapid movements of her head, gives an impression of sprightliness and intensity, and her voice is an important part of that, too—carrying easily her crisp, faintly British diction.

"I love mornings like this with the sun coming in," she's telling them. "Of course," she pauses, surveying the class with a questioning glance, her eyebrows going up, her head cocked a little to the side, "I'd love it more if we were all sitting in a cottage on a bluff overlooking the water off the Cape."

A slightly subversive remark, but she knows better than to expect these students to laugh. Even if they go to the Cape at all, for these students summer means a summer job, not rest. Perhaps she's let slip a hint of her fantasy—combining the two kinds of happiness her work brings her. Summer is her time for research—days in the library, doing lots of writing, connecting with colleagues in her field—an unusually collaborative and collegial world of scholarship in women's literature. The other kind of happiness her work brings her comes from her teaching.

In the summer she's incredibly idealistic about teaching. She has a platonic ideal of the perfect class. Everyone comes to each class. Twenty eager faces are all happily and busily engaged in growing and developing and writing. If she didn't have that kind of optimism, she would hardly get back in the saddle at all. Yet during these tense, introductory moments, all she knows about these students is in their clothing, body language, faces. Her goal today is to at least get each of these students to speak. What she does know is that if she lets them remain silent through even one class, they may set a pattern for themselves they won't later be able to break.

She tells them her name, putting "doctor" in front of it—the students inevitably will, even if she doesn't. "Let me begin by calling the roll," she says. "Please tell me if there's a name you prefer to be called."

Maximilian prefers to be called Max. And so on, through the twenty-one names on the class list supplied by the registrar.

"Amelia Goudreault? Did I get that right?" she asks a girl who, in the fashion of the day, has one ear pierced from top to bottom with many earrings. "I'm Canadian," she tells the class, "so I always go for the French pronunciation."

When she gets to Phoebe Schottenhamel's name, Phoebe's hand shoots up: "Yup, right here!"

But most of the students have raised their hands just part way, or mumble "here" or "yes."

She passes out large index cards and tells them to write their names, fold the card, and stand it up in front of them. Soon the cards with the names—some in small handwriting, some in large block letters, some first name only—stand up around the table, helter-skelter, like little white tents. "So we'll get to know each other right away." A long streak of sunlight slashes across the broad gray Formica tabletop, coming from the southeast window.

She passes out personal information sheets for each student to fill out. "The questions I've asked here are both things I'd like you to think about and things that will help me." Her voice is pitched lower and sounds stronger now, as though she's gotten "into the moment" and has found her confident teacher voice. "Tell me what other courses you're signed up for, so I can get a sense of your workload and the other kinds of writing you'll be doing. If you're working, I want to know how many hours. Tell me about the writing you've been doing in the past year. And give me one reason why you want to be an English major." The sheets, which have been passed to students on both sides of the table, have reached the far end. "Think what your goals are," she asks them. "I'm going to bring these sheets you've filled out back in December—just so you can see what's changed about you in the course of a semester."

Another student—a young man wearing a beige T-shirt with a large W on it, jeans, and dirty black sneakers—opens the door. He sits away from the table in one of the wooden chairs with its right arm widened into a writing surface.

"Maybe you could bring your desk forward so you're not . . ."

But there's no more space around the table. By now the students are writing. A young woman, Colleen, who wears a blue jersey and a single-strand necklace of tiny beads, pauses, her black pen waggling. Her reddish blond hair is long, pulled back into a ponytail. George, baseball cap still on, brim forward, shielding his face when he looks down, writes slowly, steadily. Phoebe, chewing gum discreetly, seems to be concentrating before she begins. A girl in overalls, wearing several bracelets, her Marlboro pack and lighter in front of her on the table, is chewing on her pen, her knee up against the table. *Kate* she has written on her folded card. Susie Benson has written both names large. Her long, straight, shiny brown hair is pulled back at the temples, the rest of it spilling down toward her paper as she works. She keeps a leather planner on top of her textbook and notebook. Her grip on her pen seems cramped, fierce. Her lips open and move as she writes, her eyebrows going up.

"OK," says Elaine, looking around with a half-smile. "Let's start something now, one of the most important things we're going to do here. I want you to talk to each other about your writing. Divide yourselves up into little groups, and talk to each other about what you've done over the past year." She moves around the table, counting off groups of four, pointing at them, but not touching them. "What did you write? Tell each other." Now the room is filled with the sound of five or six conversations going at once, and still it's possible to focus on any one of these conversations and pick up phrases like "enjoy writing fictional stories . . . I've been working for the past three years . . . kept a folder." The students nearest the newcomer look back at him at his desk away from the table, but he doesn't join them. He's written *Greg* on the card he's been given.

After about two minutes the voices start to die down. Max, the young man with the reddish goatee and the Rage T-shirt, sits silently, expectantly. "Have you all done your confession?" Elaine asks the class.

Now there's another latecomer, who fishes a purple pen out of her backpack. She wears glasses and brownish lipstick. She has on a yellow T-shirt with a cartoon chicken on it, and her jeans seem new, or at least deep blue, not faded or "stone-washed," and are pressed with a crease. Her black lace-up shoes seem new, as well. Glancing at her class list, Elaine asks, "Are you Rosalind?" The young woman smiles and nods and receives from her professor copies of the personal information form and the syllabus.

Meanwhile the voices have started up again. "Have we moved on to our favorite recipes?" Elaine asks, as though she isn't sure the conversations are still about writing. "Let's backtrack. You all know you have voices now, so let's look at the syllabus." While she's saying this, she's passing out copies, and as the students get them their heads lower to look at the several typed pages. "One of the things I really want to do is get started on time," she tells them. "If you look through this syllabus you'll know we're going to be very busy. I've written to all of you—would you mind closing that door?" The girl nearest the doorway slides a metal trash basket out of the way and the door closes by itself. "In my letter I told you about what we're going to be doing this semester, the book we'll be studying to begin with. Stop me if you have questions. This syllabus should be with you at all times. It's full of necessary information. How to get in touch with me, for example." Her left thumb goes out like a hitchhiker's. "If you see me walking across campus you can go, 'Yo! Doctor Beilin!'" The students watch her solemnly. "But," she points out, "the syllabus also contains my campus extension and E-mail address. If a crisis happens, come to me if you don't know where else to go. We can give you lots of support if something like that happens. The thing you should *not* do," she glances around the room, her head turning in small increments, "is to say 'Egads! I'm having a crisis.' If you see me walking on campus, don't hide behind a shrub. Don't just disappear. It's never over till it's over."

Now, in going over the syllabus, she explains that Essentials of Writing will be their introduction to academic writing on the college level. "You'll discover, as you move from department to department, that you have to learn new rules." And she doesn't mean just different rules for citing sources, MLA versus APA, for example, but even different concepts of what an idea is.

Kate rests her head on her fist, the syllabus reflecting in her round eyeglasses. "What you have to do as a writer," Elaine Beilin continues, "is figure out what the situation demands, which rules of writing apply. What we'll be laying out in this section are some of the rules, some of the conventions of writing about texts." She promises them many different kinds of activities: class discussion every day, group work, library work, individual conferences ("You and I will talk at least twice in the semester"), oral reports, short assignments, and a series of essays. Then she starts to tell them about the book they will begin by reading, David Hackett Fischer's *Paul Revere's Ride.*

"Did some of you wonder why we're using a history text?" She looks around the table, but there are no hands, no answers. "I teach British literature. I teach Shakespeare, women's literature, so I kind of wonder myself. I thought this was a good read. In my own writing, I write about women writers, historical figures." She pauses here, too, as though someone may want to ask a question, but there is, in the room, a kind of ground bass of the profoundest reticence and silence.

"We're interested in what makes a text. We'll be using Fischer's book in lots of different ways. As a text, first of all, to which we simply respond. How did I feel after I read this chapter? Did I finish it at midnight and fall asleep? Did I get up at six, just like Doctor Beilin, and say, 'Wow, this chapter was great'? The actual narrative goes to page 295, and the next 150 pages are footnotes, charts, and appendices, so we're going to talk about what kind of book this is as an academic artifact."

The students' heads are still. Phoebe has stopped chewing her gum. Rosalind scratches her chin with her little finger. Her nails are neatly manicured but seem to have no polish. On her left hand she has a ring with a modest-sized diamond, an engagement ring.

"How many of you know that Paul Revere wrote his own account of his ride?" No hands, a few shrugs. "I didn't know Paul Revere was a writer. In fact, though, he wrote three different versions of his ride. They're published, in a pamphlet I've ordered for you, alongside photos of the original documents in his actual handwriting. Some of you have probably read "The Midnight Ride of Paul Revere," Longfellow's poem?" One hand goes up, Amelia's. She's wearing a black scrunchy as a bracelet on her left wrist. "We're going to read that too. So we're going to be dealing with many different kinds of texts. That word's from the Latin. It means 'that which is woven.' As writers you're going to be weavers of texts. I hope this way of looking at things will inspire you." She looks around, her head cocked, her eyebrows raised. "Anyone want to comment? Did I ring any bells here?"

"Are we going to be doing this book the whole semester?"

"Good question, Phoebe. You might want to look at page two on your syllabus, toward the bottom—end of October. You'll be doing a research essay in some way stimulated by something of interest suggested by the text. At that point, let's talk. Do you want to go on with Fischer? If so, you'll write your final two essays on it as well. If we as a group feel we don't want to go on, at that point we'll go on to something else. Short stories, maybe. Or a novel. The last thing I want to do is keep going when we've decided we're finished."

George raises his hand now. He's kept his baseball cap on, brim low, concealing part of his face. "This isn't about *Paul Revere's Ride*, but what about the field trip?" He's talking about the field trip required for Essay Four.

Elaine Beilin explains that the historic events Paul Revere participated in took place in several of the towns of this particular region. She tells them they'll choose the place they want to visit, either alone or in a small group. "One obvious possibility is Revere's house, the only seventeenth-century house left standing in the city proper. You'll get to go to the North End and have a great pasta meal on the way back." Or they can visit the actual sites of the battles in Lexington or Concord. Or they can go to the Museum of Fine Arts, where portraits of all the "major players" are hanging. "If you're interested in art," says Elaine Beilin crisply, "you can have a field day on your field trip. Find someone who has wheels. Or use public transport. While the weather's beautiful what could be nicer? Any questions?"

Elaine has different ways of using this phrase. Sometimes she'll interrogate the class with her glance for as much as a minute, and perhaps a hand will go up. This time, though, there's not much of a pause—as though to say, "No more questions for now about that."

Another latecomer comes in, a young man in jeans with a red backpack. "Are you an English major?" she asks.

He shakes his head.

"You're going to have to find another section." The young man leaves. "You're so lucky to have two great bookstores in the neighborhood. It's English major heaven. Start at Borders, that's my favorite." She goes on to explain how they're going to do their oral reports in teams, so there'll be "someone to cue you in, hold you up, give you a cup of coffee." Around the large table there's a stirring of heads—some shaved close near the ears like Andy's; some of the women wear big plastic hair clips to pull their hair back. There are earrings through the tops of their ears, as well as through the lobes. Andy, too, has a small gold hoop in his left ear. "Twice a semester, you'll write a self-assessment. Class attendance is required. I will keep an attendance sheet." Elaine knows that sometimes students neglect classwork, especially if extensive preparation is required. They put the time they save into their jobs, and seem to feel they'll earn more than enough to pay to retake the course in summer school.

"If you're not here," Elaine stares at them, her face serious, half-way towards a frown of loss, "you can't participate."

Jeremy removes his sweater. Underneath he has on a plain white T-shirt, scuffed jeans, and a long, thick stainless-steel key chain that goes into his pocket. The number "4010" is written in faded blue ballpoint pen ink on the back of his right hand.

"I feel as though I've talked too much, so I'm going to stop," says Elaine Beilin. "What we're going to do now is a little more writing. Anybody feel you want to get up and stretch? Yeah, get up and stretch." Four students stand up; the others, including Jeremy, stay put. It's apparent now that Jeremy's hair has been sprayed a yellowish green. He's taken off the pilled woolen watch cap he's been wearing halfway over his ears.

"My preference is to whoosh right through," Elaine continues, "but if I see that we're all flattening about now—and they've turned on the heat so we're all dying—you can send me little signals." She points her finger toward the ceiling. "SOS!"

Outside the window it's a late summer morning in New England. Not far from this classroom, on the night of April 18, 1775, the night of Paul Revere's ride, when the men had gone off to fight, someone in the Belknap and Edgell district of Framingham started a story that unknown blacks were coming to slaughter them (though all the blacks in Massachusetts at that time were patriots). As in 1775, the Framingham area, and the entire area west of Boston from which Framingham State draws most of its students, is largely white. Because they appear to be white and on the whole dress as if they're middle class, it would be difficult to detect from their appearance that this group of students could be in any way culturally deprived, and yet from Elaine's perspective they generally are. "A public school teacher takes for granted being involved in the kids' lives, aware of the kids' immediate background," she's told me. "She'll slip the kids lunch money. When you're teaching college students, that assumption disappears. We think we're looking at adults, that social environment is irrelevant, that they're entirely—and merely—thinking beings. That's an assumption I've shared, but which bears examining."

Elaine has seen that even the students' ability to think can be switched off by feelings of inadequacy. "I learned a lot about how students read when I taught Milton's *Aeropagitica* last semester. 'God, it's so hard to read,' the students told me. 'You're right,' I said. 'You're absolutely right. Milton has written these sentences, but you have to machete your way through them.' Now Milton was an elitist—he believed he was the smartest man in England—but, even so, he believed that in writing a pamphlet like this you had to show off your learning. By absolute serendipity, just then, we were looking at a place where Milton explains how writing pamphlets means you have to bandy quotations with people who are far less intelligent, but then we looked at places where the writing is lucid—with metaphors that are brilliantly clear. 'Look at the lesson here,' I told them. 'When he's writing in a conventional style, when he's conforming to a seventeenth-century genre, that creates the reason for the difficult prose. But when he's writing as our passionate poet he uses metaphors—these gorgeous metaphors. So don't you dare blame yourselves. This *is* difficult material that we have to decode.'"

She learned something more about the *Aeropagitica* that time around, and something about the students as well. "Students blame themselves because they don't understand the text, instead of either blaming the writer, or figuring out why the syntax is the way it is. Look, you're asking students what they can achieve in thinking and writing skills, but a lot of it is really encouragement and reinforcement. 'You're doing this really well, why don't you do more of it?'"

But to reinforce what's positive, the students first of all have to be there, Elaine observes. "The uphill battle at the beginning is getting students to come out of their passivity or lethargy or fatigue and really become members of the class. One of my students told me, 'You know, a lot of us have a love-hate relationship with you, Dr. Beilin. We love you, but you make us work so hard, you're so tough, and we don't like you for it.' I do like it when people like me. Still, I'm not in teaching to be liked. I do meet resistance. I challenge students, set high goals, and then with some students I have to backtrack. But that might be exactly what they need, and then they're off."

Her greatest fear now, at the beginning, "is that the chemistry won't be right. And they won't want to talk. That's my chronic fear. I cannot bear to have silent students."

It's now 9:30 and the course is just an hour old. After this brief break that isn't really a break—only four students have stood up to take a stretch, while the others remain in their seats around the table—Elaine Beilin introduces the question of how it is possible to describe someone in words. She asks the students to take about five minutes to write a description of someone they know, and then reflect on the techniques they found themselves using. Almost all the students start to write right away, many of them on the first pages of brand-new notebooks. Loud voices can be heard in the hallway, but it's hot, so the door, which was opened during their brief break, remains open. Phoebe seems to be finished. "When you're finished," Elaine tells them, "think about what was involved in writing those sentences. Make a list of three things—practices, strategies, ways—that you think contribute positively to making an effective portrait in words. Keep going if you can think of more." Then she leaves the room for a moment, on what she calls her "eternal search for chalk," since she intends to list their ideas on the board.

Everyone's ideas. For ten years or more she's been reflecting on the importance of an inclusive teaching style, an issue that arose initially in sessions on campus devoted to getting work by women into the curriculum. Two visiting scholars came, Susan Van Dyne and Marilyn Shuster, and one of the things they talked about was the connection of an inclusive teaching style with the development of an inclusive curriculum. The technique they suggested was to ask questions and then have students take some time to write down answers, and that's something Elaine Beilin has done frequently in all her classes. One benefit of the technique is that it stops students who think very fast from dominating the conversation. That's one of the reasons she's chosen the Paul Revere book, too. As a Canadian she can pretend that she's a bit "clueless" about U.S. history, though she isn't at all. Still, it's not her field, so in a sense she'll be slowing herself down, guarding against the danger of overwhelming the students with her own ideas, and giving them the opportunity to be the experts. Another benefit is that writing first, before a discussion, builds the confidence of some of the more reticent students. Elaine sympathizes with students who need to think things out before they speak. When she speaks out at college meetings, she likes to feel sure that she has something to say, and not just some half-worked-out idea. Still it seems clear, even on the first day, that some students are far more confident (and thus seem more engaged?) than others. Phoebe, for example: she's finished her writing efficiently and is now going through her black canvas tote bag, signaling her readiness to move on

When Elaine returns with her chalk she sets up a list on the board of the students' ideas, writing at the top, "Techniques of Description." After asking her first major question of the class—"What can you do to make a portrait in words?"—she draws her arms around herself and waits.

"Use adjectives that aren't tired, that are alive," May says.

"We're into metaphor already," says Elaine Beilin. "Great." She writes "alive adjectives" on the board. "Like? . . ." She turns and glances around.

"Chirpy," says Max, the young man in the Rage T-shirt.

"Explain chirpy."

"Outgoing."

"That was one," Elaine Beilin says. "Certainly not a tired one."

"And they don't need to be 'chirpy' either," says Phoebe. "You could say putrid, too." She seems to be on guard lest "alive adjectives" might mean only positive ones. "Maybe vivid is the right word," she suggests. "Even if you're describing a pile of vomit, you want to use something that vividly gets that across. Sorry about that," she says, looking around.

Amelia suggests that you could describe how someone makes you feel.

Elaine writes "feeling," and Amelia half-smiles.

"Feelings could be anything from hate to love," says Elaine, her voice softening. She pounds her fist into her hand. "Are you going to write about something you're indifferent to? What kind of writing will that produce?"

The students go on to talk about hair, smell, size, sound, while May, shaking her head, says she prefers to use emotions, "the way someone makes you feel, or the way you make them feel. I used 'caring' and 'generous.'"

"Well, you have to use important information," says Phoebe, "not just pointless nonsense."

"I liked the word you used before," says Elaine Beilin. "Pertinent. You have to choose pertinent details. But something Phoebe decides is pertinent may be different from what Francesca decides. Let's push that a little further." She asks them to think of the many details they might note about someone in line at a supermarket.

"Maybe he angrily stomped down the aisle because he couldn't get what he wanted," Phoebe suggests.

"Say the person is overall a positive person," says Susie. "You could say her hair was shining."

"Oh, I love that," says Elaine Beilin. "Could you say how that helps? It relates to our personalities, doesn't it? How did her hair get to be shining? Sun? Light?"

Susie nods. But no one picks up on this by speaking.

"Ah, yes. Think of me sitting there, with sun gleaming behind me. Or how about, 'She sat in the cavern with her hair in knots?'"

"Different details would give the description a whole different tone," says Susie.

"That's exactly the right term."

"How about habits?" asks Andy.

"OK. How do you get across someone's habits? This person always counts her change."

"Or like you," says George. "You like waking up early, and coming to school all happy."

"You could also write about negative traits," says Marion, smiling back at Elaine, "so they're human."

Now Elaine asks the class to focus on the portrait on the cover of their text, John Singleton Copley's 1770 portrait of Paul Revere. She holds up a slightly larger color print of this painting, from Boston's Museum of Fine Arts, and passes it around the table. She asks them to begin a description of the portrait in class, then take it home and polish it, "so I have a first impression of you as writers."

For the third time in this two-hour class the students are asked to write. Rosalind looks up into space, not at Paul Revere's picture. Phoebe, chewing her gum, her pen in her mouth, draws her knees against the arm of her chair, rests her notebook on her bare thighs at a tilt, and writes. As Andy writes, his eyes go back to the portrait briefly. Elaine stares at the portrait herself. She opens her red glasses' case and puts on her glasses, to examine closely the image on the book cover. The image of Revere seems oddly classless. It's unusual to see an eighteenth-century portrait of a man who isn't wearing a coat. Paul Revere is in shirt sleeves, but he's clearly no ordinary workman. His pleated shirt is clean, and the work table on which he's resting his right elbow reflects him in its polished mahogany surface. His brow seems broad and intelligent. His hair, shiny and brown, seems to be his own, not that of a wig, and his cheeks are ruddy. His right hand holds his chin, while in his left hand he's grasping a rounded silver teapot. His strong fingers, with their short nails outlined in stain or polish, are doubled by the shiny surface of the silver. A man in his mid-thirties, he seems to be a prosperous member of the artisan class, yet the dignity his face reveals could be that of a statesman.

A rumbling like a ship's engine is coming through the open windows, if not actually through the walls—the air-conditioning unit for the neighboring building. Rosalind holds her copy of the Revere book up at an angle as she writes her first sentences on a blank notebook page. Her legs, in their dark blue, carefully pressed jeans, are crossed. As Jeremy bends over his writing it's apparent that his white T-shirt isn't completely plain but, decorated by himself with Magic Marker, says "Mo-Fo" with dots inside both O's. "I'm going to interrupt you," Elaine says into this silence, "so we can talk about this."

"Are we supposed to write about this as though we don't know who it is?" asks Lee. She has what looks like an expensive haircut—shoulder length and blunt cut, bleached almost white-blond.

"You don't have to have background," says Elaine. "We can start by just looking at the picture. Turn into words something that's visual. Anybody want to share with us the things you see?"

"His face is half in shadow," says Lee.

"Great."

"His eyes are glaring," says George.

"Yes, absolutely." George seems willing to comment, but only loudly enough to be heard by her and others close by. Elaine decides to say something about it. "George, you want to throw your voice."

"He seems to be deep in thought or concerned about someone," George continues, a little louder.

"Belinda?" This is one of the first times Elaine Beilin has called on a student who has not raised her hand. Andy, who is bright-eyed, and alert, clearly wants to participate. Phoebe is probably the most vocal. George, whose face remains half-hidden by his cap, seems more worried than confident, but is also involved. But some, like Belinda and Marion, seem hesitant to speak, even though they don't seem to be frightened when called on.

Belinda, a pretty girl, a little heavy-set, with long lashes and a turned-up nose that seems formed in one gesture from her cheeks, stares for a moment longer at her book's cover. "It's just kind of plain," she says. "Yet he was supposedly such a great man. He could have had a lot more things around him, yet he just chose that pot."

"Good, Belinda. But throw that voice."

"He looks like he's thinking," Belinda continues, no louder than before. "But it looks like a set-up kind of thing."

Elaine squints at the portrait, too, then nods. "Francesca, what did you think?"

Francesca, sitting next to May, has been silent for most of the class, avoiding her teacher's eyes. She has curly light brown hair and wears glasses. "He seems to be thinking of something, maybe staring out into space."

"Anyone else?"

"He looks like he's gloating," says Lee.

"As though he knows his place in history," says George.

"Pretty big," says Andy. "Very distinguished, and knows how people are feeling."

Max speaks up for the first time. "He looks really confident and full of himself."

"His cheeks are all red," says Phoebe. "Hot?"

"Maybe you're just transferring how you feel," says Elaine, referring to the overheated classroom. "There's lots of good stuff circulating here. Now you have to figure out how to turn this into paragraphs. Try to get the rest of us to see the portrait the way you see it. Type it up, and leave it outside my office by Friday." She gives them a reading assignment as well, encouraging them to "underline, score, star key ideas, then put them in your own words." Then she tells them that this kind of organization will help them further along, in Essay Three, which will require them to become book reviewers. For next week, she wants them to read the first forty pages and summarize. "I don't know why Fischer doesn't number his chapters, but it drives me nuts." Then she checks to see if they know what she means by a summary.

"A brief synopsis," says Andy.

"Good word! We could theoretically summarize the whole chapter in one sentence. No examples, no details, just the main idea. Essentially, I'm asking you to practice taking notes, to see what kind of note takers you are."

She excuses them, and with their backpacks slung onto one or both shoulders, with the shuffling of many chairs, and the banging of the chair arms, they file out. In a few moments the room is empty, and Elaine Beilin heads down one flight to her office on the first floor. In the hour she has before her next class, she reads over the student information sheets. She discovers that some of the students know very well that they have had trouble speaking up, but she's encouraged to see that they're hoping to use this transition to college to grow beyond that. Marion has written: "I'm known as a shy student, and I want to change that now." When she reads Jeremy's sheet, she notes the cramped print, the strange spelling and phrasing. She makes a note to refer him to the writing center, suspecting the possibility of some kind of learning disability. The work he does outside class and hands in—typed, spell-checked, possibly proofread by someone else—might be OK, but she'll watch his in-class writing carefully. If there's a problem, she'll ask him to come in right away. On these pages, with their various handwritings and colors of ink, she sees lots of spelling problems, lots of enthusiasm. The word "improve" keeps appearing. "Brush up on my skills . . . like to be successful . . . to the best of my ability . . . improve my writing . . . move on to creative writing courses."

The supposed distinction between creative and analytical writing is something Elaine determines to address fairly quickly. She wants them to see that the analytical writing they're doing in this class *is* creative, and some of her future assignments will clarify that. "Widen my vocabulary . . . enhance my reading and writing skills." Some of this may be for her consumption, but some may be genuine. Kate has written, "I'm a bookworm," a phrase Elaine hadn't known they still knew, let alone used, and it makes her smile.

Andy's sheet catches her attention. "For the past year I've been playing around with my movie script, sometimes every day, sometimes once a month." Susie has said she wants to be a "fictional novelist and a professor of English." And Belinda "would hope to write for a magazine as well as songs." George, who sat in class with his Atlanta Braves cap on, as though sitting on the bench ready to play, not surprisingly, wants to be a sports reporter. When asked to describe his goals for this class, he responds: "To improve my writing; as far as grammar and vocabulary goes, and also to expand my ability to write about various things." Then, on a new line, he has written, "Also to get an A," underlining the desired grade twice.

Despite her patter about being a morning person, Elaine has gotten only four hours of sleep, and is "feeling strung out." As usual, during the first five words she uttered in class a couple of hours ago, it seemed to her that she wouldn't get anything out of her mouth today. But now the class has happened, and every one of the students has actually shown up. She has seen their faces, and, for brief moments, at least, heard their voices.

2. GRADING PAPERS

AFTER THE SECOND week of classes—the class meets Mondays and Wednesdays for two hours—Elaine Beilin has already identified some voices she wants to hear a little less of. One of the groups she's set up hasn't been taking its in-class discussion assignment seriously. One time they were talking about coffee, and a couple of students, Andy and Lee, were having a private conversation. Andy, she's discovered, likes to say things in an undertone that he thinks the teacher is not going to hear. He's the kind of student who probably kept his high school classes in stitches.

Professor Beilin wants to put him on notice that "that's not what we do in college classes." She makes a point of quoting to the class something valuable Andy has said, just to show him that he doesn't have to spend his energies making funny remarks. She's also going to make sure she puts him in a group that has some well-focused students. Not with Lee, who might even be his girlfriend; she will definitely put them in different groups. In a class this size—all twenty-one on the class list have been showing up, and no one has dropped—she can have three large groups, each one seeded with several strong students. Already there are seven or eight she can identify as focused: Claudia, Susie, Rosalind, Greta, Francesca, and Phoebe, for example, would all be very dependable.

One student, Mary, concerns her in a different way. She's already had a word with her, asking her, "You're not feeling too swamped, are you?" Mary seems very withdrawn, and Elaine is wondering whether something's bothering her. Back in the summer, they'd had a conversation during advising and registration, and Mary had been quite responsive then.

Then there's Jeremy, who just sort of sits there. Elaine has picked up some things in his written work that make her wonder if he'll need extra help. After class she has asked him if he has any writing difficulties, and he has told her only that he sometimes makes spelling errors, or omits words. But he has become extremely defensive right away. She's decided not to push it but she's put him on notice that if the next paper, the first formal essay, shows the same problems—omitted words, unidiomatic phrases, ungrammatical sentences that fall apart—she'll ask him to come to a conference. In class he sometimes looks as though he's there, and sometimes he looks as though he's in his room listening to rock music. His odd appearance in class is hard to interpret as well. She's seen spray-painted hair on students before (though not this particular shade of yellow green), but is it a sign of his adjustment to college life, or his increased alienation from it, that, despite the humid late summer weather, he's taken to wearing a maroon wool watch cap that covers all but his face?

Finally, what is she to make of Kate? Her first written exercise hasn't turned up yet. In Elaine's opinion, she's stalling, basically. Well, it's only the second week and she'll give the class the benefit of the doubt for now, but Kate is going to reach her limit really soon. Elaine is determined that Kate will have to choose her priorities. If she plans to work all those hours—forty hours at her waitress job and her clerk's job at the 7-11, she reports on her survey sheet—she'll still have to figure out how to put the time in on her school work.

Elaine Beilin is up by six every day in the week, and on some weekdays even earlier—before her husband, Bob Brown, a scientist, and her two daughters, Hannah, seventeen, and Rachel, thirteen, have gotten up, and, thus, before anything else is going on in her house. In good weather, she likes to work on the screened porch off the dining room in their white three-story Victorian in Needham, about twenty-five minutes from the college. This weekend, she's been able to put in several hours each morning on this class. She can rarely grade an entire batch of papers at one sitting, needing at least fifteen to twenty minutes per paper to think about whether the students have fulfilled what they set out to do, and more time beyond that to correct their errors.

Though she finds herself writing repeatedly, "Please look at the directions you were given," all in all she's pleased with their first written assignments. She's asked them to write a description of Paul Revere as he appears in the Copley portrait, adopting at least one suggestion from the list of techniques for effective description they'd put on the board. She sees many technical flaws in their writing that she would have discussed with them if they'd been sitting there with her, but at the very least they all seem to have something to say. And for Elaine, that's the key question. Has the student put something of herself in the work? Academic writing, for her, requires the assertion of personal judgment and concern. The writer might not use "I"—but still her presence and commitment should be felt through her choice of words.

As she scans the papers, she starts to see the Revere portrait through the many pairs of her students' eyes. "A man sits with a silver teapot in hand seemingly lost in thought," begins Mary. "Possibly he is pondering the line of the silver or even matters of greater importance that will shape a young country." Mary, who attended a small and probably demanding and strict Catholic girls' high school (Is this why she's seeming so withdrawn?), is able to write cogent prose that can be read without distractions (not surprisingly, since her SATs, Elaine happened to notice, are in the 700s, unusually high for this college). Mary's paragraph continues in its precise, fluid way, concluding that the portrait is "an effort to show the man as great" without forgetting "his humble beginnings." She then adds, as a final sentence, "Surprisingly the subject bears a striking resemblance to a young Bob Hope." True, but doesn't comparing a person's appearance with a celebrity's obviate the need to describe anyone, Elaine asks in small handwriting crowded to fit into the space left at the end of the line: "What specific details remind you of Bob Hope—is there any similarity of character?"

"Not a single hair on his oversized head even contemplates being out of place," Rosalind comments. Rosalind, with her engagement ring, her choice of pressed jeans, her responsible night job supervising eight people in the office of a mail-order support-hose firm, has followed instructions carefully, unlike many of the others, and has put the list of the techniques she's used on the page with her descriptive paragraph. (With many of the others, Elaine has had to guess which techniques the writer thought she was using.) Rosalind, who is already twenty-one, and has been working full time for several years, has struck Elaine as being driven by desire and determination. Elaine notes Rosalind's use of strong verbs. Paul Revere's neck is "constricted" by his collar; in his right hand he "grasps" a silver teapot. To Rosalind, it seems as though someone might be scheming to steal Revere's pot, and Elaine agrees: "Yes—there's a possessiveness to his grasp."

Claudia starts off slowly. "Such a great figure in History," she complains, "becomes no more than you and me in a simple, dull portrait." In truth, if Claudia were in the same room with Revere she, with her large green eyes and her almost blinding sweep of waist-length white-gold hair, might get more attention, particularly from men. She's headed for a career in modeling, she hopes, and eventually in newsreading. Born in Brazil, she skipped a number of grades in transferring to the California schools, and is now barely seventeen, probably the youngest in the class, but also seemingly the most cosmopolitan. Though disappointed at first with the figure Revere cuts, she warms up to him a bit, conceding that he's "very eye captivating." In Claudia's writing, as in her speech, a slight flavor of the exotic can be heard. Even though Revere has a very ordinary face (that is, she wouldn't condescend to go out with him?) she grants that he appears to be a good person, "since I do not find a look of malice in his eyes."

Phoebe, not surprisingly, has written one of the most vigorous descriptions. For her, Revere is a "fiery man, inside and out . . . one who could not contain his fierce emotions, for they spilled from his tossing soul through widened eyes like the crimson blood of a fresh wound. Thoughtful, staid, and focused, Paul Revere was truly a dangerous thinker of his time." Elaine doesn't quite know what to make of the combination of "fiery" and "staid," but she's glad to see Phoebe's all-stops-pulled-out attempt to assert a view of Revere's character, even if some of it might fall over the edge.

Jeremy's description of the Copley painting, on the other hand, seems to present a problem. "Within the photo," he begins. How can he think the Copley portrait is a photo? Yet, on reflection, perhaps it is not that uncommon for students at Framingham to make surprising mistakes about genre and historical period:

> Out stares a man of particular importance. Yet such a distinguished man would not be depicted in such a plain way. Characteristics such as his loose coutence, in such other important historical figures a man would be straight and strong of the face. Thus upon this weak face the artist placed the effect of shadowing. Perhaps to create an illusion thus making this so-called flaw unnoticeable to those who would not dare to study the portrait.

Elaine knows better than to try to correct everything here. For starters, she's looking for something positive. "Good observation," she writes in the margin next to Jeremy's remark that if Paul Revere's vest were buttoned, he'd seem to have higher social status in his time. At the end, Jeremy writes, "Whatever it is that occupies Revere's thoughts must be of particular importance fore he is not concentrating on the work at hand. And it is all of this that leads opinion to view Paul as one who knows his importance in time but perhaps a simple life." Elaine comments, "You save the most important point till last—a good technique." But she does not comment here on the strange way this young man uses language. She only writes, "Please stop to speak to me for a few minutes after class." Jeremy, with his knit cap (that he puts on, she thinks, because he wants to hide) and his closely shorn hair (the yellow-green hair seems to have been cut away between the second and the third class) and his red canvas Converse high-top sneakers with little holes forming near both of his small toes and his incongruous brown sweater (worn *under* his T-shirt, despite the heat) and his long stainless-steel key chain hanging in a low loop from his waist, has the look of a fugitive creature who might easily run off if accosted too energetically. Yet Elaine is already drawn to him and believes there's something there, something to "bring along," if she can.

Elaine Beilin was like many of these young people. The child of immigrants to Canada from England, she credits Canada's excellent low-cost higher education system (specifically, the University of Toronto) for her own start in life. She, like Mary, was at first loathe to speak out in class. She, too, like Kate, worked her way through school. But school, it seems, was easier to work one's way through back then. With her scholarships, Elaine at first had to work only during summers. After her freshman year, she worked as a chambermaid at Lake Louise in the Canadian Rockies. Back at school, during her sophomore year, she had a job in the admissions office as a telephone receptionist. Her expenses were low since she had almost no social life, at least not during her first three years at the university. It was only during her senior year, when her social life picked up and her expenses increased, that she needed to take a job off campus. She waited tables at La Crêpe, a job that she didn't mind, though she never liked the color scheme. *Attractive* orange uniform she used to wear—that's what she'd tell people if they asked her to talk about it.

She was young, just seventeen the May before she began her freshman year (equivalent to sophomore year at American colleges). She couldn't afford to live on campus in a dorm, so she was living in the "student digs" area, living from hand to mouth on $15 a week, half for rent, half for food. School had been a very serious undertaking for her, and she sees that in many of her students now. It was certainly not a go-to-college-and-goof-off-time. It was survival time. But what distinguished her from many of her students was that going to the university had been like going to heaven. She'd had one teacher in grade thirteen who'd been especially encouraging. Her parents had thought it would be best for her to go to the local teachers' college as a way to get a secure professional job relatively quickly. In her parents' view, she was too bookish, needed to get out into the world. She'd gone for an interview at the local teachers' college, and the principal, bless him, had said, "No way. Go to university first, then come and see me about becoming a teacher. Stick with grade thirteen, and then university. And then, if you still want to be a public school teacher, come back."

As for her teacher, Mr. Henderson, he'd taken to calling her a culture vulture. "There were a few seats in the front corner of the classroom," Elaine explains, "where he put the 'culture vultures' of the moment." Since she was a culture vulture, he'd throw books at her, three a week. "Oh I think you should read *Pride and Prejudice* this week, and now I think you should write a paper." Even after she graduated, he'd given her a reading list for the summer! And, of course, she got through most of it. So university was what Mr. Henderson had been preparing her for. It had been total bliss, and she'd wallowed in it. And because she was an English major, she basically did English. About five year-long English courses, Greek and Latin classics in translation, some French, and Italian, and no math or science. No general education courses at the University of Toronto. No course like Essentials of Writing, either. All that was supposed to have been taken care of before you came.

In 1965, when Elaine began at the university, her family had been in Canada for only nine years. Her parents had come from an English culture that didn't suggest that lots of people go to college, although her father did have an engineering degree from the

University of Loughborough. After serving in the Royal Air Force, he had entered the retail business, first in England, then working for Sears, in Canada. As she looked at her own students, she saw them going through many of the same stresses she had encountered, coming from an environment where parents didn't indentify with a college culture. That, ultimately, was why so many of these Framingham students had moved away from home. Their parents didn't understand that their kids would now have to spend five hours studying every day, or didn't understand why their child had chosen a particular field: "Why are you an English major? What can you do with an English major? Why don't you go into business?" Though Elaine's parents never suggested she go into business, she kept seeing students who replicated the main outline of her story—who felt isolated, somewhat the way she herself had long ago, or perhaps even more.

What seems certain, though, looking at Elaine's own academic writing of thirty years ago, was that she was focusing all of her energies on becoming part of the academic milieu. In one of her papers written during her first year, "The Lure of *Hamlet*," she set out her task by saying:

> All this proves that there are certain qualities about *Hamlet* that appeal strongly both to learned scholars and also to the theatre-going public at large. If we are to concede that this particular play is more popular than any of Shakespeare's other plays, including his other great tragedies, we must discover the essence of Hamlet which has motivated so much enthusiasm.

It provokes a wry grin on her face now to observe her seventeen-year-old self joining the great critics of the day in attempting to discover the "essence" of *Hamlet's* appeal. Clearly, too, the "appeal," which she proposes to study from the perspective of a disinterested academic, is a projection of her own enthusiasm. Though she refracts her insights through quotations from many prominent critics, her own star-struck love seeps into her prose when she refers to the play's "special allure." Fascinated by the contradictions and ambiguities of the prince himself, she writes:

> . . . he reaches a thrilling height of passion with his:
>
> . . . Bloody, bawdy villain!
> Remorseless, treacherous, lecherous, kindless villain!
> O vengeance!
>
> (II, ii, 591-3)
>
> The spectator is lifted up, his emotions strung to the pinnacle of Hamlet's outburst, and then he is dropped into the clever intricacies of Hamlet's plan to unmask the King.

But at seventeen, Elaine had her reservations about Prince Hamlet as well. She found his "obscene remarks to Ophelia (II, ii, 115-121) amusing but really not fitting for an innocent girl and once-loved mistress." Conceding that audiences have been glad to find that Hamlet has a "highly-developed sense of humor," she still felt this "ready wit" poses a question "in the spectator's mind as to the appropriateness of the humor." Having explored some of the complex responses audiences have to Hamlet, she returns to the main source of his allure: "It is important to notice . . . that one can never remain emotionally uninvolved with Hamlet: it is either affection or displeasure, but never an indifference to what he says or does."

Here, clad in the circumspect language of academic understatement, speaks a young student who is alight with love for what she is reading, and in her prose at every moment is the kind of claim she wants her students to stake as well: she wants them to convey a sense of how much all this matters to them even though academic writing doesn't seem to focus on the self at all. We expect of young writers of academic prose that they will struggle to see which of their responses chime with those of other readers.

"All people," wrote Elaine years ago, "see the basic virtue of Hamlet battling himself and Claudius, and the terrible waste of goodness in his death." Surely she smiles, too, to watch her younger self throw up her hands at the end and confess that even in twenty-four pages (double-spaced) she may not have found the whole answer. "One still wonders if the right chord has been struck which will help to describe the enticement inherent in *Hamlet.* Ultimately, perhaps one can only be grateful that this unique masterpiece was written."

Despite this seventeen-year-old's failure to penetrate the entire mystery of *Hamlet's* appeal to both reader and audience, her teacher at the university found this a commendable effort and graded it B+. And except for "dissected" being written "disected" (one spelling error in twenty-four pages, with no spell-check program in those days) and the use of "Oedipus" as an adjective, there are virtually no errors. Elaine knows that perhaps only a few times has she encountered among her own freshman students one who might be capable of writing such a paper.

She doesn't only mean the technical ability and correctness—a good sign, certainly—but, more than that, the quality of being thrilled to be reading and writing. One of her first students at Framingham, Hilary Hodgkins, had that. After she'd dropped out of Yale, she'd come back to school at Framingham State, waiting tables at Ken's Steak House, trying to make it all work. Hilary lived one summer in the third-floor apartment on the top floor of the Beilin-Brown's house in Needham, and now she and her husband are expecting a baby while Hilary is attending law school. Oh, yes, every once in a while Elaine sees a student who has the English-major bug. "They love it, they just love it," she'll repeat to herself (the "it" being the reading-writing thing). When she sees this, she feels a kind of fierce pride of discovery, of exultation. She knows she connects with those students.

Kate Velasquez has loved to write, she tells me, since she learned to talk. (By the second week of the semester I've begun my one-on-one interviews with students, and I've started by asking them their history as readers and writers.) Kate was reading very early. She remembers reading pop-up books about dinosaurs even before kindergarten. And she was writing very early, too. In sixth or seventh grade, she started to write poetry and fiction. Her mother, who, as Kate is doing now, works as a waitress, was also an early reader, and has written a few books of poems, not yet published. Her mother never got the chance to go to college. Kate's dream since middle school, she tells me, has been to come to Framingham State, though her adjustment has been far from seamless. She's already dropped one of her four courses, Computer Applications and Fundamentals, even though she expected it to be a "blow off." It met late in the day, and Kate couldn't stand spending so many hours on campus, waiting around. Both Kate and I can see that her dream-come-true is already disappointing her; she tells me how lonely she feels on campus.

Elaine notices this too. Often on her way in or out of May Hall, she sees Kate sitting by herself on the rounded brownstone steps. If it's still morning, when the sun is behind the building and the steps are in shadow, Kate may be wearing her black leather jacket with its constellations of silver studs. Her brown wavy hair will be neatly pinned back with some glittery barrettes. With no make-up, with her slightly protruding upper teeth (she's probably never had orthodontia), with her oversized round eyeglasses over her big blue-gray eyes, there's something in the young woman that's appealingly reminiscent of the child she's so recently been. She'll be sipping coffee from a paper cup with a take-out lid, smoking her Marlboros with her lighter on the steps beside her, and Elaine will wonder what this young woman is thinking. Like a person who's scared, she looks only straight ahead, except when Elaine says hello.

Kate's desire to write, which she connects to her early love of reading, was of great importance to her when she reached adolescence. In junior high school, she wrote and wrote, but the only writing anyone ever saw was for classes. In her view this writing didn't matter; it was mere "words on paper." Anything Kate has written that in her view has had real meaning, no one has ever seen, not even her mother, who would only worry, since she is her mother. Kate has been depressed at times, and she has put all these feelings into her "real" writing. But her mother noticed that she was feeling depressed even though she had never seen this writing, since Kate frequently spoke about suicide. That "scared the hell out of her," she tells me. Kate's mother managed to get counseling for her.

Kate believes that she even scared her high school creative-writing teacher. Her assignment had been to write a story four pages long. Kate had put in a lot about sex and violent death and had been "very descriptive." She doesn't think her teacher, who was a substitute, a new graduate of Rhode Island College, got past the first paragraph. After that, according to Kate, "She didn't read a single thing I wrote. She just put an A on top of the paper and handed it back without ever making comments." Despite the good grades, Kate says she was hurt that the teacher hadn't read her work—although I wonder about that. There's something about Kate that makes me think she'll settle for scaring people, if she can't get them to like her. But Kate does seem sincere in her complaints about her high school, as though she was hoping someone there would pay attention to her intelligence by challenging her academically. As Kate stated on the information sheet she filled out during the first class, one of her motives for wanting to become a teacher herself is that she wants the students she will teach "to get a better education than I did in High School."

Kate is undoubtedly right that she was short-changed by some of her teachers. Yet Elaine wonders if Kate will be able to do much better than they did if her skills don't improve. "Boston was a tinder box from the very beginning of its existence," begins Kate's first paper. "Nothing of power or strength could break through their barrier of defense." Elaine cannot imagine what the connection might be between these sentences. Still, she is touched by Kate's account of herself on the information sheet, particularly her answer to the question, "Please describe the writing you have done, whether in school, at your job, or on your own." To this, Kate has responded:

> I keep a journal
> poetry
> short stories
> started a (hopeful) novel.

And she is encouraged by Kate's brief, earnest-seeming response to the final question about her goals, which is, "To improve my skills." At least Elaine and Kate are on the same wavelength about that.

For their first required 500-word expository essay, Elaine has given the students three possible topics, all connected to the opening of *Paul Revere's Ride*: They can analyze Fischer's claim that Boston "became a tinderbox" before April 1775; they can analyze the character of either Paul Revere or General Gage, as Fischer presents them; or they can analyze the effectiveness of Fischer's narrative techniques. To succeed at this task of academic writing, Kate will have to see how self-expression can take the form of having a clear, even bold idea, and then supporting it with logic and evidence. For example, does Fischer indeed demonstrate that in 1775 Boston was a tinderbox waiting to be ignited or doesn't he?

Kate doesn't seem to have been ignited by this task, at least judging by the results. Her typed essay is designated "Essay 1" but has no title. It seems as if Kate has simply gone through the motions of typing something, anything, but that she really doesn't care to exert the effort to link one thought to another. "Although a tinderbox is inflammable, there is always a way to set fire," Kate concludes. In the margin Elaine writes, "your meaning is not clear." And at the bottom: "Kate—. . . Most of your essay is a narrative account, summarized from Fischer. You need to ask *why* and *how* Boston was a 'tinderbox' (and perhaps define the term) in order to develop an *analysis* of this material." If possible, Elaine would like to straighten out this problem right away. "Please come for a conference to discuss the paper," she writes below her comments.

When she gets a chance to speak with Kate, though, she's even more urgently concerned about Kate's work situation than about her writing. Things couldn't have started worse for her this semester. She didn't get any financial aid. "They lost my application." She had to borrow $1,000 from her mother. Kate's father, a self-employed carpenter, needs a new van, so she has to pay her mother back soon. She's worked forty hours in the past four days, including one sixteen-hour shift on Sunday. She got home at 11:30 and finished writing her paper at 1:30 in the morning. In Kate's life, financial crises sweep in like the hurricanes of old, before there were weather reconnaissance planes or radar. She's found herself falling asleep during class, and may have to drop yet another of her courses.

When Elaine asks Kate if there's anything she can do to help her, Kate answers, "Just go easy on me." In truth, as Kate has acknowleged to me, that may be part of her problem, just how easy her high school courses were, the lack of demands put on her in the past. In Elaine's view, Kate is an extreme case of the absolutely number-one problem: students working jobs too many hours and not having the kind of time college-level coursework requires. When Elaine asks Kate if she's giving herself enough time to enjoy anything she's doing, Kate says flatly, "No." And Elaine feels bad for her. She tries to encourage her. "Clearly you're very bright," she tells her. "Clearly you get a lot out of what you do." But not any fun, of course. Elaine angrily reflects that the solution to Kate's problem would be better funding for students who go on to public higher education. They should be getting grants, like kids in England. There, if you've got the smarts to go to college, you get a big subsidy from the state.

But then, too, of course, none of this quite addresses Kate's failure to analyze in her paper. The more Elaine looks at what Kate has written, the more she begins to suspect that Kate hasn't bothered to obtain the definition of *tinderbox*, and so the very essence of the metaphor she's supposed to develop is a mystery to her. Doesn't she own a dictionary? Or is she simply used to not understanding words? Elaine wonders whether "tinderbox" for Kate might mean a sort of "pillbox"—a fortified place where you keep flammable materials, but which is itself fireproof? Had Kate worked ahead of time, she might have discussed this passage with members of her group. Or even if she could have picked up the phone and spoken with another student, this might not have happened. But with her long commute and heavy work schedule, Kate is studying in a near-vacuum. And the difficulty she's having with the book seems to be making her hostile to the whole task of writing about it.

"This paper," she admits to Elaine, "is not the best I've ever done." She's not usually this cynical, she says, but she thinks the paper stinks. Jeremy, she knows, wrote nothing but positive things about the book. But Kate, though she concedes that the narrative passages make the book interesting, doesn't like the way Fischer mixes vivid narrative writing with what she usually thinks of as "history" (by which she means fact), and says that this makes the book confusing for her.

Elaine disagrees, having picked Fischer's book because, in her opinion, "it's a darn good read." But she's not sure whether Kate is just provoked to hostility by her difficulty in coping with Fischer's language (however readable it may seem to Elaine) in the scant time she's allowed for her reading, or there's a deeper conceptual, developmental issue. Could it be that Kate can't process the combination of imaginative writing and historical fact?

Whatever the reason, Elaine can sense that Kate might have to be dragged kicking and screaming into this material, and into academic writing as well. Indeed, she's damned if she's going to let Kate slide by on what she already knows, already can do. No, Kate is going to learn to analyze, to think in her writing, not just to express her feelings. But Elaine's determination to teach Kate to write clear, logical, forceful academic prose is complicated, just at the moment, by her instinct that, for now, Kate needs a friendly face to connect with—a teacher who likes and believes in her. Mixing substantive criticism with encouragement is the challenge here. And in their first brief discussion, Elaine can see that encouragement is what is most needed first. Later, then, she'll have to sort out all the possible factors affecting Kate's writing: lack of time, lack of motivation, lack of adequate standards in high school, lack of vocabulary? And not just a lack of vocabulary, but some missing piece of cultural equipment that would tell Kate that she must absolutely know all the words she's reading, or how can she understand anything? Behind the eight-ball financially and culturally, what if Kate concludes in her secret self that she is behind the eight-ball intellectually? Yet she has to cover up with a kind of defiance, leaning back in her chair in class, her black leather jacket still on, her body language conveying an impression that she wants none of this.

Yet she wants so badly to "improve [her] skills." For now, though, Elaine Beilin will just try to perform first aid on Kate's self-esteem and hope to tackle the tough questions about her academic writing more vigorously later, if their relationship develops more trust.

Though a departmental regulation requires Elaine to assign a minimum of five short essays and one longer, documented essay based on research, even before the first official essay comes in, Elaine has already assigned and collected three written exercises, all of which she has evaluated with extensive comments. Indeed, students like Phoebe, who are well organized, throw nothing away, and intend to revise some papers to receive a better grade, will accumulate more than a hundred pages of writing during the term, all of which Elaine has seen, corrected, and commented upon—a substantial workload for the students, a near-staggering one for the teacher. Elaine is teaching two other courses this semester as well—the standard load at Framingham is three courses that meet four hours each week—and even in literature courses she asks for frequent written responses from students. As Elaine puts it, "There are many times in the semester when a professor will use every waking hour to work on student papers, and some when she ought really to be asleep."

By the time the first essays come in, Elaine is no stranger to these students and their writing problems, but this will be the first time she has asked them to generate and support a clear idea in a formal paper, however short. To stimulate original analysis, and to avoid any possibility that students may simply buy papers or borrow them from upperclassmen and hand them in (How many term papers about anorexia nervosa must be circulating in the dorms?), Elaine gives the students a choice of quite specific topics, all related to their highly idiosyncratic assigned reading. What the students assert, they will have to prove with evidence. In addition, she will be looking for a statement of the paper's main argument at the end of their introductory paragraph.

One of the mantras in Elaine's writing classes is that she wants each essay to have a "substantive, arguable, and explicit thesis." In high school, teachers may sometimes be satisfied with the first, or the first and second, of these qualities: essays for English classes have to have an important main idea, and, most teachers would feel, the idea has to be something that *needs* to be argued, that is open to dispute. But for the argument to be explicit, the student will have to have done careful thinking and shaping, and this is not something that can be accomplished in the single-draft writing most students—especially most students like Kate, who are in a hurry—resort to. Once the student has written her thoughts, and explained her evidence, she may realize that she needs to go back and make her thesis more explicit, or she may sometimes need to reshape her thesis altogether. But will she have time? And even if she does, she knows the teacher wants the thesis to be expressed in a single sentence, and this sentence often ends up overloaded and garbled.

It seems to me that because Elaine's students know so well the crucial importance of this single-sentence argument, they often bring too much pressure to bear on it (and themselves) in trying to craft it (leaving all sorts of loopholes, lest they say something wrong—or, often, not knowing just what abstract term can tie together all they want to include). The sentence, then, often collapses into virtual incoherence, losing its grip on standard idiom and grammar. In other words, the students are in approximately the same situation as that of a new speaker of a foreign language trying to express something important not covered by the phrase books he's studied.

That's something a teacher with Elaine's experience is going to expect, of course. Her task in grading these first papers is to try to read the thought that might be buried in the language—or, in some cases, to try to push a half-thought (or less) into something fully developed that can be clearly expressed. She has to pay attention to the surface—and keep her patience in order to respect these first efforts.

Susie Benson's paper runs aground just when she tries to construct her thesis sentence:

> The definition of a tinderbox according to Webster's dictionary is a metal box that holds flint, tinder, and steel used to start a fire. In the biography *Paul Revere's Ride*, written by David Hackett Fischer, Boston is referred to as tinderbox. It is essential for us to recognize why he used this metaphor and how it relates to the elements of the time. Before April of 1775 Boston was referred to as a tinderbox because it was constructed by potential aspects that could make it become a vulnerable society.

Susie's eyes, and the subtle, fleeting responses Elaine can see on her appealing face, suggest she's involved, or wants to be. Susie has written on her information sheet: "My future goal is to become a fictional novelist as well as a professor of English or at least an educator of this subject." And in answer to the request that she briefly describe her goals for this class: "I would like to be able to talk about my opinions on a subject and support myself successfully. Also, I would like to learn as much as I can at the college level English course. To gain confidence in what I have to say." Susie, with her wide, well-proportioned face with a large brow, looks as though she might be one of the daughters of Paul Revere. But she stumbles even in her informal written comments on the form.

On the first paper, her confusion is even more clearly apparent. What concerns—and intrigues—Elaine Beilin about Susie's performance is that, in the brief discussion they'd had in class, Susie seemed, of all the students, the one who most clearly understood what a thesis had to be: "A thesis has to be debatable, something you can argue."

As she writes a final comment on Susie's paper, Elaine wonders how the very person who nailed it—a thesis is an idea, something you can argue about—could write, as Susie did, "Boston was referred to as a tinderbox because it was constructed by potential aspects that could make it become a vulnerable society."

She underlines "constructed" and puts a question mark over it. In the left margin she writes, "This verb is not clear in this context." Then she underlines "potential aspects" and writes in the right margin, "two vague words together—you need to explain more concretely why Boston was a 'tinderbox.'" And on the last page she writes:

> Susie—Your idea to define the parts of the tinderbox and relate them to specific aspects of the situation in Boston is a good one. I think you need to draw the analogy in much more specific and concrete terms, however. The last sentence of the first paragraph, which should be your thesis, doesn't actually state a specific reason why Boston could be considered a tinderbox. What were the "aspects" of the situation that made the situation so volatile? Without that clear, specific reason in a thesis statement, you can't guide or focus the discussion of events in the subsequent paragraphs. . . . The gist of your idea is creative and potentially illuminating, but needs careful elaboration.

Then, thinking she can make more headway face to face, she writes,

"Please come for a conference to talk further about this essay." And she goes on to the next paper.

Elaine feels that she usually has one or two students per class who know how to write—in this class, Phoebe, probably Rosalind, too—and about eighteen who don't, but who fall short in entirely different ways. Amelia seems to glide into academic writing in a relaxed and comfortable way—which is exactly the problem. For Amelia, a paper seems to be a bit like a letter to someone, a little too chatty and breezy to be rigorous. The child of divorced parents, Amelia wants to reconcile two contradictory views of General Gage presented by Fischer: Is he a "virtuous victim of corrupt advisors" or a person "void of a Spark of Humanity." How could one man be both? "These as well as other questions," she writes at the end of her introductory paragraph, "are what I'd like to answer as I go."

This is too casual for Elaine, who writes in the margin, "state your thesis here." If Amelia avoids taking a stand, this might reflect the attitude this bright, imaginative, and witty girl has taken toward school so far—and maybe toward life. She is, as she has told me in an interview, on an independence kick, not wanting help, advice, or discipline from either of her parents. Not even waiting for college, Amelia moved out on her own halfway through her senior year in high school. The writing she's done so far has been published in the high school literary magazine and has been, she acknowledges, a good way to get out her feelings of confusion. She knows she's already spending too much time sleeping, missing 8:30 classes, as though not quite knowing how to deal with being on her own, even though independence is her top priority. The hemp-colored sweater she wears day after day and the line of earrings going all the way around her right ear convey the impression of a girl who may be on her own but may not yet have learned how to take care of herself.

Elaine, though, feels enthusiastic about the challenge Amelia presents. She views Amelia's decision to tackle a difficult question in her paper as a sign of real potential. At the bottom of page three Elaine circles a C+ and writes:

> Amelia—I enjoyed the way you took the challenge of reconciling these contradictory views of Gage. Your questions—Could he be both or could he have changed so rapidly?—suggest many possibilities for interpretation. In an analytic essay, your next step should be a *statement* of your main idea—in this case, *your* solution. Tell me your best thinking in a nutshell so that I can follow the logic of the subsequent analysis.
>
> The second paragraph does relate to the concept of Gage as a "virtuous" man, although you also introduce the issue of how he is *now* remembered. Is this relevant to your topic (it might be by the end of the analysis)? Your minnow simile perhaps refers to his being a "virtuous victim," although you don't clarify who the "sharks" are—the "corrupt advisors" or the colonists. . . .
>
> In your last paragraph, you give more evidence of his "virtue," this time from a sympathetic Englishman. So, it seems that you favor this more positive view and might have articulated it at the beginning as your thesis? Then you could clarify *how* and *why* he was misunderstood by the colonists. This is indeed the argument Fischer proposes in his Introduction, as you say. Was he such a "minnow," though? Remember how he executed his own men, for instance?
>
> In a sense, you've assembled many of the parts for a thoughtful, interesting essay on Gage. With a concrete, specific thesis, I think you could focus and organize this essay more successfully.

Having written that, Elaine adds yet another paragraph telling Amelia where in their *Writing Essentials* book she can get help with comma splices. The grade may be mediocre, but, in Elaine's view, the student isn't. Paragraph by paragraph, she is urging Amelia to reexamine and sharpen her argument—and to know her argument by the time she writes the final draft of the paper. Like the relentless surf against the sand, persistent, forceful questioning may shape and smooth, given enough time. Other instructors might have made a few suggestions, corrected a few faults, on the theory that the paper should be written again anyway. Just how much, they might ask, is a student able and willing to absorb? Elaine Beilin, though, will always convey one essential message to the students, and that is how seriously she takes each of their efforts to write.

Even though the course is only beginning, Elaine already knows that certain students—whether because they are more mature, more motivated, or more dependable—are going to do well, no matter what their skill level now. Phoebe and Rosalind, if encountered only through their writing, might seem to have different abilities. But as early as the first few weeks of September, Elaine already knows they will absorb just about everything she is capable of teaching them. Phoebe's writing may falter at certain moments, but it is fluent, with varied sentence structure and effective transitions. Rosalind, on the other hand, seems to get confused by a difficult idea for which she does not yet seem to have the words or for which she has new words whose meanings she does not yet completely understand:

> Paul Revere's character is extremely complex thus far in David Hackett Fischer's narrative. The most appropriate way to describe him would have to be as "[a] venturous conservative" (Fischer 5). He was venturous in the way he rebelled against the laws he believed to be wrong. At the same time, he was conservative, in that he never questioned the principles he believed to be true. The character Fischer creates is in constant conflict with himself, or at least he seems to be from the onlooker's point of view. However,

> Fischer makes it evident that Paul Revere felt no conflict within his persona.

In her opening, Rosalind has tripped over the word "persona," which many students tend to confuse with "personality" or just plain "self." Still, Elaine is quick to see something outstanding going on here. For one thing, Rosalind has seized on the complex idea (quoted by Fischer, but actually from Tocqueville) of the American character being that of a "venturous conservative." It's not surprising that Rosalind, without much background in the history of political ideas, should then get lost in the terms "radical," "liberal," and "conservative." Still, Rosalind has a mind that is ready to tackle such ideas—eager, for example, to understand the patterns of history—but she has an undernourished or rusty academic vocabulary that can't quite represent, or even misrepresents, what she wants to say.

Both Rosalind and Phoebe are somewhat older than the other students. Phoebe, who is nineteen, says she was put into first grade a year late—a decision she's still happy about, since, bright as she is, she's never wanted to overstress. She says she chose Framingham State over Brandeis University, her older brother's choice, because if she were paying that much tuition by taking out loans she couldn't let herself get a grade lower than A+. Rosalind graduated from high school at eighteen, but had to go to work. At twenty-one, she is the night manager for a mail-order supplier of surgical support hose and incontinence products, supervising as many as eight workers who answer the phones and take orders.

Responsible and intelligent, with good interpersonal skills, Rosalind is often pressured to accept more responsibility on the job than she wants. During a brief stint at a computer company, she found herself in charge of ordering $400,000 worth of supplies, though she didn't have any idea what they were for. She was so stressed that she went back to work for Comfort Plus and applied to college. She has always wanted to be a teacher, placing heavy emphasis on the value of education, pressing even her fiancé, who was working as a janitor at Dean College, to begin taking courses. Now Joey works in a computer lab as a technician and is studying for a degree. In her view, Joey was falling in with that crowd of middle-aged maintenance men, guys who were either divorced or fighting with their wives, complaining they were in dead-end jobs but not taking any free classes. "And none of them could speak," she tells me when I interview her in mid-September. "OK, I thought, time for Joey to take English lessons." She kept urging Joey, "You're getting free school, in a year you'll be so much further than they are." She now feels that she has proved to him that he could do the work, and she's sure he's feeling much better about himself.

Meanwhile, Rosalind is taking stock of her own situation back at Comfort Plus. Among the workers there, she feels she is sinking into pettiness, the way people get when they don't do anything to improve themselves. For hours these forty-year-old women will discuss minutiae, acting as though they're fifteen, forming cliques, gossiping. Well, Rosalind loves poetry, and loves trying to figure out what a difficult author might mean—that kind of thing. True, she's sometimes finding the Fischer book "wicked dry," but then he'll throw in something that sparks her interest.

For example, she finds the chapter about John Hancock so amusing that she reads it three times. "Such a funny little man," she says of this patriot who was also the richest man in New England. And then there's the anecdote about Hancock's trunk full of valuable revolutionary documents that Paul Revere, cursing no doubt, had to drag off the scene before it was captured by the British. "Why didn't Hancock just put the trunk in his coach?" She's become very interested, too, in Margaret Gage, wife of the commander of British forces in the colonies. It's possible that Margaret Gage, an American, supplied her countrymen with valuable military intelligence, that she was one of the secret heroes of the Revolution. But no one has documented this yet. Rosalind would like to study this more at some point, but she thinks it will be difficult to find out about, since most (male) historians seem to have ignored Margaret Gage.

Then, too, Rosalind's been moved by the sense Fischer gives of the real violence and risk the colonists had to suffer. "I never appreciated the American Revolution before, how it was real people, husbands and fathers and sons, guys dying on their own doorsteps. Oh my God, I kept thinking. That is so horrible. It's war!" But when Fischer just starts "listing facts like an encyclopedia, with no descriptions to match to the names," she fears she'll lose her mind—though Rosalind—being Rosalind—believes that she should slow down for these "boring parts," lest she miss something crucial.

With what determination, now, she is reaching for the light! "Paul Revere," she writes,

> could not speak well, and was not well educated, yet he was an extremely intelligent man. As a child, he and his friends got together and created the "Bell Ringer's Association". They proposed that they would be in charge of ringing the bells at the North Church. They even drew up their own agenda and created a mini-government structure. The idea of structure itself is conservative, but the structure they created was a kind of democracy, hence being a venturous concept. Later in life he joined the malitia, believing strongly in Freemasonry.

Elaine corrects the errors here, almost automatically after so many years of grading papers, while she disciplines herself to keep her mind on Rosalind's argument. "These are two different organizations," writes Elaine in the margin. And she draws a line under Rosalind's statement that "structure itself is conservative" and puts a question mark over it.

Despite her errors (which don't figure into Elaine's grading) and the flaws in her argument, Rosalind gets a B (the same grade as Phoebe) and some support from her professor. After praising her for taking up a complex idea and "thoughtfully" exploring it, Elaine briefly explains the difficulty with Rosalind's use of the word "conservative," a word whose "connotations . . . are complicated and shift through time." In her lengthy comment in handwriting that is smaller than her usual script but still takes up two-thirds of the last page of Rosalind's paper and one-third of the back), Elaine says: "I would ask you to consider . . . that a conservative *could* question his/her principles (and a liberal could—or couldn't—too!) and that structure is not necessarily only a conservative idea. Nor is upholding the law."

But for all her nudging Rosalind to become better informed, to think harder, Elaine Beilin feels that Rosalind will succeed. She can already recognize in her that love of being part of an academic community of inquiry and debate.

3. IN THE LIBRARY

A STEADY RAIN is falling on the day of the library visit, thunder having rolled through at about six. Traffic on most of the highways is jammed, the cars in long gray lines, ineffectual headlights on. Ten minutes before the class starts the lights are on in May 213 and Elaine Beilin is there already, chatting with George, Francesca, May, and a few others. She's holding up a recent *Newsweek* article on Margaret Gage, offering to pass it around. As others come in and the 8:30 hour approaches a silence seems to develop in the room, and Elaine Beilin again seems to be talking across it, her voice a thin bridge spanning a chasm.

Claudia, who commutes from Shrewsbury a few miles west on Route 9, hasn't shown up in class yet, and her group is supposed to give an oral report. Elaine decides to wait a few minutes for her. She asks for volunteers to talk about their provisional topics for the research project, and Phoebe's hand goes up. She's thinking of studying the music of the Revolutionary War. Susie is curious about where the practice of tar and feathering comes from. "I mean, what idea could one have had that you'd tar and feather someone?" It's something she thinks she'll look up. "And when did they stop? And why?" Francesca says she's interested in the myths that have grown up concerning Paul Revere's ride. A silence again descends on the room. Rosalind, who commutes down crowded Route 128, comes in rain-soaked, her dark hair in loose, stringy curls.

Elaine tells the group waiting to report that since Claudia's

517-FELD

not here yet they'll postpone their report till next week. "So next Wednesday, we'll double up on the oral reports." In addition, there's a lengthy reading assignment. Elaine is asking them to read the three different versions Paul Revere wrote about his famous ride. "If you like decoding handwriting, with all the crossing out, that's fine. But remember it's all printed out at the end of the book." She wants them to find places in Fischer's book where he's quoting Paul Revere's own words, to see how he's using them. Also, she wants them to check out what was happening back then in their own towns.

At last Claudia comes in. Even rained-on, she looks like the model she's thinking of becoming. Today she's wearing a beige-and-brown bulky sweater above black leggings and carrying an umbrella—the folding type everyone has, only it's brown with dark pink flowers on it, not a solid color. Elaine explains to her, "Claudia, we've decided to postpone your report."

"Oh, I'm sorry."

"Well," says Elaine. "How long is it?"

"Five minutes," she says, looking to Colleen for corroboration.

"I'll make another contingency decision," Elaine says. "Let's go ahead with it." The first contingency decision this morning has been not to cancel the library tour, although the computer system is rumored to be down. For their oral group report, Colleen, Greg, and Claudia have been asked to select a passage from Fischer, summarize it, decide what it has to do with Fischer's overall topic, and, finally, speculate about what feelings it's designed to provoke in the reader. They selected the passage several days ago when they met together outside of class, though it seems especially appropriate today:

> The Regulars stood quietly in the mud with the fatalism that is part of every soldier's life, while sergeants prowled restlessly through the ranks, making sure that every infantryman had 36 rounds and a full cartridge box. The men were increasingly miserable. It was not a cold night by

> New England standards, but the men were sopping wet and a chill wind was blowing. They began to tremble in their wet uniforms, which were uncomfortable enough, even when dry.[10]

Colleen explains that the soldiers had to wait till the road and their uniforms were dry, and then they had to wait for disgusting food. The part she thinks gets across their fatalism is the way they had to endure in miserable conditions, every soldier on his feet. Claudia goes next, to explain that this was finally the moment when the British were actually "starting something." They'd stood around town, had their egos inflated, and now they're starting to realize that things are hard. Greg finishes the report by saying that he believes that the passage almost makes us feel sorry for what the British soldiers went through, especially the description of their wet uniforms. Greg is finished quickly. Claudia praises Fischer for being sensitive and humane, since these soldiers are British. "I agree with what Claudia is saying," says Greg. "You could sympathize." Though Greg, who generally sits away from the table in one of the seats with its own desk, has said very little, he has already said more than he usually does. A young man of medium height with black, wavy hair and a pale but clear complexion, Greg seems to be very shy, or is he merely silent?

"All right," says Elaine. She isn't conferring approval. She hasn't expected the report to be quite this brief. "Take some time to think. They've picked a very interesting passage."

"I feel the same way you guys did," says Rosalind. "You think about war as something abstract, not actually how the weather was. They landed in a swamp. That kind of sucks."

"Literally," says Elaine. "Yes, those cold and wet uniforms." And then she quotes Fischer: "'designed by a demonic tailor who had sworn sartorial vengeance on the human frame.' Fatalism is part of every soldier's life. Anyone here been a soldier?"

Their faces still focused on hers, no one answers.

"Fischer's not just talking about 1775 here. What is fatalism, first of all?" She cocks her head and freezes, as a bird might if it were trying to make something out. "Got the word 'fate' in it."

Silence.

A little laugh from May. "They don't believe they can control their fate?"

"Anybody else got some thoughts whirling around?"

"I think he's saying it's going to be the same for all of them," says Claudia.

"Yes," Elaine says. "As May suggested, none of them have a sense of being in control."

"Well, you pretty much give up control as a soldier," says Rosalind. "And it's more pronounced in time of war."

Elaine nods thoughtfully. "Other comments on this passage? OK, thank you very much. Now, in order to wake up those of you who haven't quite made it yet, we'll take a walk over to the library. If you want to get together and share an umbrella, I have a couple in my office, or"—standing now at the side of the table, she looks around as the students leave, most of them bareheaded— "if you just want to be a tough New Englander . . ."

May and Francesca walk to the library together—as they seem to do almost everything. In early September, when I first asked to interview them, they asked if they could come in together. I said, "Fine," and that's what they did. In our first conversation about a week ago they told me they met during the summer at Freshman Orientation, on one of the many lines where students were stuck. One of my motives for creating this class of English majors was that I was hoping, since the students would all be majoring in the same subject, that they might find in this common interest a basis for friendship. And Elaine has designed these group reports not only to enable the students to give each other courage in what she, perhaps rightly, judges to be nerve-wracking public exposure, but also to get to know one another. We're both aware of research indicating that the single most important factor in a student's decision to stay in college or leave is likely to be whether the student has forged some kind of bond with other students or with a teacher.[11]

May and Francesca told me that when they discovered that they both liked books and writing, that they both had similar, or at least somewhat complementary problems at home—May's with her stepfather, Francesca's with her mother's boyfriend—they decided to room together. Now, when they work on their papers in their shoebox-sized room in O'Connor dorm, their desks face each other and their computers are back to back. If you had to guess, you'd think that May, who's apt to draw her hand repeatedly through her long brown hair, was the romantic one in this friendship, and Francesca, whose wavy brown hair is fairly short, was the pragmatist. In fact, though both girls have boyfriends, and they both spend time wondering if they might meet someone more romantically interesting. May prefers writing about relationships between people, delving into character. She likes boy-meets-girl romances. Francesca likes to write poetry and song lyrics, and she admits that she prefers other kinds of writing to reading something and having to analyze it. May agrees. "When I heard this whole class was going to be about Paul Revere—one person—my heart was like—" May makes a diving sound. "How the hell are you going to do a class on one person? How exciting can it be? He rode on a horse. I was thinking we were going to have a textbook and read different kinds of stuff," says May. "It's kind of nice to have variety."

Francesca, by far the quieter of the two, seems more resigned. "I thought it was mainly going to be just analyzing. In my last English class, we just had certain questions to answer. I thought it was boring. You didn't have anything creative." In Francesca's view, Elaine Beilin at least has given them "more room to put in some creative thinking." And she likes the way Fischer's style is "not just all facts," the way he "uses visualizations, so you can see like you're there." She explained that she enjoys the way facts are combined with imaginative passages. "History with a creative swing," she calls it.

"That was awesome," says her friend, turning to her with a grin.

During the second week of class, May's mother called her to tell her that her best friend had been hit by a car. By coincidence, that same week, May's stepfather also had been rushed to the hospital, but for a different reason. He had not been able to go to the bathroom at all for about four days, and it was serious enough that he was running a high fever. "They gave him two enemas," she says without smiling, "and then some human dynamite, which didn't do anything, so he took the whole bottle. Slight stuff happened, but nothing great." Her stepfather is in his late fifties, she explains, and very heavy.

Things have not been great at Francesca's house either. Her family is about to have an auction because there's not enough money. They'll be forced to move to her mother's boyfriend's house. "You have to keep those things aside," she says, glancing at her friend. "Put them on the back burner."

"Francesca was on the computer when I got the phone call about my dad and my friend, and I started crying."

Francesca is able to stay in school because of financial aid, a work-study program, a summer job, and loans. So for now she's not worried about that, but she's uneasy because she doesn't know her mother's boyfriend very well. It seems to her that he can be really sarcastic. Francesca's already had to live with one stepfather who could also be sarcastic, really cold sometimes. When she thinks about her younger sister, only seven now, she worries that this is the only way this man knows to raise kids.

"This really messes her up," says May about her friend. "Her little sister is an angel." May knows, because she stayed over at Francesca's house this summer. They rented a movie, saw another one, *Twister*, and then, she said, "we shopped our butts off."

"When we first met this summer we might have begun talking about what a 'concentration' was," says Francesca in her soft, barely audible voice, trying to explain how they became friends.

"Yeah," May says, "and I asked you, 'What does that mean?'

And we found we have so many similarities. It's so weird." She spills her hair off her shoulders.

"My dad used to be an alcoholic. Before he quit drinking, he beat my mom, and so they got a divorce."

"My biological father beat my mom," says May. "That's why I was born three months premature. So then she married my stepfather, and he's kind of an alcoholic, but he tries hard to control it."

When asked why they like each other, May answers that it's because Francesca finds her entertaining. "We go to wash up, brush our teeth and stuff. I put the toothpaste on the sink, it falls on the floor. I just kind of stare at it. She just kind of stares at it. She's laughing. I just kind of avoid that side of the sink."

And when asked why she thinks May likes her, Francesca has much the same answer. "I make her laugh, too."

On this rainy day, as the two young women walk over to the library together, they admit that they might like to talk with, say, Amelia, and Greta, too—young women they think are cool—but they also believe that Amelia and Greta might look down on them, perhaps because they enjoy the relatively quiet life in their non-smoking dorm. "Usually people who smoke are more rebellious or rambunctious," May explains. Amelia and Greta, both of whom are smokers, impress her as fast-track types.

Once they reach the library, they sit side by side in the ground-floor room in the third row of blue metal chairs facing an enormous TV that's hooked up to a computer while Ronnie Klein, the reference librarian, waits for the rest of Elaine Beilin's class to come in, shake out their umbrellas or their hair, and settle down. Even in her high heels Ronnie is shorter than any of the students. With her closely trimmed black hair and her large gray-blue eyes, which make eye contact with students in all parts of the room, she has the crisp confidence and neutral friendliness of a tour guide. The TV screen says "Hello, Welcome to the Minuteman Library Network." Ronnie Klein knows that the students are reading *Paul*

Revere's Ride, and she has prepared a bibliography of reference works tailored to their needs, figuring, for example, that they might want some background on the American Revolution.

The room is lit by long banks of fluorescent lights, with some gray light coming as well from the high, narrow windows and two floor-to-ceiling plate-glass windows toward the back. The cinder-block walls are painted white, and the concrete beams running overhead are cast hollow, like upside-down chutes. A row of computers runs along the back of the room, and in front there's a moveable green chalkboard on which Ronnie Klein has diagrammed the pull-down menus of the on-line catalog. As Ronnie talks—holding up general, then more specific reference books—Greta comes in late, and squints at the large screen.

When Ronnie types in some keywords, "Lexington Concord Battle," the screen shows the first five of ninety-five entries. The Options menu brings up a form on which students can request books from other libraries in the system, giving them access to over a million volumes. To these students, this is just what a library is, a network. Many of them have never used, or even seen, a card catalog. Ronnie shows them the *Expanded Academic Index,* which refers to 1,200 periodicals, as compared with 200 for the more familiar *Reader's Guide to Periodical Literature.* Abstracts, and often whole articles, can be brought up and printed right from the computer screen. "I don't think you realize what a neat thing this is," says Ronnie Klein. "It doesn't cost you a thing. And it doesn't matter if the library has the periodical." Greta is blinking sleep out of her eyes. By now, eighteen students are here, with only Max, Lee, and Kate still missing.

As she speaks, Ronnie Klein moves back and forth between the chalk board and the computer keyboard. With her white-flowered black skirt and her black blazer, she and Elaine (Elaine's wearing a black dress with rose-colored flowers) seem like coordinated partners, standing above the rows of desks with the students and their book bags. Together they are showing how to get started on research at a time when library technology is changing very fast. But they don't seem like spokespersons for the future. They might as well be showing these students some perfectly ordinary appliance characteristic of middle-class life, say a refrigerator or a flush toilet.

"I want to remind everyone," says Elaine, "that now you've met Ronnie Klein, please remember that even if you can't remember one of the things she said, or have a problem, please feel you can speak with her. She's a marvelous resource. See, she's smiling."

"We don't expect you to remember everything," says Ronnie. "This blue booklet here has all sorts of instructions. I promise I won't yell at you if you just want to ask me."

Andy is sitting in the first row, studying the booklet. Perhaps, without Lee there, he's beginning to focus on all the work he'll be doing. Rosalind—her fat black bookbag, the sign of a commuter, hanging off her right shoulder—goes right up to Ronnie.

Upstairs in the reference room Jeremy is investigating other colonies, his wool cap still on. He's tried Virginia, New Jersey, Maine—but no, that was part of Massachusetts—wanting to know why Massachusetts was the first to rise up in armed rebellion. "Why us?"

There's a long oak table where a number of students are sitting, but others are crouched before the low shelves containing encyclopedia volumes, or standing in the narrow areas between the metal stacks projecting from the outer wall. The reference room, too, has floor-to-ceiling plate glass in the outside corners, and narrow horizontal windows near the ceiling above the bookshelves. The walls are brick or smooth-surfaced cast concrete. In addition to the conversations among Elaine Beilin's students, who have "taken over" this space for a while—the reference room isn't that large, and it's rarely this full—there's the high-pitched Morse Code of Jonathan Husband, one of the other reference librarians, typing at a terminal. The students tend to go over to Ronnie Klein or Elaine Beilin, not Jonathan, though he stops typing and answers questions if anyone asks him.

"Start with reference works," Elaine is saying to Amelia. "Look anywhere, even in the encyclopedia. See what they *do* say. Do the Americans really say 'The British are coming?' Hey—" she spreads her hands. "If this is something that interests you, then go to the catalog. It might be fun to look in a *British* encyclopedia."

"All right," says Amelia. She bites her lip, as if puzzled.

Most of the students are by now reading from large volumes. "Anyone who doesn't know where to look?" asks Ronnie.

May sneezes a couple of times and blows her nose into a tissue. Greta is consulting with Susie. Amelia has found a volume called *Notable Americans.*

"If you find lots about Thomas Gage," Elaine Beilin is saying to Rosalind, "but one line about Margaret, keep track of that, too. That's interesting." Rosalind, who is wearing a red sweater on this dull day, is a spot of brightness under the fluorescent lights. Elaine follows her to a large biographical dictionary.

"She wasn't in there, and I was getting aggravated," says Rosalind. After flipping through the dictionary, the two women continue talking for a moment amid the circulation of students around them. Rosalind is interested in the long life of Margaret Gage, separated from her husband after the war and on her own in London. As I look at them, I imagine that Rosalind's dark, dark brown hair and fair rosy-cheeked complexion must be just like Elaine's at her age. But the similarity seems to go much deeper than that. Right now they seem to be sharing the same wry sense of fascination with the silences of history on the subject of women.

"You know, my husband Bob and I joke about something we call the Journal of Negative Results. He's a scientist, and he's always telling me it's important to note when there's nothing at all to be found on a subject, sometimes just as important as finding something. Why have the history books ignored Margaret Gage?"

Rosalind is nodding, as though something vital is being made clear to her. She's studied Copley's 1771 portrait of Margaret Gage, which shows Margaret with her head resting on her hand, her elbow on the high arm of a sofa. She's pensive, certainly, leaning against the sofa, as if in a reverie, her full taffeta gown fallen in swirls and spills around her legs, her low bodice with a little bow, her head partly covered with some stylish British version of a turban. "I've been totally fascinated with the look on Margaret Gage's face," says Rosalind. "Fischer doesn't make any comment about her expression, just something about how it's a beautiful picture of a lady. That's totally insignificant."

When Rosalind looks in the reference works here, even with Elaine's help, all they find out about Margaret Gage pertains to her father. "It just says when she was born and when she died. I can't understand why there's nothing about her." When she checks in the computer she finds a correspondence with Thomas Hutchinson, an account of which is in the noncirculating section of the Concord town library. "I want to know whether she was educated, what she did in her community. Which side was she partial to? Was she really partial to the British? An interesting woman, an American married to a British soldier."

In her own family, Rosalind has told me in an interview, her mother is the source of stability. It's she who masterminds the gift cart business her parents now own in two malls. Even though Rosalind's father helps out at one of them, her mother does all the purchasing. I suspect that Rosalind is more capable than some of the high-salaried employees at the mail-order house where she works, and, judging from her stories, more rational, too, than the temperamental man who is the owner and her boss. Now she seems provoked to curiosity about this woman who may have been so important.

Rosalind once described her freshman English teacher in high school as a very crazy woman who would throw coffee over her shoulder and never shave her legs. She interested Rosalind in Shakespeare. In her sophomore year, Rosalind's English class was taught by the school's athletic coach, a man who drilled them in grammar and made them read literature that was absolutely horrible, in Rosalind's opinion—one violent story in particular about a man who killed a child on a school bus. (Though she couldn't—or didn't want to—recall the author and title, she must have meant Robert Cormier's *After the First Death.*) "I can't deal with violence," Rosalind told me. In her junior and senior year things improved, and Rosalind had a woman teacher who was excellent. "She didn't have to be mean, just very authoritative. It was what she said, that was it. She was just lightly sarcastic. There's an art to that, and she had it down." Rosalind took advanced literature and then went on to Advanced Placement literature, reading nineteenth-century American authors, including Hawthorne's *The Scarlet Letter.*

Elaine Beilin has recognized from the outset that Rosalind is the particular kind of student she most looks forward to teaching. Indeed, Rosalind may be the most intellectually ready of this group. It's significant to Elaine that when Rosalind missed a class last week she called to apologize. As they talk, Rosalind mentions her fiancé, Joey. He's aware of just how much time and effort she needs to put into her school work because she wants to teach. "Oh, that's music to my ears!" Elaine says, and they both laugh.

As a researcher, it often seems to her that she and her husband are on similar paths. "Bob's always discovering things. He's always coming home and saying things like, 'Do you know what the mice did today?'"

Elaine's work on women writers of the Renaissance got started back in the late 1970s when she was commuting from Boston to her job at Mount Holyoke and she happened to share a return trip with Patricia Spacks, who was returning to Wellesley from a speaking engagement. Elaine remembers vividly that "She asked about my work, and then said, 'After hearing what you've said, I'm wondering about women writers of the Renaissance. Why don't you write about that?' Well, that was the moment of epiphany. The women writers of that period had been submerged. Oh, there was some excellent work done in the 1930s—two dissertations, but they hadn't been published." It is a story she often has told to students. "If you dig, you often find these trails, buried because people follow what's in the anthologies or what's being taught in graduate schools."

* * *

Belinda, with orange nails, some chipped and bitten, is sitting by herself at the long oak table while Elaine Beilin and Rosalind and some of the other students are comparing notes about what they're finding on Margaret Gage. Belinda, who also knows that she wants to be a high school teacher, is following up on myths today. The Longfellow poem on Revere, for example. She'd like to know why history books, too, tend to be so inaccurate. She's interested in why teachers don't teach the truth.

Back in Swampscott, north of Boston, her mother became ill earlier this month and Belinda was called home. Then last week she was called home again for a funeral. "College isn't agreeing with me very well," she says, smiling shyly, "but I'm caught up with my work." She's gentle, humorous, and pretty, with straight but somewhat fly-away hair—perhaps slightly hennaed—that tends to escape from its barrettes. She has a small nose—almost baby features. Sitting at the table, she's been highlighting some of the handouts Ronnie Klein gave her with a blue highlighter. Belinda has also taken some time out between high school and college—one year, working for near-minimum wage at a dry cleaner's. Now, in Framingham, she works twenty-five to thirty hours a week at the meat counter of the local Stop & Shop. "It's not too bad. I smell of deli meat afterwards." But she makes more than a dollar above minimum wage and can get time off from her boss if she needs extra hours for her studies. Her nails break at work, so she tries to keep polish on them. "All my customers at work tend to like the colors I pick." She looks at all the colors she has, and then asks herself what kind of mood she's in. Pink might be an attempt to keep herself cheerful. "Green is, like keep going, almost there. Black is a depressed week."

"And orange?" I ask her, looking down at her hands.

"That might be for fall, for excitement, or maybe anxiety."

Belinda says that she couldn't have gone on directly to college after high school. She'd applied to community college, but she now feels certain that she wouldn't have studied. All that year following high school, working at the dry cleaner's, she was free to hang out with her friends, and to write "creatively, but nothing all that good." That was her party year, "instead of doing it my freshman year." She saved a little money, although not as much as she would have liked, but it was definitely a year well spent. "A lot of kids I hang out with are freshmen. Some of them are, 'I can't believe I'm here, this isn't what I wanted.' It's not like I didn't want to go to school, but I wasn't ready and I *knew* that. A lot of my friends went to community college and after a semester they stopped going."

Her parents were disappointed that she took a year off. So were her teachers, as far as she could tell. "A lot of my teachers, they're like, 'Eighty percent of kids who don't go right away, don't go.' I knew, though, if I didn't take a year off I wouldn't enjoy what I was doing. And I think that's what school's about, enjoying what you're taking. So. I just wasn't ready. I missed not being in school, and I'd ask my friends, 'What are you doing for homework?' I missed the academic time of my life. But I can't imagine what it's like to just graduate, have that partying summer, and then hit the books right away."

Belinda's older brother, twenty-four, goes to Fitchburg State, near the New Hampshire border. He took a few years off from school as well and is now a sophomore or a junior. She has three half brothers, who are twelve, eight, and six. Neither of her parents—her father lives in Swampscott also—went to college, nor did they graduate from high school. Though nearly everyone who's heard of her town thinks it's affluent, and half of her contemporaries back home do not have to work, both of her parents work in factories. This semester all but $500 of Belinda's expenses will be covered by financial aid. The remaining $500 has been covered by her mother, and Belinda has already planned her Christmas present to her mother this year: paying her own tuition bill. But, right now, she's finding that her books are much more expensive than she expected, and she's had to put them on her Master Card.

She wants to get involved with activities—the student

newspaper, for example. But that's just more of a time commitment than she can make right now. She still wants to set aside some time to spend with her campus friends, though none of her friends has a car, and it's difficult to get anywhere. She and her friends lead a pretty calm life, she feels. She gets back from work about eleven, and then they basically hang out on campus, watch movies, listen to music. It's not unusual, though, for her to start her writing assignments between eleven and one or two, when she goes to bed.

Belinda's happy here in the library. "I love research; I love new things." She, too, is interested in Margaret Gage, and in women writers and women in history. She's heard that that's Elaine Beilin's field, but she doesn't have much of a sense yet of what Elaine might really be like. "I still have a feeling professors aren't real. Like, in kindergarten, I used to think 'my teacher never goes home.'" Her professor in the Major British Writers course she's taking recently told a long story about Miss Piggy. They were reading *The Duchess of Malfi*, and he was telling the class that his daughter had a Miss Piggy doll and that she'd said that if the doll was going to be in the house it had to have a first name. He was relating this to the Duchess having a title instead of being considered a person. The Miss Piggy story went on for about ten minutes. He imitated his young daughter's voice. It gave Belinda a picture of him—a picture that kind of frightens her. He is so off the wall—but he's fun. Otherwise she might hate the class, she admits. Without warning, he'll start speaking Japanese, German, or French. In high school, in junior year, she read some of the same literature, but he makes it much more interesting. One problem, though, is that he doesn't seem to like Belinda's writing style. So even though it's still only September, she has already gone to see him in his office. She didn't think he could possibly know her name yet, but when she walked in he said, "Hi, Belinda, how are you?" And he was already able to give Belinda a portrait of herself.

I often hear this theme as I interview students—how grateful they are, and surprised too, when a professor seems really to be interested in them. "It's weird," Belinda tells me, "to think he knew me, even though I didn't know he knew me."

Over the High Holidays, Elaine Beilin's family broke the Yom Kippur fast with two other families they've been friends with for many years. They sat around the table with their children—Elaine's Hannah, the only senior, and Rachel who's entering eighth grade, and their friends' children, two girls, juniors, and two others who are in seventh grade—and the juniors were quizzing Hannah on what it's like to be a senior. They wanted to know about "the whole college thing."

Elaine wonders how many of her own students might be part of such discussions in their own homes. Maybe Claudia. Elaine met Claudia's mother at open house last spring. She's a journalist, and at their house, Elaine suspects, they might talk about writing, about careers. For others—like Rosalind and Belinda, for example—much of what they know about colleges, about education, had to come from high school teachers who took an interest in them, and that could be why they've both set their sights on being high school teachers. Yet both seem to be fascinated just now by what they can find out that their high school history teachers and text books never told them—almost as though the counterpoint between school discussions and home discussions, which gives Bob and Elaine's girls a sense of the fallibility and subjectivity of the classroom, never happened for them.

At the dinner table the other night the adults—a psychiatrist, an artist, an editor, and the director of the American Archaeological Institute, as well as Elaine and Bob—were all fascinated by the way their kids took over the conversation, comparing notes on teachers and workloads. The high school kids were all in accelerated classes. Elaine's close friend Sheila, the editor, one of the hosts, is a member of the same book group as Elaine. "She's the most well-read person on the face of the earth," says Elaine. "She's read everything—it's dazzling." Sheila has done a lot of volunteering in the schools. "And we were all fascinated by what's going on in that high school, and with these kids. Hannah and one of the other girls were in a play together last summer at camp. Then she's in a mock-trial club with one of the other girls. One of the girls went on Outward Bound. She just loved being abandoned on an island, eating wild berries, though as a doctor Bob wasn't too thrilled about that idea.

As Elaine surveys the students among the metal stack shelves, or leaning over the big dictionary volumes on their turntables, or seated with papers spread out at the long oak table, there's a good feeling in this close-packed room full of young people, wet clothing, and books, though she's only just getting to know them. She enjoys teaching them all the more because they probably don't have a chance to have dinner conversations like the one at her table the other night.

She's curious to observe Andy without his close friend Lee around today. He's been working with *The Grove Dictionary*, trying to find out where "Yankee Doodle" came from, and what other songs there might have been back then. He does seem to be more focused on his work today than he does when Lee is present.

Andy and Lee are a pair—in this class, at least. It hasn't escaped Elaine Beilin's notice that they like to sit next to each other in class, and that Lee occasionally gives Andy an affectionate back rub down near the base of his spine. Lee's steady boyfriend is at some school in Connecticut. That's probably where she is today, in fact—missing this vital orientation to the library, something that will handicap her now for the rest of the semester. Or she may have gone all the way back home to New Jersey where family problems have cropped up—parents who are unable to co-exist without Lee around, pulling her home just when all her attention should be on school. Even while Elaine's helping Andy by suggesting items he might look up, she's wondering about Lee: How will she be able to start her research, having missed today's orientation?

Andy has heard that the movie rights to *Paul Revere's Ride* have been bought by Steven Spielberg, that Fischer himself is writing a script, and that Mel Gibson will be playing the part of Revere. He likes the way the book makes things visual, and has actually enjoyed writing about Revere's portrait and analyzing Fischer's writing techniques. He understands that Elaine has chosen the book because it shows all the ways a writer can display a person's life.

Andy seems to be the kind of young person who has, for whatever reason, more-than-average alertness to what adults may be thinking. Others in the class have supposed that Elaine Beilin is an enthusiast about American history, but Andy is one of the few who seems to understand that she picked the book because she is not an expert in that field.

Perhaps because Andy is a teacher's son he seems to grasp what might be on a teacher's mind. At our interview, he explains teacher behavior something like this: All teachers say they don't want their students to be their friends. Some teachers actually say that they don't care whether students like them. In Andy's view, this is ludicrous, since many of his teachers have become his friends. He's gone out to lunch with them. They've given him rides when he needed a ride. "These teachers care if the students learn. They aren't just dictating and dictating. They'll ask the students their own opinions." Even his political science professor might be better, Andy thinks, if he'd just stop talking so much and ask the students some questions. He'll go into one of his long stories—something about a man delivering papers, and a cop writing him a ticket—but he'll do this for an hour, describing all the people watching the cop write the ticket. And the whole thing will go absolutely nowhere. Andy keeps thinking he'll connect it all, but the class just sits there, and it's like watching a movie when the ending doesn't work, and the audience just sits there wondering what it was all about. Then, too, he has a computer class with a professor who hands out exercises and merely repeats what they've read. Each class Andy goes to gets smaller and smaller. He puts up with it because he feels he has to go. He keeps thinking that this week the teacher will change. But he always has to motivate himself to go, because it's his only Tuesday class. Still, he gives respect to the professor, even though he knows he'll forget this man's name in a year or two.

But Andy likes the Essentials of Writing class, even if he has to work much harder than in his other classes and keep revising his papers. In Essentials, he'll be able to show the kind of person he really is.

Outside the library it's still raining, the puddles spreading on the black hardtop walkways. While Rosalind follows Elaine Beilin back to May Hall to talk further, Phoebe heads off on her own. With her black clothes, her careful makeup, and her air of cautious puzzlement—which dissolves into an unexpected articulateness and enthusiasm once she's approached—Phoebe seems to exist here apart from the other students. "So far, I'll meet someone and I'll think they're OK, and then they'll mention some aspect of their life, and I'll say, 'OK, what they're into just doesn't interest me.' That whole marijuana scene, when someone's just harping on it constantly—should I let that get in the way of friendship? I don't know, but I do, I guess. It kind of turns me off to the things we might have in common."

As for the other students in this class, so far Phoebe doesn't know if anyone in class is a potential friend. "I'm so tired this early in the morning," she confesses. "I'm not even good with names, so I wouldn't be able to name anyone.

"This school is OK," she says. "I'll give it a year. It's very high schoolish. It's cliquey." She was hoping to find new kinds of people, new ways of life. Parties, marijuana, and boys—give it a rest! A lot of girls here have turned her off. They seem so squeamish, they scream at anything at all, they live for parties—all the sorts of superficial things she thought would kind of disappear when she came to college.

Phoebe admits that she makes friends with men more easily than with women, though this isn't intentional on her part. She also knows that her near-phobia about going to the resident cafeteria doesn't help when it comes to making friends either. For some reason, she doesn't like eating in public, so she spends her hard-earned money stocking her little refrigerator with yogurt and other food, even though her board is already paid for. This "cafeteria complex," as she calls it, has kept her out of crowds in the caf', and maybe kept her from meeting more people. "I just couldn't sit there for the duration of lunch. I just don't like that scene."

One person she's met, who went with her two out of the three times she's been to the cafeteria, told her "I notice a change in you," when they go to the cafeteria. "You seem to get very uptight and almost worried or insecure." She definitely has a problem, she admits. "It's not just a fear of groups or anything. I like concerts and shows and things like that." She admits that not eating in the cafeteria is a waste of money. "So much money I'm spending on my own food." She seems to accept her own oddity, though.

Asked how she thinks others in the class are getting along, Phoebe can already identify one student who's been late with her papers and exercises. "I've spoken to her, and she is one of the people who is completely hung on marijuana. So I don't know if she's too busy with that kind of scene." Phoebe adjusts her heavy-looking black book bag on her shoulders. The rain is beading up on her plastic rain hat.

She mentions another student in class who's also very into "that kind of scene," and who, Phoebe believes, has still gotten her work done. But so far this young woman has seemed obnoxious to Phoebe outside of class. She seems to come across as someone who thinks, "I'm cooler than everyone," as if nothing can touch her. But it's not like she's a grownup or elegant; she just thinks she's a better person. "Cool," says Phoebe, as though no word could describe it better. She shrugs, then grins, heading off by herself through the rain.

That student is Lee. Maybe she does try to seem cool. But when her father brought her to Framingham State a few weeks ago, Lee told me in an interview, it was all strangely emotional, and Lee was upset for a while. Lee had always seen him as the strong one—the one who at her grandmother's funeral just stood and stared while the others were all crying—but when he was leaving her dorm room a few weeks ago he began to weep and had to stand out in the hallway for several minutes to calm himself.

Now every time she speaks to her family she cries, too. By the third week she wanted desperately to go home, but her parents have said "No, think about it a while." The truth is, though, that Lee doesn't think she adjusts well to new situations.

When I interviewed her—a few days before the library visit—Lee told me that a new problem has come up: her roommate hasn't been talking to her. This had been going on for about five days, in fact. Lee would say, "What's wrong?" and she'd reply "Nothing, I'm not talking to you." Her friends can't believe that her roommate has such an attitude. Lee supposes she's done something terribly wrong, but her roommate refuses to tell her what it is. The only thing she can think of is rather trivial: she let some people stay in their room about a week ago, and one of them slept on the floor. Her roommate woke up the next morning surprised and upset to see them. She seemed so cold to Lee. Lee has gone to her resident adviser to ask if there's something her roommate has said to the RA, anything about Lee, or about wanting to change rooms, and her RA has advised her that it will probably pass, to give it a couple of days.

So many of Framingham State's students have come from the same Massachusetts high schools that the orientation activities—pizza parties, and the like—where they force students to sit together and meet each other have helped an out-of-state student like Lee find what she calls "insta-friends." But despite Andy and these others, the loneliness persists. Her uncle—her mother's brother—lives right in Framingham with his wife, but Lee isn't drawn to them. They married when they were both about forty-five, and have ways that seem strange to Lee. Once when they were about to go out to dinner she found them sitting in the dark, "reading by natural light." She says that, though they "refused" to have children, they would treat her as their child if she'd let them. So far, if she needs to do a laundry, or if she's feeling sick, she may call them. But she misses her boyfriend, who's in Connecticut, and most of all she misses her home.

Lee misses home all the more because she senses that something there is going wrong. She thinks that her father's uncharacteristic tears may have been a signal that her departure—she's the first to go off, leaving her two sisters, one in high school, one still in fifth grade—may be triggering a break-up in the family. Lee's mother has always stayed at home, a "domestic goddess," taking care of the family, but now she's saying she might want to teach again, if she gets "horribly bored." Lee fears that her family may be starting to crack apart, as though she were the keystone, and removing her brings down the entire arch.

On the gray day of the library session, Rosalind follows Elaine Beilin back to her office. Amid the seemingly disorganized clutter of her office on the first floor of May Hall—a desk piled high with books and papers, intriguing art postcards and prints, a clothestree with a spare sweater and an upside-down umbrella, its spokes spread a little like wings—Elaine comes across to Rosalind as someone who recognizes her, who knows who she is and what she cares about. "Margaret Gage lived to ninety," Elaine says to Rosalind. "A really robust life."

Rosalind grins and nods. "Yes, she quotes from Shakespeare in context and everything," Rosalind says.

"I'd track down that passage in *King John*," says Elaine, "and find out what Queen Blanche might have meant to her. Well, if you were doing a longer project . . ." She pauses, thinking of the original research that might be done on that subject, then concludes, "But this is just a short one."

She also makes a mental note to have a talk with the students who have missed the library session today. Max—well, that doesn't surprise her. He seems so aloof, so neutral, almost as though he thinks he's on an independent track, present physically sometimes, but not really. And as for Kate, it has to be that long commute on top of no sleep after keeping those impossible hours at the Seven-Eleven. But with Lee it is something else. She decides to call Lee's dorm to see if she can find out where she might be.

Lee can seem just fine, a complete success story, and then, suddenly, there's an inexplicable faltering.

4. THINKING

IN HER FACULTY development work at Framingham State, Elaine Beilin has often given interested colleagues "Illiteracy and Alienation in American Colleges," an essay based on the ideas of Paulo Freire, which suggests a relationship between writing and political and social empowerment. It proposes that students' abilities to write even a cogent sentence may depend on whether they are ready to accept responsibility for independent judgment. Students, the authors observe, often

> lacked the confidence that they were qualified, or allowed, to make judgments that active declarative sentences required. So they didn't write them. Their *psychological grammar* was quite accurate [with its sentence fragments and run-ons]. They did not believe it to be within their power to make judgments, statements, decisions, and to act on them. Before they could find their own natural voices, they needed to see themselves as subjects, as knowers, as persons responsible for taking action in creating their world. [Authors' emphasis.][12]

Some of her early class sessions in Essentials this fall had fizzled in this regard, in Elaine's view. There was that awful half-hour when she'd felt like an automaton reviewing the rules of MLA style with students, most of whom hadn't bothered to bring their handbooks with them.

Whatever had been going through her brain? It was just the sort of class she abhorred—the professor laying down the law, the students in a stunned, inanimate trance. Maybe it had started with May, who had ventured a question that began, "When we're writing about these three topics—"

"You do ONE of the three," Elaine had said to her. "Did everyone hear that? Does that answer the question?"

Just a few minutes before she'd told them to get up and take a stretch. Then she had tried to break the assignment down for them into the smallest possible steps. They were to find a quotation to illustrate their thesis. "Be sure you put quotations marks around it." Her voice—she could hear it—had taken on a strident urgency. It was as though she had convinced herself that the papers would turn out all right if she could just give them a detailed enough string of instructions ahead of time.

Moments like these felt like teaching a kid to drive. The students had no interest in the introductory verbal instructions at all. They'd only listen when they were actually behind the wheel, panicking at a crowded intersection. On the other hand, some kids appeared to have the book by heart but to have forgotten it all when behind the wheel. Even so, she'd kept going through the points in the handbook. "Any questions about that?" she'd ask again. And again there were no questions. So she'd given them one of her quizzical looks. Out of the corner of her eye she had seen Phoebe cracking a smile. "I think the coffee's percolating. But the coffee's not quite done, is it?"

So then she'd told them to turn to the grading criteria on the back of the assignment sheet and had explained to them what she meant by a thesis. "I would just remind you," she could hear herself telling them above the rumbling of the air conditioner from the neighboring building, "that effective writing has a beginning, a middle, and an end." Rosalind was chewing a piece of blue gum, almost imperceptibly now. "Any questions about that?" she had asked again. The end was the most mystical part of the paper, she found herself telling them. What is it that creates a sense of closure?

"Mystical," she'd said, "because you need to have a sense of whether you've really rounded things out for the reader."

And then more silence, so she'd just kept marching through the particulars: typed, no exceptions, double-spaced, one inch margins. "You will have done a spell check. You will have done a grammar check, if you have it. You will have checked punctuation. You will have checked that each quotation is precisely accurate. You will also have a Works Cited section. I'll go into that in a moment. . . . On Monday, you'll bring in the final version, all typed up, ready to roll." And then she'd held up the handbook. "Inside the front cover there's a checklist. This is a very useful feature. In fact, there are twenty checklists in this book. The one for citations within the text is on page 58. Those of you who have the book turn to page 58." Claudia was working on a thin strand of her hair with her left hand, twisting it into a thread, her knee up against the edge of the table.

"OK, so I'm reading your paper and I see Fischer, page 52. How do I know what that might mean?" She had decided to stand up now. "Max, could you pass me that eraser?" She wrote "Works Cited" on the board. That was the signal, apparently. Most students were writing something down at this point. "You can write it down now if it helps you remember," she told them, "but it's all in your books." Now Claudia decided to let down her hair again—waist length, spun gold—combing it with her fingers, then smoothing it and arranging it down her back. Mary supplied the place of publication for the bibliographical entry they were working out on the board. "What's the next punctuation mark?" Elaine Beilin asked them. And Greta, in her smoker's contralto, said, "It's a comma."

"Thank you," said Elaine Beilin. "Where'd you find all this information, Greta?"

"First page," she said, perplexed.

And yet earlier in that session, Elaine says, she could have sworn that they'd really been thinking—thinking perhaps for the first time about the difference between fact and opinion. She'd prepared the ground by asking them to think and write about this question at home before class.

Clumped into three groups around the large, square expanse of the gray Formica table top, the students seemed to loosen up, their faces relaxing from the seemingly attentive (but often actually frozen) masks they still tended to assume. From different parts of the room voices started up. The group in the corner near the window with Phoebe, Susie, Mary, Amelia, and Greta seemed in full swing. Meanwhile, Greg, still sitting near the wall, couldn't seem to figure out how to connect with this group of women.

"Andy," Elaine Beilin asked, "which group are you in?"

Andy pointed to the people around him, including Lee.

Above the sound of people talking in all parts of the room, she could hear Rosalind saying, "It took me three times, taking notes. I did all the American things." She was speaking as though she'd had a real experience, something close to an ordeal or an adventure. It was time to harvest some of this talk.

"OK," Elaine said above the hubbub, "what are we writing?" She wrote on the green chalk board,

Summary vs. Narrative Techniques

intending to gather a list of advantages and disadvantages for each way of writing about events. At the end of the table near the door, Marion, Colleen, Rosalind, Francesca, and May still seemed focused on each other, not ready yet to turn away and work with her and the class. Just to her right as she stood at the board, Andy, Lee, Claudia, Arthur, Max, and Jeremy seemed silent most of the time, making, at most, a few very soft comments. Claudia seemed to be the only one writing a list.

From the third group near the window, Greta volunteered one advantage of summarizing. "You get the main facts," she said.

So under "Summary" Elaine Beilin wrote in a quick, legible hand, "Short version of main facts and ideas, quicker reference."

"How about this group?" she said after a moment, nodding towards the group nearest her, the one that hadn't been talking much. "Arthur?"

"When you summarize, you don't have to put it in your own words," said Arthur.

Wrong, of course. That was the key advantage of having them summarize: they *did* have to use their own language. Elaine waited to see if Arthur would have any second thoughts, but he didn't.

"It's already there for you," said Kate, trying to help out, "but you have to think about it and put it into your own words."

"I like what you said in the first part of that sentence, Kate. You have to *think* about a text when you summarize it. Then, as you said, it's all right there." Again the room fell quiet. "What about someone else from this group?" The quiet group, that is.

"It's kind of like paraphrasing," Claudia offered.

"You end up remembering it better," said Rosalind.

"I'd contrast summarizing, and even making lists, with highlighting," Elaine explained. Looking around the room now she could see some books open to pages lit up with day-glo yellow or pink. "Highlighting doesn't take any particular thought. By summarizing, you have to go that next step. I'd agree with Rosalind and her group. Summarizing helps you remember the material. Any disadvantages?"

Andy's hand went up. "There might still be some minor details that would be left out."

"Andy," she said. And the way she said his name made it seem as though she'd just welcomed him back from a long journey. "You made that interesting point in the last assignment we did." She turned to the whole class, trying to catch everyone's glance. "As Andy pointed out, the fact that Revere's father was an immigrant and a goldsmith was significant in forming the man Revere became. But at some point, in your summary, you have to make a choice of what to leave out."

"You lose a lot of descriptive details," said Susie.

Now Claudia's hand was up, too. "So you don't think Fischer's details contain a lot of assumptions?"

"I think he makes a lot of assumptions," Elaine said to them. "He's using facts and using what you might call historical imagination. Fischer is arguing that the way to write history is to write a narrative. Let's look. This might be a good moment." She directed them to a particular page and read to them:

> Even as General Gage knew what Paul Revere and his friends were doing, he made no attempt to stop them. Perhaps he saw no reason to try, as long as Doctor Church was keeping him so well informed. Without interference, the Boston mechanics met at the Green Dragon Tavern, and organized themselves into regular watches. "We frequently took turns, two by two," Revere remembered, "to watch the soldiers by patrolling the streets all night."
>
> In our mind's eye, we might see them in the pale glow of Boston's new street lights, patrolling the icy streets on long winter nights, their hands tucked under arms for warmth, and the collars of their short mechanics' jackets turned high against the bitter Boston wind. All the while General Gage's officers watched the watchmen through frosted window panes, then gathered around white oak fires in cozy winter quarters, and laughed knowingly into their steaming mugs of mulled Madeira. (52)

"'Oak fires and mulled Madeira,'" she repeats to them. "Pick out parts that have some historical basis in fact, and what's imagined."

"Benjamin Church was a spy who reported everything to Gage," said Arthur. "You have the footnotes in the back."

"The Boston mechanics met in a church," said May. "If you look, there's a footnote. Twenty-two. Do you want me to read it?"

"Ibid. comes from the Latin, *ibidem,* the same," Elaine explained to them. "I was intrigued by that," she said, meaning the fact that Revere had initially written that the mechanics met at the Masonic temple but had later crossed that out and written "Green Dragon Tavern." Had he changed his mind? "Almost all the time Fischer is quoting from eighteenth-century documents," she told them, and that was one of the points in Fischer's favor, in her view. "But then Fischer uses the phrase, 'In our mind's eye.' George?" Worried George, sitting with his blue Braves cap on, actually had his hand up.

"He's trying to get us to visualize the scene," said George.

"What details has he chosen? And remember," she said, "this is fiction, but he's using his best judgment as to what it would be like."

"He's using lots of . . . um words that refer to the senses," said May.

"What's implied?" asked Elaine Beilin.

"They're laughing at us," said Arthur.

"He said 'us.' He's right in there!" Elaine Beilin said. Arthur, she thought, with his Scottish family's military past, really could instantly put himself into the colonists' militia back then, perhaps without even realizing that Fischer had set him to time-traveling. She loved these moments, when they got carried away by the text, and she got carried away, too.

She moved on to the main question now. "What we're starting to do," she explained to them, "is to break down into parts the narrative technique that Fischer uses."

Claudia put her hand back up again. "He always describes, like, the background scene and the emotions."

"So he provides the setting. Are we on the street? In the country? Is it hot? Cold? All those things have got to do with setting. And that also suggests feelings, emotions being described."

Rosalind seemed to want to get all this nailed down in her notes. "Would it be characterization here where he's describing the British and the Americans?"

"Yes," Elaine said to the class, "how do you feel about Rosalind's suggestion?"

"Yeah, that's actually a very good way of giving you a group mentality," said Andy. "He uses direct quotes."

"We have to distinguish between two kinds. There's documented quotation," Elaine explained, where there's some source. "But there's another kind of quotation going on here." She started to page through the book. "Basically more like dialogue."

"Yeah, at the top of page 63," said Rosalind.

"That's actually documented," said Rosalind, amending herself. It was confusing. There was a passage of dialogue, and not till a couple of paragraphs later was there a footnote. But as she read the note, she could see that Fischer had several sources to substantiate the dramatic scene of "a man in black," a clergyman, Thomas Bernard, confronting Colonel Leslie and the infuriated British soldiers who were "pricking" a colonist in the chest with their bayonets.

"I can't find any undocumented dialogue," said Elaine Beilin after a few minutes. "Well, that's interesting. So much of Fischer's seemingly imagined dialogue is documented."

As she sat on the screened porch off her dining room, glancing occasionally at the early October morning sunlight falling on the chrysanthemums she liked to keep in pots along the base of the screens, she was going over the latest papers. Some had been a little bit funny, at least they seemed so when she wasn't feeling that she ought to bite her pen in two. Each time she picked up a double-spaced paper from the pile that was still unmarked she hoped she'd just be able to read and not stop to correct, but she was constantly pausing to try to figure out how sentences these students wrote could be edited. She focused particular attention on the final sentence of their first paragraph, where she expected to see some sort of thesis the students would support with further evidence and argument.

Most of the students had chosen an assignment that asked them to evaluate Fischer's captions. She picked up Amelia's paper and recalled a scene that had happened a few days before, when the students were divided into groups to peer-edit the first drafts. Amelia and Mary were both in the group sitting near the window at the corner of the big table to Elaine's left. Amelia still hadn't obtained a printer. She'd said her father had promised to buy her one, but he hadn't yet, so Mary was reading Amelia's paper right off the screen of her laptop.

"Does anyone want the lights on?" Elaine Beilin had just asked them. No one said yes, so she'd raised the shade a few feet more. It had clouded over outside and the light on the leaves was silver. She had sat down by herself near the other window. The big table made of six smaller tables had been split down the middle as the groups had pulled it apart, so that there was a corridor right through and Elaine could walk up and down helping, advising. Amelia's group was sitting around one of the smaller tables in their corner, but Amelia and Mary who were sitting against the wall were facing her, so she could see that something was going on there. She'd thought at first that Mary might have erased Amelia's paper by mistake.

Amelia was definitely crying. She'd wipe one eye and keep writing on someone else's paper. Her long hair was worn back, as usual, with a clasp at the back, a few strands escaping, and multiple earrings went up the outside edges of her ears like stitches.

"Amelia," Elaine had said, leaning forward, "come see me afterwards."

After class, Amelia had explained to her that since she'd been absent from the last class, she hadn't heard Elaine explain that she wanted them to write about only one portrait, not several. She'd written about four portraits. And even though Mary had said some good things about her work, she'd been overcome at the thought of having to recast the paper from scratch.

Well, if Amelia was "highly labile," as Elaine's husband would say when the stormy reaction of one of their daughters drove him to take refuge in his neurologist persona, no one in the class conveyed the pain, the frustration of being asked to think and write more (and more vocally) than Kate, her *enfant sauvage*. If Elaine were to have summed up Kate's indictment of the class so far—and, actually, she already knew that the class was Kate's favorite—it would go something like this: I don't like this book, so I don't care to write about it. All of this has nothing to do with my actual abilities (though, at the same time, I'm covering up for the fact that my abilities may not be very great).

Kate's anger seemed projected not just onto Fischer, Revere, and writing papers, but also onto the other students. In Kate's view, the other students were not participating in the class in the way she would have liked. To her, critical thinking meant sharp dialogue—maybe some idea of arguing she'd picked up from talk radio or television—but in a way, she was right: the other students didn't seem to respond.

Now, in October, the class felt more and more engaged in the careful spadework it took to analyze and evaluate Fischer's text. Kate wasn't part of it. She'd lean her chair back against the wall, her eyes closing sometimes, and seem to reject, to disbelieve everything, projecting an attitude of boredom and anger.

Maybe it had started back in September, when they began their peer editing. Kate had apologized to her group for her scribbled first draft, written, she told them, at one o'clock in the morning. Mary, with that silent smile that seemed more and more like camouflage, was examining a thin ring of green stones on her left thumb. Then she stifled a sneeze, and Kate was the only one to react, whispering "Bless you." Professor Ambacher's voice was wafting in from next door—*Now why would they do that? It's still a declaration of war . . .*—when Kate got her comment sheet from Jeremy, and started to read it. She looked concerned, but also smiled. At that moment, almost as though someone had given a signal, the class started to hum with a number of quiet conversations. And then Kate said, "Mary had a really good essay. It kept my interest more than this book." This remark made everyone at her table laugh. "I want more coffee," Kate then said, more to the universe than to anyone in particular.

And then Mary, as though making her own quiet effort to

connect, said, "When I wrote my essay, I just hated the whole thing—Bostonians, the people of Boston."

And Lee said, "That's not your fault; that's the book."

That seemed to bring Kate into the center of the conversation, especially when Amelia said, "I'm like Kate. This doesn't interest me at all. It took me three days to write this stupid paper, because none of the three topics interested me. I would rather have picked my own. There are more interesting things in here you could write about."

"Jeremy got so much stuff out of this paper," said Kate. "I don't know where he found it."

"He's just such a positive person," said Amelia.

"I'm very high about myself when I'm writing," said Kate, "because that's what I want to spend the rest of my time doing, but it just kind of sucks. It's not as lively as what I like to write."

"Yeah, tell me about it," said Amelia. "It's because you don't like the subject, you don't like the book. No sex in it. There's the petticoat. She took her woolen underwear off to wrap around the oar."

"We're making Jeremy blush," said May.

Jeremy, wool cap off, but face looking warm nevertheless, might have been blushing. "I'd like to use more descriptive words," he said.

"That's all you have to say?" asked Lee.

Elaine had come over to them then. Kate and Amelia were discussing their jobs. "I can't get out of work," Kate was saying. "I manage a restaurant."

"That's my job," said Amelia. "Foot Locker, all the way."

Could she get them back on track? "Did this group come up with any issues?" she asked.

"I had a hard time writing this paper," said Amelia, "because I had very little interest."

"Me, too," said Kate eagerly, pleased, it seemed, to have Amelia leading the charge, a temporary ally in her hostility to the work she was being asked to do, work that came hard to her.

"Did you brainstorm it here? What topics might work?"

"Make something up," said Kate to Amelia. "You're a writer."

"No," Elaine Beilin said, "that's a serious question. How about calling me? You can also call someone in the group."

"It didn't motivate her," said May.

That was back when Kate had started to wear the heavy eye liner and the carefully applied reddish-toned lipstick, and Elaine could remember seeing her sitting on the front steps when she'd arrive in the morning. She had come to think of this as Kate's outpost, where she used her smoking to keep herself from going inside where the other students were probably chatting in the classroom.

"Nobody can possibly be that brave," Kate said in class that day. They were looking at the scene where Paul Revere is detained by the British. Rosalind had been wondering how they could know whether Revere had really spoken up so bravely to the British—or had later invented the dialogue.

No one answered. "We have to rely on Revere's truthfulness," Elaine Beilin explained. "But we've already seen how things got changed, revised from the draft version of his deposition to the final version, so there is no ultimate way of telling that story. History has to bow to the pressures of how Paul Revere wants to present himself. And then Fischer comes along and we have to evaluate if Fischer has drawn an accurate portrait of Revere's character. Which words, Phoebe, seem to support your sense that Paul Revere is bravely undeterred in his mission?"

Phoebe ummmed for a moment. "I just kind of gathered it," said Phoebe. "He never said 'I am determined, I will not be stopped.'"

"Good, but what did he say? We really need words here."

"'I will tell the truth,'" said Phoebe, reading from Fischer. "'I am not afraid.'" She looked up from the book. "A person who was intimidated would maybe not feel as strong or be able to tell the truth," she said. "The fact that he said straight out, 'I'm going to tell the truth,' pretty much says that he really won't be swayed."

"Um hum," Elaine said a couple of times, nodding as Phoebe was talking.

Just then Lee spoke up, and after she read aloud some of the dialogue from the book, she shrugged. "He could have been, 'Oh my God, please,' but then written down something else."

"But remember, there were witnesses," Elaine said. "You yourself pointed out that we have another deposition, so we've got someone else who said what went on. That's why we can conclude that Fischer uses this. But Lee you've raised such an interesting point about the novel, drama, history, whatever—we're always having to deal with a narrator who's telling the story. What kind of sentences is Paul Revere given to using? What style?"

Elaine let the question hang there a moment, and that's when Kate said, "Nobody can possibly be that brave. Obnoxious."

That changed the silence. Before, they'd been in the thick of sorting things; now Kate's angry rejection seemed to have splatted down over the page, covering it with tar.

"Well, we've gone over only a few of his statements today," Elaine said. Then she took a few breaths. Generally, she knew it was best to be thick-skinned, not to take personally a student's biased rejection of a character or a text. But sometimes—and this was going to be one of those times—it was best to confront the student's distortion. "Kate, I have to disagree that he's obnoxious."

"I think I'd be a little snide," said Rosalind. "He really does know a lot more than the British think he does."

And then George said, from underneath the bill of his Braves cap, "He's in a no-lose situation, because if they're going to shoot him, why go crying like a baby?"

"He could lose his life?" said Claudia.

Then Rosalind, Amelia, George, and, of course, Kate, started to argue about Paul Revere's bravery.

"OK," Elaine said. "Here's what I'd like you to do. Take this little discussion going on about Paul Revere. Everyone take a little time to write down an idea, something that might become a thesis. I'd like you to take sides in that argument." She walked around handing out the assignment sheet for the next paper, Analysis and Persuasion, with suggestions for doing well and detailed criteria. "But look at words," she told them. "Weigh them, trying to see how words work in context. The more detailed your analysis, the stronger the case you make."

But Kate hadn't gotten it. Next week she still seemed so hostile—referring to "the Stamp Act, and all that baloney"—that Elaine couldn't tell whether she was referring to the futility of the Stamp Act (because it raised no revenue for the British) or to the baloney of trying to analyze the way history is written, the way it comes to us. On that day, Elaine herself hung fire—that's what she usually preferred, to let the class discussion itself correct the excesses or idiosyncrasies of a student's interpretation. And that approach paid off, because that was the day Kate was set straight by the class. Kate had read aloud a passage in Fischer that made no sense to her. Lord Percy, Kate read aloud, "was appalled by what he took to be the narrowness of New England ways, and genuinely shocked by the mobbings that he witnessed in Massachusetts. His outrage was not that of a modern liberal, but of an eighteenth-century gentleman who came to regard the people of Boston as a race of money-grubbing hypocritical bullies and cowards, utterly devoid of honor, candor, and courage" (237).

The part Kate couldn't process was the way Fischer combined "bullies and cowards." In her view, you couldn't "use those two words next to each other; they totally contradict themselves."

Then Greta had said, "Don't cowards generally pick on people who are weaker than they are?"

Later, when they were meeting in their group Jeremy asked Kate, "Were you a bully or a coward in high school?"

"Bully," said Kate, without hesitation.

By the time the class met again, Elaine had read over at home the students' assessments of how the class was going so far. Fourteen out of the fifteen students who'd filled out their sheets said that the short written assignments she'd been giving in addition to the papers had helped them look more closely at Fischer's words. "One person," she told the class, deliberately looking off at some neutral space along the wall, "said the assignments were not helpful at all."

She knew that that person was Kate. Kate had made a special point of coming up to her after they'd written their assessments and showing to her just which sheet was hers. Elaine looked around, scanning the room. "Anybody got any ideas about what could make the class better?"

And that's when Kate threw out her challenge to the group. "Will someone *argue* with me?" She'd been leaning her chair back against the wall, as she often did, but now she was leaning forward over the table, looking at the other students with a crooked smile that seemed to suggest that she was half-joking, but underneath fully exasperated. "I like to argue, but nobody will argue with me."

This was pretty rare, actually—for someone to turn to the group and hold a mirror up to them. Elaine was worried for Kate, who didn't need to do anything more to make herself feel lonely on this campus. "Kate," she said, "it would help if you'd show people *how* to respond to you." The room was silent then—dead silent, almost as though people were breathing shallowly, moving less. "You have to learn to use the 'because clause'—you know, 'I don't like this *because*.'"

Elaine looked around the room again, and finally at Kate, who seemed to have taken that in with a slight nod, pacified, perhaps, or—for the moment, at least—not inclined to say anything further.

The mid-October morning of Elaine's scheduled conference with Kate has turned out to be gray and a little misty, but the trees outside Elaine's ground-floor office are still mainly green. As usual, her desk is loaded with papers, her glasses, a tea cup, a Thermos. There's a picture of Toni Morrison on the wall above her and a small, subtly colored transfer print given to her by Jim Eng, one of the professors in the Art Department. Elaine is wearing her blue blazer, with a picture-pin on the lapel. The pin, made by a woman friend of hers back in Needham, is an image of a Native American princess. When Kate comes in Elaine swivels her chair over from the computer in front of the window back to her desk and turns away from the clutter. Before conferences, while she's thinking about a multitude of other things, she always seems to find part of her brain in which to form a strategy. Knowing what a student ought to be told is much simpler than figuring out how to tell her. Maybe Kate likes a debate because she has a certain brashness—rare here—a willingness to speak out. But none of her spunk will ever get her anywhere unless she knows how to back it up with information and reasoning. Then, too, she'll have to learn to come across to people as reasonable, not just angry.

Kate has on her black leather jacket with the silver studs. She carries a black leather bookbag. Her glasses, which are riding on top of her head, are covered with tiny beads of mist, and strands of her hair are wet. Her carefully applied makeup, including thick eyeliner and lipstick, doesn't succeed in making her look older or more sophisticated. Her large eyes and the slightly protruding upper teeth that never had braces actually make her face more unpredictable and appealing—as though she's not quite old enough for her adult teeth.

"These aren't typed," says Elaine when Kate puts her folder of papers into her lap.

"I write in longhand first," Kate explains. "And then, when I have time, I go to the high school to use their word processor." She watches Elaine picking up the papers and pausing briefly over some. "My mother will buy us a laptop and printer for Christmas."

"Is it right," says Elaine, still glancing through the folder, "that I don't have some of the assignments?" She turns to her green grade register on her desk. "I don't have the fifth and sixth. You really need to stay on top of the assignments. If you do, the practice will get you in the state of mind to do critical analysis."

"I probably have them in my papers," says Kate, looking down at the folder in Elaine's lap.

"Well, so if you can get me that self-assessment . . ."

"I'm hoping to get it done this weekend. I'm going to Lexington Green with my mom." Elaine Beilin seems to smile a little at this, though it doesn't change the basic expression of concern on her face.

Elaine asks her if she's yet had the time to go to the writing center for her first tutoring session.

"No, but I'm doing it next Friday," says Kate.

"So," says Elaine, as though she's refraining from pointing out that since this is Thursday, next Friday will be eight days from now, "have you worked on revising any of these essays?"

"No," says Kate. "I'm going insane."

"Well, I really think you should work on the third essay," says Elaine, "because that's the one with the most potential." She asks Kate to read her the first paragraph out loud.

As Kate reads, she finds out that she's left out some words. "Oops, I don't know what my sentences were supposed to be." She squints at the paper a moment, as though it's a strange object. "Not the best thing I've ever written."

Elaine laughs. "I would guess not."

"That kind of sucks," Kate decides, letting the paper fall to her lap.

"Who was your chosen audience?"

"Anyone who was reading."

"No, c'mon, you can do better than that. Someone who reads *The Gatepost? The Millis News?*"

And here Kate shakes her head, as if she's her own haggard parent hearing about her wayward daughter. "I have no idea."

"Well, that's why I put that as number one," Elaine explains, pointing to her own comments at the end of the paper. "What I hear is confusion about your audience. Part of the paragraph is very formal. 'The claim that has been stated in the above paragraph,' and so on, is a kind of classroom writing, but part is more personal and informal."

Kate is smiling a little, but her face seems less animated, almost pained.

"Can you think of particular people in class that you could direct this essay to?" When Kate doesn't answer, she continues. "Fischer's telling the story created problems for you as a reader of history."

"Kind of, yeah. To be totally honest, I didn't really like it." Kate's expression still doesn't change, almost as though she's waiting to see how her professor will react.

"But your responsibility to your reader is not just to say 'I don't like it,' fold your hands, and say 'talk among yourselves.' Your responsibility is to say I don't like it *because*. I know you can do it. When I heard your group pushing you the other day, you had something to say. '*Why* don't I enjoy it?', ask yourself."

Now Kate's expression modulates into something more mischievous, a grin that seems to imply that she's going to shock or at least discomfit Elaine with news she doesn't want to hear. "Rosalind is pretty much the only one who says she disagrees with what I said."

"Well, Amelia just wrote a very strong essay on the strengths of the book," Elaine says. Her voice sounds reasonable, patient, just a little quavery with the effort of remaining so. "Amelia did make the point that there was some bias in the book." She then tries to persuade Kate to "write the paper for Rosalind. How would you do that? You might want to jot some things down here."

Kate's taken off her leather jacket. She works for a few minutes, commenting on this passage from Fischer:

> As Paul Revere stumbled through a maze of burial mounds and sunken holes, perhaps he had a moment to think about the men and women whose mortal remains lay beneath him in the ground. Inconceivable as it may seem to their degenerate descendants, the Whig leaders of revolutionary America often had these periods of reflection. They took a long view of their temporal condition, in a way that Americans rarely do today. "Think of your forefathers!" John

> Quincy Adams urged his contemporaries, "Think of your posterity!" (175)

Then she reads what she's written aloud. "I think what I wrote was right. If you were walking through a cemetery to see if Hancock and Adams were, excuse my French, bitching and moaning at each other, would you really think of such things? It's totally unlogical."

"Well he does say 'perhaps.' I want you to be clear on what you're objecting to. I have no beef about what you're objecting to, but it's how you build your argument. He's saying 'maybe.' What's wrong with a historian saying 'maybe?' What should he have said?"

"Nothing. I can't put what I'm trying to say into words."

"Well, what you said in the paper was, 'Why not write, "Paul Revere was thinking about Adams and Hancock and how to deal with them if they hadn't left?"' But Fischer's point is that Paul Revere thinks differently than we do, that he's so imbued with seventeenth- and eighteenth-century texts, which were all about mortality. That's really part of his argument, that Paul Revere really did inhabit a different world. I was surprised you didn't jump at that rather gratuitous comment about 'degenerate descendants.'"

"To tell you the truth, I didn't know what 'degenerate' means. This is really sad, isn't it?"

"No," says Elaine, undeflected. "If we knew what everything meant we wouldn't need dictionaries."

"No, I mean that I have to count my ABCs to look things up."

Elaine gets Kate to read aloud the passage in Fischer.

"So," Elaine asks her. "Who is Fischer alluding to when he says 'degenerate descendants?' Who are their descendants?"

"Puritans," says Kate.

"Who are the descendants?" asks Elaine again, without astonishment or impatience, but with a certain grave alertness, like a physician noting a limb that may be broken.

"Parents?"

"No." Elaine leans forward as Kate reads from the dictionary. "So who are these?"

"His children," says Kate. When she gets no immediate response, she tries again. "The Whig leaders? You're losing me."

"I'm simply asking, who's Fischer talking about in that sentence?"

"Americans today."

"Yes, so Fischer says Americans today are their descendants. So he's saying readers of this book, even."

"That makes a lot more sense now."

"OK, so what do you say now?"

"It's better than I thought it was."

Elaine laughs. "He's using your kind of language, Kate. So here's a historian who's not saying 'Paul Revere went through a graveyard thinking about his British captors,' but 'Paul Revere went through the graveyard thinking in a way his degenerate descendants wouldn't ever dream of.'"

"I'm totally shocked," says Kate, "that he said something I kind of agree with. I mean, kinda, kinda. Well, I don't care," she says, but then she seems to recall something about herself. "No, it's wrong to say I don't care. It happened, and without it a lot of things wouldn't have happened."

"What is it that you like about this statement?"

"Negative!" says Kate, without hesitation, almost gleefully.

"Do you have the idea that people today are not very reflective? Can you talk about that a little for me? What are people interested in today?"

"Themselves," Kate answers quickly. "How to put other people down and further themselves, no matter who they have to step on?"

"Sounds like you have some interesting stories to tell," Elaine says, nodding, considering. "We'll leave that for another time. Sounds as though there was something you liked in this quotation. But you kind of missed the point about the paragraph when you wrote about it, didn't you? You need to say, 'Why did I quote this?' and take the time, even though I know you're pressed for time, to look these words up in the dictionary. That's what makes things boring. You disconnected with this guy." Here Elaine pauses a moment. "Look. You've got a very good brain. You can get by by making wisecrack remarks. But I think you can do tremendously good work if you take the time to say, 'OK what is he thinking?' Because you can still be critical, but by starting the process of saying 'Why am I critical?' you embark on a discovery of yourself. What are my values, what do I like to read? What moves me? What appeals? What bores me? I'm not saying every part of this book is fascinating. There's some part of every book where our eyes glaze over. But you dismiss things too quickly."

Kate stares steadily and seriously at Elaine, who asks her to read the passage again.

"Now when he says 'Paul Revere stumbled,' that's part of what you think of as storytelling. That's what I expected you to jump all over. 'Wait a minute! How does he know?'" Her voice assumes a tone of mock-protest. "Now that's where it seems to me you could write something interesting about—what would we call it?—narrative license? You see what I'm saying?"

"Yeah," Kate says, a little doubtful.

"It's the forest and trees thing," says Elaine gently. "You've picked out some trees, but you didn't see the forest." When Kate nods, she continues. "Let's go back to your introduction. Can you rough out a few sentences for me about what you'd want to get across to the reader? And you may want to do a little pro and con here. Just start writing."

"It's the thinking that's the problem here," says Kate, more than sobered, maybe actually saddened with herself.

Though Elaine Beilin's desk is loaded with a clutter of papers, her officemate—who is on leave—has left her desk neat, with a glass-covered blotter, a pile of colored paper clips in a clamshell box, an "in-bin" with just a few papers, an electric pencil sharpener, a digital clock, and a box of pink tissues. As Kate writes, Elaine is musing about something, staring at Professor Thomas's desk. She writes a brief note to herself. Kate reads three sentences that clearly describe how Fischer's writing that Paul Revere "stumbled" brings the narrative alive, but changes the history. She looks up from her paper.

"You have to really logically work this through," Elaine insists. Her voice is calm. "You have to decide whether the book is *filled* with these kinds of sentences, things that are pure imagination."

Kate seems to be listening but doesn't answer.

"Do a data hunt. Look for three or four representative sentences on that model." She assumes a Kate sort of voice—or the voice of Kate when she's feeling brash and defiant, which isn't now. "This is what's bugging me, there are so many sentences like that one. But it may be," she says, returning to her own voice, "that you won't be able to find many of them, so maybe something else is at issue. Maybe you can find fifteen pages that move the book over from historical narrative to some sort of fiction. You don't have to rant. You can find evidence. I don't know what you're going to find. I will be *extremely* interested in what you are going to find. Is this characteristic or is this exceptional?"

"OK," says Kate, and nods.

"Is it an important event, going through a graveyard?"

"No," she says.

"Can you think of a really important event?"

"When he got captured."

"Great. Go look at that chapter and see what kind of writing Fischer's doing there. It's really a matter of analyzing evidence, to see if you can make your case stick. Now that's the place where I remember him using a lot of Revere's words. You can talk about what's legitimate and what's fictional. I'd really like you to do this revision soon—while you're still thinking about it. But I also want you to be fair, Kate. Say that what I've discovered, the more I look at this, is that Fischer and I may be on the same wavelength. Tell what you think is good about the book, because it doesn't necessarily detract from your negative criticism. Somehow, I know, in your hectic schedule you need to make some time to do this sort of thing, because you're selling yourself short if you don't. I really want you to do well, because I have an inkling that you can. Do you have that—" She stops now because it's beginning to look as if Kate's eyes are welling up.

"I'm thinking of dropping out," she says, and it tears out of her like a sob. "I don't like people here. I don't like what I'm doing."

"I'm sorry about that," says Elaine. "Sometimes you have to figure out how to make a positive experience out of something negative. One way to do this is to try to shape up the discussion in the class."

At this point, Kate is crying so openly, her eyes overflowing, her face red, that Elaine begins to search through her drawer for some tissues until she recalls seeing some on her officemate's desk. She hands her one, and Kate is wiping her eyes on the pink tissue.

"I'd be really sorry if you dropped out," says Elaine. "What can you do to make this experience more positive for yourself?"

"I can't think of anything," says Kate. "My history teacher, I just want to kill him. He doesn't even know my name."

"Sometimes it does help to go talk to a teacher," Elaine says. "Even if he seems unapproachable."

"He started talking about his coffee cup today, and about the Sixties and Seventies and how it was a waste of time." She sounds at a loss, disgusted.

"We have to find a way to be in the game," says Elaine. "I noticed your body language the other day, leaning way back, resting against the wall. Like I'm not part of this."

"No," says Kate. She's not crying anymore, but the tissue is wadded into a clump the size of a plum. "I was comfortable."

"Well, I'm glad to hear that." She pauses a moment, as if deciding whether Kate can take any more self-scrutiny just now. "My sense is that you're saying 'I'm not committed to this.' If you are, though, not only I but other people and the class will be out there to meet you. If you said, 'I want to do this work,' you could be in my office every single day and work on it. But if you're sitting in class writing a poem, it's really going to seem boring."

Kate is just nodding now, her appearance almost back to normal, except for slightly reddened eyes.

"I'm really encouraging you not to drop out. You'll find this is why you came to college. You can correct me on this."

"I'm uncomfortable around the people. I couldn't wait to get out of high school, so I wouldn't have to be around people like that. Everybody's stereotypical," she says, but then shakes her head. "Not as much in our class. But the people on the lawn, they kind of give you these strange looks. This guy on the front stairs here—he was sitting in my seat, too—gave me this dirty look, like I was a leaf on the ground. OK, did I breathe wrong? I've wanted to come here since 7th grade, and now I don't want to be here."

"Well, first semester is really hard," says Elaine, "and maybe nothing is going to live up to those expectations."

"That's the reason I came here," says Kate. "The best English department in the state." This comes out so emphatically it sounds like a declaration.

"Well, I'm glad to hear it," says Elaine, finding the compliment pleasing, but somehow funny, too. "I want you to have a good old jaw with your adviser. You have all the makings of having a really positive experience here. You can be that person you want to be. Rosalind wrote the same thing, on that sheet I gave out the first day, about wanting to teach so she could do better than some of her teachers in high school. You've got my interest right away." She mentions the counseling service, too—how it's free. But Kate was in counseling at a miserable point in middle school when she was self-destructive, talking about suicide (though not really planning it) and writing poem after poem she wouldn't show to her mother. Her mother set up counseling for her. But that was then. She doesn't want to go back to that, doesn't feel she needs to.

When Kate's got her leather jacket on, and has left, Elaine just sits in her swivel chair a few moments. The major issue, she's convinced, isn't that Kate is rejecting the text so much as that Kate isn't allowing herself the time she needs to read it. Education takes time, and Kate's not giving herself the time. She'll need—if she can accept the need, and the help—both the writing center *and* the counseling center, because it's really a question about her identity that's upsetting her. And though she's very pressed for time, she also doesn't have the discipline. That's a hard lesson in coming here: you have to have more discipline because the workload is heavier, and you have to give up things.

The doorway seems empty for the moment, and Kate's chair has returned to being simply a chair. Elaine turns to her Shakespeare syllabus to see which group is due to report later this morning. But Kate does not leave her mind right away. She needs to talk to her about where she gets her strong desire to be here, what her reading has been, what's moving her. Essentials of Writing may not be a great course for eliciting that, especially this section, because of her choice of text. All of this may be very different from what Kate imagined herself doing. Earlier in the semester, when Kate was talking about working forty hours, her appearance was a lot plainer, she looked exhausted, her hair was kind of messy, and then, at some point, Elaine remembers looking twice at her because she got all glammed up. Perhaps that's a good sign. Anyway, this conference has been such an instructive thing. That wisecracking kid with a chip on her shoulder is jelly. Confidence 101, she thinks, not for the first time. That's what they ought to call this course.

5. EXPOSURE

SITTING IN THE dark with her Essentials of Writing students, watching the slides of the Copley portraits of these elegant and substantial figures from the past, Elaine Beilin is thinking of all she has planned for class today, and that the talk by Doris Birmingham, their guest speaker, might be running a little long. On the screen, with her two projectors, Professor Birmingham from the college's art department is showing them Copley's portraits of American tradesmen and merchants, sitting stiffly, unsmiling, in borrowed finery, resting their elbows on borrowed furniture. The painter, an autodidact, was trying to do his best to copy the British portraits he'd seen only in engraved versions, she tells them. Americans are the ultimate self-made people, yet only in Paul Revere's portrait did Copley depict a man in work clothes. Revere is shown with a silver pitcher that reflects each finger of the hand that made it, that *grasps* it—to use Rosalind's word—the same picture that's on the cover of Fischer's book. Doris Birmingham, standing behind her projectors, her face lit from below, is telling them that Copley—the American Copley—was an artist who was interested in painting what he saw. He had no hierarchy of interests, according to Professor Birmingham. Everything in the picture is painted with exactly the same intensity: fruit has the same detail as a face, as a chair. "In European painting at that time, though," she continues, "there's an awful lot of invention. There's this fluffy kind of painting; there's a certain freedom, a razzle-dazzle devil-may-care manner in the way an artist paints a dress or some curtains."

As she listens, Elaine Beilin forgets for a moment her constant anxiety about not having enough class time for what she's planned. Mainly, she's remembering her art history classes and how much she loves what art historians do. Most of the students, she guesses, have never taken a tour with a docent in a museum; and few, if any, studied art history in high school. Nor, for that matter, have many of them been taken to the theater or to concerts.

When she was growing up in Canada, her uncles listened to the Metropolitan Opera radio broadcasts sponsored by Texaco on Saturday afternoons. In high school, she took operas out of the library and copied the librettos. She knows that if she had to name one person who has shown her simply and purely what a teacher has to do, she'd name Mr. McDonald, her eighth-grade music teacher. He'd been slender and worried-looking (he'd looked, actually, a lot like the official pictures of King George VI), but no one had tormented him, despite his shyness. For an hour every Monday and Friday, he'd enchanted and amazed them—getting them to sing opera. Asked once to write about a teacher she remembered, she'd picked him. In opera, she'd written, she found "the good, the bad, and the risqué." She found "loyalty, betrayal, and sensational love poetry." But she also found "complicated worlds in which virtue was not likely to be victorious . . . and very few happy endings." Only in eleventh-grade French class did she discover novels "that could match the intensity and the heat inhabiting any opera."

But then there was the time when she and her family were coming as immigrants from England to Canada on a steamship, traveling, she guessed, third class, and she'd sneaked up to the first-class movie theater and seen Laurence Harvey's *Romeo and Juliet.* To this day she can remember every moment of that film, though she was just seven at the time. With her short brown hair, wide face, and intelligent eyes, she must have looked a little like Anne Frank—impish, precociously wise, taking everything in. One moment of exposure had changed her life. She'd never forgotten that movie, perhaps because she'd known she wasn't supposed to be there. Indeed, maybe her whole education was like that.

For Elaine, school is where the self is formed, and learning is just as likely to run contrary to the grain of parents' wishes for a son or daughter as it is to be sanctioned by them. Perhaps that's why she takes her teaching as seriously as she does—and why she attributes some of the students' difficulties to their parents' not understanding how much time it will take to succeed. She wants to civilize these students, of course, for all the well-known practical reasons, though when she hears herself say that, it immediately evokes shades of British India. But, much more than that, she wants to do what Mr. McDonald did for her.

Elaine watches her students as they stare at a Reynolds portrait set beside an American Copley. One thing versus another. Two projectors: the minimum any art historian would need to make comparisons.

Now Doris Birmingham is describing the sad, successful conclusion of Copley's long life. He married a Tory woman whose father owned the tea that was dumped during the Boston Tea Party. He couldn't stand the thought of an approaching war in this backwater of an English colony, and he had a strong desire to go to England to learn to become a better painter. In England, indeed, Copley changed—he soon learned how to make what he wanted to see rather than to match what he saw. Doris Birmingham shows the students a portrait of Mrs. Seymour Fort, in which there's an impressionistic spontaneity in the painting of the dress, drapery, background. "In the end," she concludes, "Copley was very proud of achieving what he achieved, but died a very sad man in England, and regretted leaving America. He thought his American works were better. You'll probably find quite a lot of writing comparing this, how they shake down in terms of quality. And now I have to stop," she says.

The still-darkened room has returned to what—even now, well into October—is still its default mode of profound, embarrassed silence. These students, Elaine can only hope, will talk more toward the end of the semester. Still, when she asks for questions, there aren't any. Patience, she tells herself. All she can do is to move on in her usual efficient, fast-paced way. Her younger daughter Rachel's bat mitzvah is coming up in less than a month. "The reticent cannot learn; the hot-tempered cannot teach." That's what it says on the very first page of the prayer book, a quotation from *Pirkay Avot, The Wisdom of the Fathers.* She wishes the students would be less reticent, but she's schooled herself to be calm about it, too, rarely losing her temper.

Kate, whose mood seems to have bounced back since their conference, asks about the "formulas" that Copley followed. She seems to be inquiring about just how much of a hack he had to be, always putting in the same tables, the same bureaus, the same lace bonnets. Rosalind puts her hand up, too. She's curious to know what Professor Birmingham makes of the portrait of Margaret Gage.

"She's kind of leaning and dreaming," Professor Birmingham observes, "a convention that comes out of English portraiture. It comes down to gender perceptions: Young women were supposed to be kind of simpering and dreamy. It's an early form of romanticism, suggesting the feelings, the inner life of the subject. There's a whole series of—we call these things conventions, or motifs." The room is still lit only by the bright rectangles the slide projector is casting on the blank, white wall. Doris Birmingham's and Elaine's voices are coming out of the darkness from behind the students.

"Is it also a convention," Elaine asks, "that, as in nineteenth-century photography, people didn't want to be painted smiling?"

"Well, that was partly practical," Doris Birmingham explains. She means that subjects were told not to smile lest they blur the images, which required long exposures. "But, yes, you wanted to present yourself in a really dignified way. I can't think of any smiling portraits."

"The *Mona Lisa* isn't really a smile?" says Elaine Beilin.

"Yeah, it's a—"

"—smirk."

Doris Birmingham pauses. No other hands are going up. Both professors wait, but there's no point in the two of them continuing to conduct a dialog. "Perhaps I should leave these here," says Doris Birmingham, referring to her two projectors on their cart. "If I try to move them now, people will get all discombobulated." She squeezes around the corner of the table to leave.

But before this talk fades from her students' minds, Elaine wants to see if they can draw a connection between the way Doris compares pictures and the way they've been comparing texts. She snaps on the fluorescent lights and the room seems, at first, bleached, almost colorless. "Take a few minutes to write down anything you heard that you think is similar to what you might do in textual studies," she tells her class. Then she goes out, and it's quiet in May 213, the seminar room on the second floor, with its large gray square table about twice the size of a ping-pong table, a table so big that papers getting passed over the center sometimes get stranded. A student might have to crawl over the table to retrieve them.

Before long Elaine comes back into the room, sits down at the end of the table opposite the door, and watches her students writing. Jeremy, hat off by now, pulls back from the table, musing. Mary, still one of the quietest students, but one whose sweet, responsive smile continues to make it clear she's engaged in everything that's happening, seems now to be in a brown study, eyes saddened by something. Claudia has wound up her waist-length blond hair into a kind of knot held by a large plastic clip at the back of her head. Max, who is left-handed, writes steadily, deliberately, slowly. May and Francesca sit side by side, as always. Marion, whose contact lenses are in today, making the pupils of her brown eyes seem enlarged, is glancing around, her expression sharp and alert. As Mary begins to write, her face softens. The sun is very bright again, even though the blinds are still halfway down. A shaft of light is striking Colleen's red notebook, kindling it.

This is Wednesday, and the final drafts of the papers are due in Professor Beilin's mail box by Friday. "Has everyone got something to help you go on with revisions?" she asks the class. "You can also contact each other, or contact me. So before Friday, if you want, come to my office." Some chairs begin to move. It's almost 10:15. Belinda starts to leave, but then looks up at the clock on the wall—not that it's ever any help, since it usually seems to be about six and three quarter hours fast—and sits down again. "You could help me put the tables back," Elaine says. They've been doing group work, splitting the large, gray table into the six smaller tables from which it's assembled.

May stands up to help shove the table. Her ID and cafeteria cards are hanging on a long strap around her neck. "You're slow," she says to Francesca.

"I'm usually last," Francesca agrees. "I'm going to go home and have a sleep. Everybody tells me, don't start saying 'home' to mean the dorm."

"Is this your coat?" Elaine asks.

"She's asleep," says May.

"I wasn't going to mention it," says Elaine, "but I came to school the other day with one blue shoe and one black shoe. I haven't done that since I had babies. Then I never knew what I looked like."

May grins at her, and Francesca smiles her sadder, more private smile. Soon the room is emptying out, and Elaine's alone, gathering her papers. She thinks about Mary's lisp, and how much less pronounced it was today. She must have a way of controlling it. And Jeremy, she thinks. Jeremy! What happened to him today? He took his hat off! He's here! He's present! And then she thinks about that particular moment, near the end of class, when the room was humming with their voices, and she was looking over at the group near the door. Rosalind was working with Phoebe, and confident, articulate Andy, from New York City, was talking to Susie—dutiful, cheerful Susie—about her paper. And she was thinking, *Do you know? Do any of you know how beautiful you are?*

When the field-trip papers come in, she finds herself giving the highest grade to Rosalind, who went up to Strawberry Banke, an historic district in Portsmouth, New Hampshire, and had very little good to say about it. In her essay "Strawberry Banke: A Journey Back In Time Or An Egregious Waste of Money?" Rosalind makes an argument and supports it. "The overwhelming majority of the staff was surprisingly indifferent, and came across as being mediocre in their knowledge and not very helpful at all," she writes at the end of her first paragraph. "The effects of the sites mediocrity also came across strongly in the atmosphere and physical condition of the houses and the land."

"Clear thesis, strongly stated," writes Elaine Beilin in the margin.

Rosalind's prose is stilted, to be sure, and in her overreaching—she seems to take such pleasure in the word "egregious!"—she may lose her grip on small details of grammar and usage and can be wordy. Elaine corrects "the effects of the sites mediocrity" to "the mediocrity of the site," but doesn't hold this awkwardness against Rosalind, understanding that it may well be the result of her attempt to find some higher level of language that she feels will enable her to assume the authority needed to criticize. Perhaps at some later point in her life she will feel secure enough to say "shabby" or "unkempt"—forceful Anglo-Saxon adjectives. For now, Elaine merely corrects the most awkward places as she reads primarily to see how Rosalind has structured and supported her argument.

It isn't as though these students haven't been anywhere before—though most of them have never traveled widely—but, more important for her purpose in this assignment, Elaine wonders if they have ever felt that they had a right to be critics of what they saw, backing up their strong opinions with evidence and details? How many times has she overheard a student's near-inarticulate reaction, "it sucked," followed by a shrug. She finds it interesting that they don't seem to approve of much of what they see. They can't screw up at their own jobs (lest they get fired and have no money for, say, car insurance), so they expect others to do their jobs well also. For example, Rosalind describes the woman in eighteenth-century costume who seemed to know little about the history of the neighborhood:

> She was the first I encountered who was less than helpful and enthusiastic. She looked grimly at me when I began to question her about the location of any houses that might be relevant to the American Revolution. Upon my reminding her in what years the Revolution took place, she told me, much to my disappointment, that there were only two houses in the whole lot that would be pertinent. I then went on to question her as to where Fort William and Mary was. Her glazed eyes looked upon me with contempt as she did not know to what I was referring. The fort is a historical site from the Revolution and is still accessible today, as I came to find out later.

Upon my reminding her in what years the Revolution took place . . . Rosalind has been reading eighteenth century depositions, like the ones Paul Revere gave concerning his famous ride, and she sometimes echoes eighteenth-century syntax. Well, someday she'll settle into her own style. But, most important for Elaine, Rosalind has given evidence for her claim about the mediocrity of the staff. The two gentlemen, she concluded "were the only two worthy souls there that day." *Worthy souls!* The grade, despite the need for much line editing by Elaine, a rarely given A-. (In her self-assessment, which comes in a few days later, Rosalind has written that "anything less than an 'A' disappoints me. I am just now beginning to figure out how to balance school, work and my fiancé.")

In the "Suggestions for doing well" sheet she hands out for each assignment, Elaine tries to make her evaluation standards as transparent as possible for the students. She doesn't want a mere narrative or travelogue; she wants a main idea, just as though the students were writing a critical essay about a text. Item 1: "You'll need to use your observing eye to provide supporting details and images, and your selectivity to include only those that help to convey your *main point* about the place." Item 5: "Write a thesis (main idea) that states clearly and explicitly what you think the historical significance of the place is or what its main effect on the visitor is." Indeed, perhaps because they must argue a thesis, some of the essays, including Rosalind's, are far more critical than they might otherwise be. Greta, for example, visited Paul Revere's house in Boston's North End:

> Cobble stone streets, the hum of tourists; Yes, we were close to Paul Revere's house. As we approached the back entrance to the home, I expected to see a well-restored and an expansive display of the belongings of this legend. I have to say that I was disappointed by the outcome. The house was very small and many of the artifacts were not those of Paul Revere's. They were either pieces resembling the time or were left behind by the previous owner. The home did have a certain out-of-this-time feel. Too bad it was not the time of Paul Revere.

She goes on to say that "the kitchen could have belonged to anybody," and that "the next room was a waste of my time" because "the room actually represented the decor of the previous owner."

Although Elaine is basically positive about this essay, she suggests in her comments that Greta could have looked harder for items that did indeed reflect Paul Revere's life ("Did you see the bed which his mother and then his children slept in?") and also that she could have reflected more on how an historic site might better give "a sense of life *lived* at the time." Elaine suspects that Greta, who has recently been expelled from her dorm on a few hours' notice, may not have been in a particularly appreciative mood when she went on her field trip.

Last week, a gray-haired policeman—portly, rumpled, wearing

one of those complicated belts that have so many compartments and a plastic hat protector like a kind of shower cap to keep the misty rain off—had been waiting outside the classroom. At the time, it seemed as though someone in Greta's family might have had an emergency—an accident, some sudden illness—but it later turned out that slender Greta with her tall dancer's figure, her big eyes, and her smoky voice had been brought up on assault charges by her roommate. Certainly none of this was on Elaine's mind when she made her way past the policeman. As she is trying to expose them to art, history, music, literature—what else are they exposed to?

Greta still works in the bridal shop in Norwood, her home town. "I dress women," she explains to me during our October interview. "The dresses are really big. You flip them over your head, put the women in them. Like the eighteenth century. The worst is when they lie to you about their size." Despite her wide smile and big gray eyes, it's hard for me to imagine Greta in the context of anything bridal, with the multiple earring holes along the outside of her ear, her pulled-back hair, her bitten nails, and her strong smell of tobacco.

"If I had ever had any notions of having relations with women, they would have been erased," she tells me. "Oh god, they wear g-strings and don't shave. Half of them don't wear bras. You get all excited when you see a woman who has a slip on. She came prepared."

Greta was already working at the bridal shop at sixteen. "'What bridesmaid dresses will complement this,'" they'd ask. "I didn't really care, but the work paid pretty well. I'd been working piercing people's ears, and I never got my raise, so when a girl told me about her job, $7.25 an hour, I thought, 'I'll take it.'" Greta is sure she could write a novel about the shop. "Charles, the guy that works on tuxedos? He has this fork, and keeps it on this dusty, grimy shelf. He'll eat potato salad, and then just put it back on the shelf." She cringes, but then smiles. "So disgusting. The only other guy is an ex-boxer, Mr. Mann. He goes around hitting on you. And the owners are, like, on crack or something. They don't use their real names. They're called Mark and Sonia, but their real names are Harvey and Cindy. One day I'm fixing a mannequin and they're, like, 'I'm not dealing, I'm leaving. It's a beautiful day.'"

At first Greta was expelled from the dorm for having a bong. I have to ask what that is. She does a double-take, then grins. "That's a water filtration system for use with marijuana," she explains. "And my roommate brought it to the attention of the RA," the resident adviser, an undergraduate herself. Greta explains that she didn't have any marijuana in her room, but this pipe had marijuana resin in it. "I assumed their confiscating the bong would be the end, at least till after a hearing. I didn't know I'd be kicked out that night. They were in our room for about an hour, and then later they were paging my name. Then they came back again, and said, 'You're not allowed in any residence halls.'" Greta shrugs. She seems dismayed, but also amused.

"When I was allowed back to the dorm, I asked my roommate, 'Were you the one who told on me?' She said, 'No.' She let me borrow her shirt for the prehearing conference. I didn't want to wear her shirt—I just wanted to beat her up. So I yelled at her, 'I can't believe you didn't come to me first.' I told her, 'I hope you die a horrible, miserable death.'"

After she yelled at her roommate, the campus police came back for her and escorted her to a meeting with the dorm director. Her roommate had already been to him, charging her with physical assault. "I should have nailed her when I had the chance," Greta says. According to her, the dorm director told her not to bother to explain, saying "You know what you did. You're being kicked out for the weekend." She says the explanation for all this was that she was branded a drug addict who beats people up.

"Then I had my hearing," she continues, "and got every sanction you could get. Five weeks out of the dorm. No contact with my old roommate. Disciplinary probation for the rest of the year. I had to go to the weekly alcohol-rehab group, the only person there on pot. Which made everyone laugh, because my last name is Weed. I even have to split the semester phone bill with my roommate."

To Greta's exasperation, her roommate left the dorm as well. "The dumb little wench up and left, and goes and commutes because she couldn't handle it. People were making fun of her. People found out what she did and were making fun of her. I was actually perfectly calm through the whole thing, refused to let anyone see they got the better of me. That day the campus police came to the classroom? They came to all three of my classes because someone said that I was using my ID to get into Towers and they wanted to get the sticker off my ID. I was absent that day, so people in all my classes kept saying to me, 'Did you know the cops were there?' The cop who came to my room the first night said, 'If I'd have known all this stuff would happen to you, I would have said I found the pipe in the hallway.'

"My family was psyched," she says. "My mom yelled a little bit. After they got mad at me, they got mad at the school."

"Your father, too?" I ask.

"My father didn't know. I haven't talked to him in years, since I was eleven. My mother's boyfriend didn't say anything. My mother smacked me around a little bit. I don't care. She pushed me. It wasn't like she was beating me up. I didn't blame her for it, or say it was a physical assault. She said, 'I could have come up to school with you. I could have gotten you a lawyer.' But," says Greta, "I couldn't." Greta doesn't think she would have been allowed to have a lawyer in these proceedings. "Lawyers are against the law there," she says.

Greta plans to live at home through the spring semester, taking only three classes so she can work from 3:00 till 8:30. She shrugs and smiles. "I love my mom to death, but not to live with. My family's wicked poor, anyway," she says. Right now she's getting a ride Mondays and Wednesdays with her mother's boyfriend, and on Tuesdays and Thursdays, Jen, a girl who lives in Needham, drives to Norwood to pick her up and take her to the college. "I'm waiting to hear from financial aid," she says, "so I can buy a car to get me back and forth for next semester. I'm hoping to take Shakespeare, or history."

This young woman—the only one in her family her mother thinks is trying to do something with her life—is getting good grades in Elaine's class and in her other classes as well, despite her expulsion from the dorms. She and Rosalind are in another English Department course, Approaches to Literature, and in their section the professor is stressing oral interpretation. When I visit the class, I watch Professor Mark Seiden and his friend Bob Buckley, an actor, divide groups of students into "teams," and name them for the poem they're doing. The "We Real Cool" Team performs their interpretation of a Gwendolyn Brooks poem. The blonde—who goes outside, then comes back through the door and announces the poem's title and the poet's name—has borrowed a pair of "shades" from one of the men in the class. This group is all female, all white. Other than Bob, there seem to be only two other black people in the room. Hard to imagine the girls in this group imitating the young black males, the "we" of the poem. Yet as they recite, each taking a line, the poem takes on a strange new subject:

> We real cool. We
> Left school. We . . .
> Sing sin. We
> Thin gin. We
> Jazz June. We
> Die soon.

So say these white girls, whose lives may or may not be much safer.

Despite all that's happened to Greta recently, she tells me she's hoping not to miss any more of Elaine Beilin's classes, which she always finds worthwhile. Ever since Doris Birmingham came to class, she's been thinking about art history. "That discussion had a lot to do with thinking about questions similar to the questions we're asking in literature: What does this mean, what's the tone, what era was it painted, and why was it painted that way?"

Greta is taking an Introduction to Painting course, too. "With my art class," she says, "we went to the museum, which got me thinking what art means to people. We saw the Grant Wood at the Worcester Art Museum—the show that has his version of Paul Revere's ride, by the way—and if you get really close to his work you see that it's made of lots of little dots that form into a picture. We've gone to the Boston Museum of Fine Arts several times, too, and I hadn't gone in a couple of years. I used to go with family and friends. When I saw the Copley portraits, I remember thinking it was funny that his subjects were all trying to look rich, but in the end they all looked the same. Like, the wooden table was a prop to make them look wealthy, but they all got to pose with it. Anyway, those trips broke up the monotony of day-to-day school. It brings you back to elementary, middle, and high school. Then the art historian came, and I found myself thinking, That's an interesting career. To be able to look at art, and do the same kind of criticism and research that people studying English do—that seemed really fun. I remember looking at the Paul Revere picture, the really big one on the screen, and thinking about the difference between how it looked on screen and on the cover of our book, and how important it is to see the real thing."

Marion, too, has gone to the Grant Wood exhibit in Worcester. "I always thought of art as boring and meaningless," she begins her essay. "It was always difficult for me to understand it." However, when she hears that Grant Wood's famous *American Gothic*, as well as his depiction of Paul Revere's ride, can be seen at the Worcester Art Museum—the second-largest art museum in New England, and only a few miles from her home in rural Paxton—she decides to find her way there.

She enjoys the half-hour video about the artist's life, the various books about him on display, the biographical material accompanying the versions of Wood's self-portrait, and writes that, in general, "The exhibit was well-organized and very helpful."

Her essay, though, is only moderately successful in Elaine's view:

> Marion—This essay is beginning to take shape, and if you thought of this as a draft, you could go on to fulfill its *real* potential. The first thing to do is to write a specific, explicit thesis: *define* the ways in which the show differed from your expectations—or state the ways in which your perception of art (or this kind of art) *changed.*

Unlike Rosalind, or Phoebe, or even Greta, Marion has never considered herself an A student. Though she gives Elaine Beilin no cause for any particular concern, Elaine still wishes that Marion could do better. Whatever Marion's problem is, it's certainly not a chaotic family life. Marion's consistent good grooming—straight, shoulder-length hair always neatly brushed; sweaters or blouses, not T-shirts—whether she's wearing her contact lenses or her glasses, suggests the solid, loving household she comes from.

Marion's father, who teaches auto-body mechanics at the regional technical high school, sounds pretty close to the ideal father, in fact. He introduced her to Shannon, who'd been one of his students at the technical high school. Shannon had been working over the summer in the high school administration office, and when he found out Shannon would be a sophomore at Framingham, Marion's father assured her that if the two girls met they'd be best friends. "Call her," he said. "She's really nice."

"This girl is going to think I'm a loser," Marion remembers feeling. "She's going to think I'm a spoiled little princess, or pathetic." (Later she found out that Shannon had the very same self-doubt.) "Anyway, I called her, finally, to shut up my father. We were on the phone for an hour. She gave me advice about the dorm, about buying books. She was, 'Yeaah, come down some time.' She seemed pretty nice. A couple of weeks later, a couple of weeks before school started, we went shopping and went out for lunch. And then she told me what day she was moving into the dorms, so I was walking around with May and Francesca and I figured I'd go see her. 'I'm so glad you came,' she said to me. That told me we were really going to be good friends."

Surrounding Marion's life, I begin to realize, is a strong safety net of people who care about her. And this especially includes her father. Recently someone close to Shannon, an old childhood friend, committed suicide—a kid Shannon had grown up with. Shannon's mother found out about the death and knew Marion's father was headed for Framingham to pick up Marion. "Could you just tell Shannon to call me," the mother had asked him.

When Marion's father arrived at the dorm, he and Marion paged Shannon. "She comes down all happy," Marion recalls, "and I didn't know how to act around her, how to act when a kid you grew up with committed suicide."

"I'll call her later," Shannon said, when she got the message to call her mom.

"I think you should call her now," said Marion's father.

"I felt uncomfortable," Marion recalls, "but I'm glad we went up to her room with her. We stayed about an hour. She was crying. My father had his flashers on, and his car battery went dead. We had to call a tow truck to get it jump-started. That made Shannon laugh," says Marion, shaking her head. "It's going to be a rough semester for her. I know I wouldn't have wanted to be alone, if I were her. It was really nice of my father to let his car battery die."

Even Greta, whose home seems like a gallery of wistful failures, thinks of herself as a strong student, while Marion conveys the sense of someone not quite born into her adult self. Marion has identified her strongest subject as English, and meeting Julia Scandrett, the English Department faculty member in charge of student teachers last spring at open house, has helped her decide to become a high school English teacher. "I was really quiet in high school," she recalls. "People thought I was shy. We had to do these personality posters—representing what we think we're really like—and I was the last one to be called up in front of the class to explain my poster. I'm talking, and people are asking me how come I didn't talk before."

Here at Framingham, Marion lives relatively quietly—she recently transferred from Towers to Horace Mann, because most of the people she's friendly with live in this quieter, smaller old-fashioned dorm—and she doesn't have a job here. At first she worked in the cafeteria on Mondays and Wednesdays, but she didn't like coming from a two-hour class and having to deal with hot, smelly food and rude people. She was working in the residents' cafeteria, slopping food onto plates, and one kid found a long black hair in his food.

"'Look at that! Look at that!' he kept shouting, and I'm, like, 'Does that look like it's my hair? Well, don't yell at me. Go back and yell at the cooks.'"

Now Marion goes home Thursday night (a typical pattern at this college) and works Friday, Saturday, and Sunday—about fifteen hours in all. Her father picks her up and drops her off.

Perhaps the best way to describe Marion's goal so far is that she's going to make sure that she doesn't do badly in any of her courses. Having gotten two C's on the first two psychology tests, she's determined to spend more time on that course and get a B. In Western Civilization, a lecture-style course, she's doing all right by committing the main facts and ideas to memory. In Elaine Beilin's class, though, she's begun to get an inkling that she can reveal a brain of her own. She remembers when they were talking about John Hancock's seeming more concerned with a salmon than with the fate of the American Revolution, and everyone wrote the same thing: he's a spoiled little baby. The first thing that popped into Marion's head was that she didn't care, that she was more concerned with the good he accomplished for his country. Marion didn't expect anyone to say, 'Wow, that was really interesting.' But perhaps it was May who'd said—and someone else agreed with her—that she really liked what Marion had said. And they'd had a little debate about that. Then—right then—she'd felt intelligent.

She'd said honestly what she'd thought. This growth isn't showing up consistently in class yet, but it's happening inside Marion. And, Elaine can't help hoping, some day it may surface in her writing and speech. "I need to hear *your* voice, your guidance in every paragraph to explain the relevance of the information or reaction to your overarching purpose (thesis)," she writes at the end of Marion's field trip paper. "I sense that something significant, even exciting happened during your visit. *Reflect* on it and *explain* specifically *what.*"

Indeed, in Marion's writing about Grant Wood, one can sense a half-formed identification with this artist:

> Born in a small farm town in Iowa in 1891, Grant Wood's life ambition was to be an artist. What can be better than getting paid for working at something you love? That is exactly what Wood thought and so, he set out to fulfill his life's dream. Being a timid and quiet child, Grant Wood's only way of expressing his feelings was in his paintings. Art was his creative and emotional outlet. . . . Although he enjoyed France, he returned home to paint the things he knew. Among these things were farm scenes. He painted landscapes, farmers, animals, townspeople, social gatherings, and family. Wood was most comfortable painting subjects that he was familiar with. His works have a sort of emotional quality, marked by somber faces of the hardworking citizens of his hometown.

What does Marion from rural Paxton see in the "somber faces of the hardworking citizens?" Does she see her own neighbors, parents, herself? For the first time in her life it begins to dawn on Marion that some people find a way to work joyfully, intensely at something they love.

6. A SMALLER TABLE

IT RAINS OVER the weekend, but by the time class begins on Monday, the third week of October, some blue is beginning to show through the heavy clouds toward the southwest. Too late, because Route 9 has been flooded, and Elaine Beilin has had to detour around this main road. She arrives a few minutes before the class starts, pauses in her office only to shed her raincoat and hang up her umbrella, then heads up the stairs while discussing the commute with Marilyn Harter, her colleague who lives only about ten blocks from the college. Just twelve students are in the classroom. She asks them if they had trouble driving. Claudia, who has to come east on Route 9 from Shrewsbury, says it wasn't too bad. Kate tells a horror story about an accident and traffic jam on Route 495—but Kate is safely here.

Surprisingly, most of the leaves are still on the trees and still green. Elaine notices this at first from the classroom doorway, looking out through the two large, high windows at the towering maples in front of Dwight Hall. Just then the bi-weekly freight train that serves some of the factories downtown sounds a long blast on its horn. Today Elaine's dressed more for the approaching winter than for fall: black pants, black turtleneck, and a dark red-and-black houndstooth jacket, something like a man's sport coat, which she decides to leave on as she sits, as usual, at the far end of the room, in front of the windows, and takes attendance.

She's glad to see Jeremy. Jeremy's field-trip paper has come in on time, but when it was time to begin the next assignment, the research paper, which must be thought about way in advance, Jeremy suddenly seemed stalled. His paper was supposed to be something about battle movements on Lexington Green. He didn't have a question, didn't really know what to do. Elaine told him to come and talk about it. He wrote her a poignant note instead. "I don't think I'm doing very well, and this is always something that seems to happen to me." It reminded her of the note he wrote on the student information sheet the very first day. "This subject—English—seems the only one open for me for I have never done well at much else." She stopped him in the hall one day when both of them were headed to other classes. "Come see me," she said.

"I'll take help anywhere I can get it," he answered.

But he didn't come.

Still, if he won't come for a conference, at least he's here. She surveys the room to see who else is here. Phoebe is here, as always, in black, finishing off a small box of Lucky Charms—but not yet Rosalind, who also has a long commute. Amelia's wearing a Boston College cap this morning, brim forward. Andy, Mary, Susie, Marion, Belinda, Arthur—all of whom live in the dorms—are here, but May and Francesca, who also live in the dorm, must be exercising their prerogative to be absent. And, alas, no Lee. Rarely Lee, these days. And George, too, has begun to fade away, though he seemed to have started the term with such determination and energy. And no Greta today, either—her complex system of getting rides from home having broken down, evidently.

She begins by asking the students what they learned from giving their oral reports, and what suggestions they would make for the next time they have to advance an oral argument.

"Not to repeat yourself," says Andy.

"Why does that happen, Andy?" she asks.

"I had everything in my head and nothing came out. I kept saying the same thing."

"You're a bit hard on yourself," Elaine says, looking at the others. "What could you do?"

"I guess be better organized," says Andy. "Put down topics."

"Topics is what I've found works best," she nods. "Rosalind?"

By this time, Rosalind has arrived, her umbrella dripping from the long walk from the commuter parking lot, and she has taken her customary seat midway along the side of the table in front of the chalkboard. "Even writing down one word," says Rosalind, agreeing.

"In your notes sometimes I see sentences written out nicely and articulately," says Elaine Beilin, "and what do people end up doing? Reading. Looking at the paper. Not really talking about the topic to the class. So Andy's suggestion about word cues is often helpful. Other suggestions?"

Amelia, who's leaning back against the wall today, Kate-style, the brim of her BC hat low over her face, begins to recount how she once taught her high school class for two days. "You have to keep it interesting," she says.

"How?" asks Elaine.

"Find a place that you care about," says Amelia nonchalantly, still leaning back. "If you care, you can find something to stir people up."

"Make connections," suggests Claudia.

Phoebe's hand is up now. "A lot of people didn't want to make eye contact, so they stared mainly at you."

"Yes," Elaine says. "It makes me extremely self-conscious. But it's hard to break the habit if you're used to classrooms where the focus is on the teacher." She looks around at them. "Can someone tell me what the difficulties are in trying to make contact with other students? When you talk in the cafeteria you make eye contact. How about one of those cafeteria skills translated to the classroom?"

Amelia, leaning back still, drinking from her bottle of mineral water, makes some kind of remark Elaine can't hear.

"Well," says Elaine after a silence of several moments, "you could say to yourself, 'Everyone in this class really likes me.' That might help. Let's try to make eye contact and really engage people. This," she says, moving some of her books directly in front of her, "has been a small homily on making eye contact. And being interesting."

At this point she begins the main business of the class, setting up a discussion of Henry Wadsworth Longfellow's "The Midnight Ride of Paul Revere." She says they'll go around the room and each person will read some of the poem. "Let's see, one hundred and thirty lines, divided by thirteen people—that means we can each take exactly ten lines." She gets up and walks behind Susie and Phoebe and Marion to get to the door, closing it, "in case it gets really loud and exciting." Then she assigns them their sections. "Claudia you read down to 'all is well.' Arthur you read down to the end of that stanza. Phoebe take it down to 'saddle girth,' Amelia take it to 'fire and load.' And I'll do the last one. Don't ask me to repeat which ones you've got." She leans back in her chair now, and laughs. "Take a few minutes to think how you're going to read them expressively."

After a while, they begin:

> Listen my children, and you shall hear
> Of the midnight ride of Paul Revere,
> On the eighteenth of April, in Seventy-five,
> Hardly a man is now alive
> Who remembers that famous day and year . . .

Marion, the third reader, can't be heard above the racing engine of a truck below their window. The students read in a mechanical and singsongy way, all except Rosalind, who's been practicing reciting poetry all semester in Professor Seiden's Approaches to Literature class and gives her stanza real life. Elaine's eyebrows go up, and she smiles. Jeremy can hardly be heard. Andy, of course, is loud and clear. But then Arthur, too, is loud, clear, and surprisingly expressive. Kate can't be heard except as a murmur. Elaine finishes, reading the poem's final stanza slowly, without irony:

> So through the night rode Paul Revere;

And so through the night went his cry of alarm
To every Middlesex village and farm—
A cry of defiance and not of fear,
A voice in the darkness, a knock at the door,
And a word that shall echo for evermore!
For, borne on the night-wind of the Past,
Through all our history, to the last,
In the hour of darkness and peril and need,
The people will waken and listen to hear
The hurrying hoofbeats of that steed,
And the midnight message of Paul Revere.

"I remember a TV version of this," says Amelia, after the brief silence that follows.

"My husband remembered a children's book, Robert Lawson's *Mr. Revere and I*, told from the point of view of Paul Revere's horse. He kept a copy of it from when he was seven." Elaine holds the book up, then passes it around.

The students begin to say what they like about the Longfellow poem, particularly the rhyme. "I can't write with rhyme," says Kate, "but I like it."

"Me too," says Amelia. "It keeps the flow going."

"The rhyme makes it easier to understand," says Claudia.

"For example?" asks Elaine.

"Just the first stanza, and also the end," says Claudia. "Sometimes you really have to look into poetry, but this is really basic."

"Longfellow would be overjoyed to hear you say that," says Elaine, nodding. "Notice *hear* and *year* are connected to *Revere.* Why would Longfellow have wanted—that's actually the easiest rhyme to come up with. Why would he have wanted those words to rhyme?"

"He was writing how Paul Revere spread the word around about the British," says Claudia, "so he'd want to suggest that people listened to him. And this was a 'year' that he wants us to remember."

"So I think you spoke very accurately when you said rhymes make it clear."

"Those rhymes come back at the end," Amelia points out.

"And has anything been added to the meaning?" Elaine asks. Behind her the sun breaks out for a moment, a silvery light on the trees. Claudia leans back and with her fingers strokes her long hair out to its full length. Rosalind stares at the rings on her left thumb and three more on the fingers of that hand, including her engagement ring. On her right hand, she has only one ring, a kind of wedding ring. Claudia tells the class about how Longfellow was walking through the North End when he got the idea to write this poem.

Three people—Elaine is glad to see—volunteer to read the paragraphs they were asked to write about the poem, while the rest of the class takes notes. Rosalind argues that literature is a way to go back in time. This poem, written in 1860, told the truth of the events as people thought about them then. This, she says, gives us a clear grasp of the parallels between history and literature. What historians are claiming today could change tomorrow. Belinda recalls having to get up and recite this poem back in seventh grade. "I prayed the teacher wouldn't realize my lips were moving but no words were coming out." She goes on to say that they had no reason to ask her to memorize wrong multiplication tables, and yet they asked her to memorize this.

"We only had to memorize the first stanza," Rosalind recalls.

"He was a horrible teacher," Belinda says.

"Anyone else have to?" Elaine asks. Lots of people now are talking at once.

"I went to Catholic grade school," says Rosalind. "I remember doing Frost and Longfellow. It was a big thing—memorizing and reciting. We had a contest. I remember getting up and doing it. I notice that at work I can picture things, and remember them—we have these order forms—and I think that's what it was from. Memorization is a good tool."

"I can't memorize to save my life," says Kate.

"Constant repetition bores you," says Amelia to console Kate.

"There's a long tradition for saying poems out loud," says Elaine.

"I had to memorize a ten-line poem first year in high school. I couldn't follow it."

"They did the poem so well in that Paul Revere cartoon on TV," says Amelia. "I thought it was great." Then she points her pen at Rosalind. "I have a question for you. Did you like the poem, or not like it? Didn't you say something about how the poem changes the historical facts?"

"That doesn't mean I didn't like it," says Rosalind.

"It seems to me this is supposed to be for children," says Amelia, "more than adults. Other than the final lines, it seems like something adults wouldn't care about."

"It has a fairy-tale style to it," Jeremy says.

"What does he mean by 'children?'" Elaine asks.

"Other generations?" Rosalind says.

"The last stanza is the least known," says Andy. "By that time, most children have fallen asleep from their bedtime story."

"I thought the last part was written really well," says Rosalind.

"Yeah," Andy agrees. "It brings across the main point, 'A cry of defiance, not of fear.'"

"What I'm hearing," says Elaine, "is that the last stanza is written differently."

"I don't think it was written for children," says Claudia. Her hair is now wrapped around her left shoulder like a scarf.

"I hope he wrote it for children," says Phoebe. "It's really trite. Cockadoodledoo and the cow."

"Wait, you lost me there," says Elaine.

"Just that the things he harps on seem trivial. He could have heard a mooing cow and a goat. I totally gathered it was written for children."

"What do you do with the last stanza?"

"Maybe he felt silly," says Phoebe, "and tried to write something normal. I don't think it's beyond children's understanding."

Elaine looks around at the class. "That word 'message' has more meaning at the end than at the beginning. What do you think the message of Longfellow's poem is, as distinct from Paul Revere's message? Why should children listen and hear this story?" She seems relaxed in pondering this, and waits for anyone to speak. "Did he reach you at all with a message?"

"It seems like he's just summing it up," says Phoebe. "He went here, then there. The end just seems to sum it up. It's a little bit longer, it's worded a little differently."

"What are some of the words he's repeated from stanzas before," asks Elaine, "or are the words different kinds of words, which is what I'm hearing from some of the others?"

"Just particular words?" says Phoebe. "Here, he likes that word 'Paul Revere.'"

"Yes!" says Elaine. "Twice in that stanza."

"He says 'steed' a few times in that stanza," says Phoebe.

Elaine leans her head on her left hand. "Are these words different?"

"'A cry of defiance and not of fear,'" says Rosalind. "That's like a contrast. It gives Paul Revere a character, which we haven't seen before—some kind of personality."

"I'm not sure I know what that midnight message is," says Elaine.

"That's true," Rosalind says, "he never says 'The British are coming!' I don't know where I got that idea."

This question—of the poem's meaning—is left suspended. To convey that she's not the keeper of any "hidden meaning," Elaine decides to allow the confusion to linger for the moment, like a light cloud of smoke hovering where a real fire has been ignited. They seem to come alive when the topic is literature—a group of English majors. Maybe it will be good to switch gears with the reading, as soon as they're done with the research paper. She's been thinking about that.

Now, though, she wants to organize those who are here into two debate teams. She asks them to think of the poem as part of a high school curriculum. She's already drawn up a sheet with two teams. "It might help to pull the tables out so you can sit around them," she says as the students divide, half to the corner near the door, and half to the corner between the chalkboard and the window.

"I drove home from Maine last night at nine," says Claudia, who has a boyfriend up at Bates College. "It rained so hard. They got rain after we did."

"I hope no one's going to the Boston Public Library in this," says Elaine.

"I think May and Francesca went to the World Series," says Colleen.

"Well, that's two counts against them," says Elaine. "They got to go to the World Series. And they're not here."

The students are settled around the two smaller tables they've detached from the usual large gray table; Elaine explains to them that they're to debate the question of whether to include this poem in a serious curriculum for the tenth grade. These hypothetical students will be taking English and history at the same time. Rosalind, Susie, Colleen, Phoebe, Andy, Belinda, and Marion, in the corner near the door, should plan how to support the proposition, and Kate, Mary, Amelia, Jeremy, Claudia, and Arthur in a corner near the window are to form the opposition. Elaine places herself near the other window, and watches both groups. The loud laughter coming from Kate's group isn't caused by her—she's writing something at the moment. Mary is sitting silently, with her pen upside-down. Near the door, to Elaine's left, Rosalind is talking to her whole group about how ninth grade is when students start analyzing. Marion suggests that studying this poem would be a good chance for the English and history departments to work together. Near the window, to Elaine's right, the "con" group hasn't settled down to a pattern of letting one person at a time speak to the whole group. Instead, Kate is talking while Arthur is talking. "Oh boy," says Amelia leaning her chair back against the wall, and hiding her face in the wide sleeves of her sweater, "I can't really contribute."

While the group near the door is still letting one person speak at a time, with all others attentive and taking notes, the "window" group falls silent, except for some giggles, as though the students have reverted to helplessness. Kate starts chatting about her freshman year in history, how they were left with a two-hundred-year gap because they got behind schedule. Clearly, Elaine notices, they're not on task. "I found out Paul Revere was captured," says Kate, "when a customer came in and told me." Arthur is talking to some of the others in the group, his back toward Kate. "To tell the truth, I didn't know it was Paul Revere who warned the colonists," Kate continues. "I thought it was Sam Adams. I never read this poem till I read this book," she says, pointing to Fischer's history.

Elaine decides to go over to this group. "OK," she says, leaning over Kate's shoulder, "you have a couple more minutes to put your argument together."

Near the door, Phoebe is addressing her group, while the others are all taking notes. Though she's gone back to her seat, Elaine focuses almost entirely on the "con" group, with Kate in it. Now Kate and Jeremy are both talking at the same time. "Did anyone go to private high school?" Kate asks.

"I went to private high school," says Mary.

"Well, there goes my point, shot to hell," says Kate.

This is the first time Mary has spoken in this group, but even though they're just chatting, no one follows up Mary's comment by asking her about the school she went to.

Elaine can't help wishing they would. She feels that Mary is academically so solid, but socially so vulnerable and at risk. What is it that her quiet smile, her watchful eyes are saying—or masking—as she confronts this class, which must be so different from her small parochial high school class? You'd think Kate would be looking around to see who else is feeling left out besides herself. Yet she's just holding the floor, telling the others about all the kid stuff at Paul Revere's house, all these little toys. Amelia seems to be half-listening, her hat brim is now skewed to the left. Maybe Arthur, at least, is starting to apply his mind to the debate. "I think it's more interesting to find out that he didn't get to Concord," he's saying. "That he was captured."

"Do we have our points in order?" Elaine says to both groups. "That's the final thing you should do—make a list." She walks over to check on the "con" group, though she knows that they couldn't possibly be prepared.

"We can make stuff up," Kate says, as though to reassure her.

"Well," she answers, "most arguments are made up. But the ones that succeed have to be good ones."

The students reassemble the table into one continuous plane of gray Formica, and, sitting at opposite corners, begin to debate whether the tenth graders they're imagining should have to deal with "The Midnight Ride." Elaine asks them to alternate, one reason pro, one reason con, giving everyone a turn to speak. "But listen to each other," she says, "so that you can think of ways to respond." It's not clear that this is the sort of thing they ever did in high school—at least, not frequently.

Marion begins by saying that her group thought the poem would be a good introduction to a course that has to do with the topic of the beginning of the Revolution. "It's fictional, so it would also be a good way to get into poetry, killing two birds with one stone." As she speaks, Marion is looking diagonally across the table at the other students in the con group, not at Elaine.

"We said one reason it shouldn't be taught," says Arthur. "When you're in tenth grade, you're starting to get into complicated poems, and you'll look at this, and it's geared towards little kids, so you'll think, 'Oh yeah, it's an easy grade,' and you won't take it seriously." Arthur sounds like the wise, older catcher advising the pitcher—his cap on backwards.

"I think it would be a breath of fresh air," says Rosalind. "It brings you into the literature of a time following the revolution when it was still pertinent to ask what the generations following thought about it."

"But it's really teaching you inaccurately," Amelia counters. Perhaps it's that she lets her chair swing forward away from the wall, or that she speaks up so quickly Rosalind hardly has a chance to finish, but her comment draws a laugh from her own group. "It makes you think he didn't get captured. And there are other characters involved who are never mentioned. If you're doing this for history, people will get the wrong view."

"You could study the inaccuracies of it," says Colleen.

"You've studied it in seventh grade," says Claudia. "You already know it's wrong, so why bring it back again?"

Now it's Phoebe's turn. "At this age," she says, "you could see it in a whole new light. You won't see it the way you saw it in seventh grade. It would give you an opportunity to analyze what is truth and what is fiction."

"Wait," says Kate. "You're fifteen, and you're telling me you want to analyze that? You're full of it."

"If you're going to have poetry in the tenth grade," Belinda argues in a calm voice, "it better be interesting."

"Even this morning," Kate says, forgetting it's supposed to be someone else's turn, "when we were discussing this poem, I was thinking about who I'm seeing this weekend."

"I'm *shocked*," says Phoebe, "at that statement." There's lots of laughter.

Rosalind takes over now. "You could show about how history changes. This is a completely romanticized version. But it's valid to show how history does change. So it's valuable in that way."

"They don't teach that in high school," says Kate. "I didn't learn a lot of things that you should learn. I know it was my fault."

"But I'm saying this is a tool you could use," Rosalind says to her.

"In history," Jeremy says, "I'm there to learn the facts. Everything has to be important! Amelia was saying you won't think about what's true and what isn't, you'll just accept it—"

"You're on the same side," Elaine reminds him.

"You're not just reading facts, you're reading things that interpret. And next year you'll get a different interpretation," says Colleen. "This would prepare you."

"Why not take two different textbooks then?" asks Amelia.

"Because then you're not dealing with two different cultures," says Colleen.

Elaine has been hoping to see Mary get into this debate. "Most kids know about the ride," Mary says at last. "So it's not really an important issue, how the interpretation changes."

Marion begins to explain her plan of how the English and history classes could be put together, with the history class finding out the facts, and the English class "would take over the literature part of it—including Fischer's book—and stories, both factual and fictional about the Revolution. And that," she concludes, "would be an interesting way to find out about the difference between fact and fiction." Though some students have used a middle term, "interpretation," in Marion's mind there is only a clear dichotomy. Phoebe is the only one who seems to be acting at times during this discussion, as though the debate is a performance. "So it would be *very* beneficial," she's saying, in a gentle parody of a stuffy teacher's voice. But then she seems to dive in. "Longfellow," she says, "is an historically interesting figure. It's much more significant to pick a poem of Longfellow. He's someone you could investigate. He's right in the area."

"Yeah," says Claudia, "but you can't analyze this poem. There must be some other poem he wrote that would be more effective."

"People learn in different styles," Phoebe counters. "Some people would get more out of reading poetry in different styles."

"Why don't you teach the depositions," says Amelia from under her cap. "Look how those have changed from version to version."

"Because they're so boring," says Rosalind, laughing.

"Anyone want the last word?" asks Elaine, looking over at Jeremy.

"I don't care," says Jeremy.

"Well that was wonderful," says Elaine, looking around at the whole group. "I think we should record the debate and send it over to the high schools. It would be good for them to hear it. Don't forget," she says, as the students take their book bags and jackets and begin to migrate out the door, "rough draft of the first paragraph of your research paper, due on Wednesday next week."

Wednesday they spend more time on the Longfellow poem. Elaine chooses three statements from their papers. Marion: "Longfellow is trying to expose the beauty of the moment." Phoebe: "The poem has little depth, and thrives only as a children's poem for amusement." Claudia: "Longfellow wrote the poem to entertain, and arouse patriotism, not to seek the truth." She asks the students to go back to the poem and find specific lines, statements, words that support one of these ideas. Many of them quoted lines in their papers, but didn't spend enough time explaining why their quotations supported their arguments, so she wants them to practice using evidence to support specific claims.

Monday they go to the library again, and by Wednesday when their topics for the research paper are due, nearly the whole class is present; only Lee, George, and Donna are still missing. The room is so crowded, in fact, that when Elaine arrives she has to sit on the side of the table in front of the chalkboard, not on the side in front of the windows, as she usually does. Maybe it's only that she's seeing the classroom from a slightly different angle, but she notices that the table seems to have become much smaller.

She doesn't know whether other teachers feel this, but when she starts out in the fall it seems as though the table is very large—and then as the semester goes along people seem to get closer. As she tries to explain it to me, she stretches out the fingers of both hands as though gathering something, pushing it into a lump like clay or yarn or dough. "The students," she says as though it surprises her, "are actually talking to each other."

7. RESEARCH

OR IT COULD be that the table seems smaller because this is the day she's decided to spend some time telling the students something about herself. She's decided to tell them about her most recent research project, an edition of *The Examinations of Anne Askew*, who was born in 1521. "She wrote an autobiography of her very short life when she was called up before the authorities as a heretic. She was burned at the stake at the age of twenty-five. That caught my attention right away," she tells the class during their last meeting in October.

By now the leaves on one of the large maples in front of Dwight Hall—the red-brick three-story administration building in the center of campus that looks like a typical 1930s high school with its large clock over the central entrance—are beginning to yellow, while the leaves of the one beside it are turning reddish brown on one side of the tree. Though the lawn in front of Dwight is half-covered with leaves, the lawn behind May Hall, with its 1970s minimalist tripod-like aluminum sculpture, is still intensely green. The campus has a late-autumn somberness—a place you'd come to work, but not to hang out. Elaine can see all this out the window today because she's sitting in front of the chalkboard, between Jeremy and Belinda, and it's when she sees the students gathered around the table from this unfamiliar angle that she first notices how much smaller the table looks. Almost all the students are here, and the room is so crowded that when she came in she had to say, "Someone want to make a place for me?"

"We're going to spend the next three classes on various aspects of research," she tells them. Generally, freshman English programs at any school require the so-called research paper, a documented paper designed to familiarize the students with the conventions of citing sources and with the techniques of using the library—and even, recently, the Internet. It seems as though such a paper has been part of the academic landscape forever, but it first appeared in the early twentieth century, accompanying the growth of American academic libraries. Early models, however, were not highly argumentative or interpretive. In the 1950s and 1960s, the assignment assumed a service function, in response to complaints from professors in other disciplines that undergraduates didn't know how to support an academic argument—how to find things out for themselves, how to document, how to quote.

Professors throughout the country have recently begun to assign collaborative research projects in their classes, on the theory that students need to learn cooperatively, and that students with different strengths, at different developmental levels, will assume appropriate roles in the collective effort. Elaine Beilin doesn't see it that way, however. Though she's assigned plenty of group work of that sort, she wants all of her students not only to know how to gather information, but also to put the stamp of their own minds on the material, as Fischer has done with his highly readable but heavily documented book.

The students, though, dread the prospect of doing such a paper, and Elaine knows that. Almost all have been assigned just such a paper in the junior and senior year of high school—or so they think—yet they are apt to complain that their teachers never really explained how to do research, or else that they were taught a different format, a different way of organizing, a different set of criteria. Well, the weather has finally lost its beguiling Indian-summer charm—Elaine Beilin can hardly remember a year when the trees kept their leaves this long, or the lawns stayed so green—

and she feels that today she's reached the rolling-up-the-sleeves part of the semester, and also the part where both teacher and student are likely to feel the strongest sense of fatigue. For her, the semester has its rhythm, and she watches herself and the class for signs of flagging spirits. If that is to happen, she will have to change something about the class to renew interest—the students' and her own.

Though the research paper is required by the department, it's actually at the core of her Essentials course. Research, in fact, is at the heart of her life. She and Bob, in their different fields, live to discover, to get to the bottom of things. Today, she has decided to bring to class a copy of the just-published Anne Askew book and to tell the students something about the research that went into it—and what research has meant in her life. Even though last Wednesday's class—the Longfellow debate—went so well, she's glad the room is more crowded today. Perhaps nothing she can tell these students matters more to her than what she is telling them now.

Anne Askew was burned at the stake in 1546 because she refused to acknowledge that the sacramental bread literally, rather than merely symbolically, became the flesh of Christ. She was asked such profound questions as what would happen if a mouse should eat the Host. Would it receive the body of Christ? Read as literature, her account of her interrogation provides a self-portrait of a clever and learned young woman whose weapons were her almost total recall of the Bible and her subtle irony. She didn't confront her inquisitors so much as evade, parry, and counterthrust. In a sense, students who might not understand how Fischer's history could also be read as a literary text might not read *The Examinations of Anne Askew* as a work of literature either. Yet, for a scholar studying these early women writers in English, this text matters. First of all, the book was quite well known through the first half of the nineteenth century, until the so-called English literature canon (of virtually all male writers) was established at universities and in anthologies and textbooks. Also, *The Examinations* portrays a woman about to be executed, in part for assuming an authority forbidden to women in the past—a right to read and interpret the Bible and draw her own inferences about the nature of God.

If Elaine Beilin's choice of an academic career was initially developed in opposition to her family's advice, and her later research has run counter to certain fashionable theories about women's writing (because the pious writers whose works she explored in *Redeeming Eve*, to the disappointment of some critics, didn't fit the "mad woman in the attic" mold of 19th century women writers), then surely Anne Askew is a kind of sister. What comes across most clearly in Anne Askew's sixteenth-century text is the character of this woman of conviction, courage, and knowledge—just the kind of character Elaine would like to see forming in her students. Research, then, isn't some kind of hollow ritual. Research—that is, formulating questions, gathering information, and clearly and persuasively asserting what you believe—is at the core of academic citizenship, and, for that matter, of full adulthood.

It is not likely, she knows, that all of these students—or even most of them—will be successful in progressing that far in their first semester. For some, the breakthrough may have to wait for Literary Study, a course they may take next semester, or in their sophomore year. For some, effectively writing about research may have to wait till they're seniors, when, with enough hard work—by them, and, in many cases, the professor teaching the course—all of them will be able to do it. That is, all of those who will still be enrolled—about half. But then, she's not satisfied to accept the results of probability. She wants them all to be there.

"You do need to spend the time between classes collecting the materials and really reading them and thinking about them," she is telling the students. But will they believe her? Will they actually put aside jobs, parties, and even some of the catching up they're probably having to do in their other classes? She gets up and writes *TIME* on the blackboard behind her seat.

"Like you," she says to them, "I started doing research in elementary school. I discovered I really loved it." She can see

Rosalind nod. "I loved being in the library. And I still prefer the lower stacks, pawing through things. I ended up researching in the Harvard library, where the dust is so thick I have to take Handiwipes with me."

She thinks she knows some of the thoughts Anne Askew must have struggled with when, a young mother and a woman of keen intellect and deep powers of spiritual reflection, she faced the prospect of early death. But of course we do not say—sometimes we would not even know how to say—what causes us to devote ourselves to one project rather than another. Anne Askew left behind her account of her "Examinations," and that Elaine Beilin was determined to make available to modern readers.

"My task," she explains now to her students, "was to write an introduction so an undergraduate, a sophomore in college, would get something out of it. So I knew my audience. I can't tell you how much easier that made it. Every time I came across information, I asked myself whether the sophomores I was teaching would understand the historical context, the technical religious terms. The answer was 'sometimes yes, sometimes no.'"

There's a stillness in the crowded room, perhaps a kind of perplexity. This ten minutes is the longest she's ever spent talking about herself. "There were some things that helped me tremendously," she says. "First, I cared about these people. I read this woman's work and it blew me away. I wanted to find out about her, about how people lived in her time, what people thought about. So that really drove me and motivated me. The other thing—and I was trying to think what motivated me through endless drafts and redrafts—was that, in a nutshell, I wanted to get a reaction from my readers. I wanted them to say, 'This is an amazing writer, an amazing woman'—to realize that this woman has meaning for them in 1996 even though she lived in 1546. A lot of this I was working on while I was teaching, while I was doing family stuff. So I needed motivation, I needed that—you know what. So," she says, grinning at them, "that's my little autobiographical piece."

She looks around. "Anyone want to give some parallel experience?"

"Did you bring the thing?" asks Phoebe.

Elaine Beilin holds up the Oxford paperback.

"It's in that book?"

"Yeah, sure."

"Oh, can I read it?"

"Sure," says Elaine Beilin. "I tested it on my market—asked for volunteers from my Literary Study class. Three students read it and gave me feedback. I thanked them right there in the Acknowledgment." She holds up the book, a paperback with an old-fashioned, all-print brown and tan cover. "Most of the book is Anne Askew's work; she's the main focus. The first part is my historical introduction. Then a textual introduction—just like the one Fischer did in his book—where I explain where I found this stuff. I had read an important book about the city of London in Anne Askew's time. The author was an eminent don at Oxford, but I phoned her in a pleading voice, and she was pleased to be called. I asked her how she had been able to date the interrogation of Anne Askew in her book. She said that the interrogation was recorded in the city of London records, and she gave me the volume and page number! 'Thank you, bless you,' I told her, 'I'll send you a copy of the book.' So it's really helpful to find someone who knows. Rosalind is studying high school history textbooks, so I said to Rosalind, 'You ought to talk to Dr. Grant—the education expert in the History Department.' Marion's working on fashion, so I told her to go talk to Professor Taylor, who actually *makes* eighteenth-century-style costumes."

Rosalind raises her hand. "Are we writing this paper for the class?"

"I think that makes sense," Elaine Beilin says. "Where are we now? Week nine? So we have that common body of thinking and reading now." She looks around.

"Why was she burned?" asks Kate, letting her chair, which has been leaning against the wall, tilt forward.

"She was one of the first Protestants."

"Oh, a Protestant thing," says Kate.

"Late in the reign of Henry the Eighth."

"That's really odd, because Henry's daughter was a Protestant."

"One of them," says Elaine Beilin. "He had two daughters. If Anne Askew had lived for six more months she would have been safe for six years, till Henry's Catholic daughter took over."

"Protestant and Catholic is not that different," says Kate. "I'll never understand that at all. They shouldn't have burned someone just because of that. It's ridiculous."

Kate sounds as though she should have been asked to vote on the matter. But the judgmental streak in her comments doesn't bother Elaine. How can it, when this student, passing such harsh judgment, was in tears in her office not long ago?

"In some ways," Elaine explains, "it's like what you're reading about the American Revolution. You remember that little phrase, 'an Englishman's home is his castle.' Americans thought of themselves as English, until the Revolution called into question those categories. The British became 'them,' the Americans, 'we.' But clearly that was not the thinking at the time. So it's a matter of historical perspective. We look back now and say, 'How can this be?' But that's why you have to go and look at the history."

Kate's nodding. Her indignation seems to have lifted, and she's ready to focus her efforts on the paper. "Where do you start?" she asks.

"That's the trouble" says Elaine Beilin. "But if you have access to a computer, you can call up Infotrak. As Ronnie Klein said, you can—with care, with critical thought—use the Web. You can get into a rare book collection. If you've been doing that, and—" she looks around, "you run into issues, let's talk about that."

She passes out a work sheet with questions designed to help the students narrow down and define their topics. As the sheets are going around the table, she says she wants to make a point about attendance, "which seems to be good today." When she has their attention, she continues. "I know some of you are going full speed ahead, and others are still saying 'Where do I start? Help!' We'll work with wherever you are. So be sure you come to class. It will be helpful, even motivating, to see where other people are." She explains that the essay she's asking for is relatively short, only 1,500 to 2,000 words, or about five double-spaced pages. "So make sure your topic is focused." She also wants a minimum of three primary sources or three secondary. "Some of you," she says, "will be looking at an unmediated source. You'll be the person looking at it and analyzing it. If you work from just three, I'll be happy. That's fine. Some of you are looking at secondary sources, and the rule of thumb there is never use just one source. You see the logic in that. Some of you have pointed out to me the difficulty of working just with Fischer. I've brought in Esther Forbes's book on Paul Revere. Anyone remember what Fischer says about her work in his book?

"Well," she continues, "he doesn't like it. He mentions her as one of the people who've romanticized Paul Revere. But that made me very curious about her. So I felt I wanted to see some of the things she wrote to see how she was different. Fischer does credit Forbes with starting a new interpretation of Revere's significance. I'm going to try to read this passage in a neutral voice, but I'm going to fail." She picks up her copy of Fischer's book and reads to them:

> The architect of this new interpretation was Esther Forbes, a New England novelist who turned her hand to the writing of history with high success. It was one of the more improbable pairings of subject and author—a masculine figure whose life had been absorbed in the hurly-burly of politics, war and business; and a New England spinster who worked beside her aged mother in a quiet alcove of the American Antiquarian Society. (338)

"Now was I neutral as I read that, or did you hear a slight exasperation coming through? I'm indignant," she says, "that if you want to write about Paul Revere, you better not be a spinster who lives with her mother. What does that imply? That it takes a man to understand Paul Revere? I don't *think* so! What's a spinster?" she asks.

"An unmarried older lady," says Kate.

"Good. But I don't think so!" she says again. "My daughter's reading *Johnny Tremaine,* and I noticed the copyright is under her married name. So, he's got it wrong! She *wasn't* a little old spinster!"

"I can argue with that," says Kate, agreeing. "I met an older guy who said Fischer sucks. 'Fischer sucks!' he told me. 'You should read Forbes.' He was pointing out a hundred things wrong. Like Fischer saying that there were no left and right shoes."

"But notice what's happened here," says Elaine. "Fischer's kept the discussion going. That's what it's all about: keeping the dialogue going. We're always walking in someone's footsteps, but we're saying, 'Time to make a left turn or right turn, or time to stand ground.' Fischer would whip documents and depositions out before you could blink an eye. He really could. Academics love to argue."

"I'd just sit there and keep smiling," says Kate.

"It seems he has a different opinion about how significant the ride was," says Rosalind. "Most of his book is about the social world. The ride wasn't that important. Revere gets caught after he warns five people."

"Thanks for getting me back on track," says Elaine Beilin. "Forbes and Fischer have very different goals. He's talking about Paul Revere as revolutionary networker, absolutely essential to this historical moment. Forbes is a social historian, interested in the fabric of everyday life. Absolutely right. But this is getting back to my point about using a number of sources. We can argue. The man you ran into," she says to Kate, "is very knowledgeable and clearly has a different view. So go to Fischer, check out Forbes. Colleen, you're writing about poetry. Forbes includes little poems; Fischer wouldn't be interested in that. So you've got to balance." She makes a balancing gesture with her hands.

I'm curious to know what the students felt about Elaine's "little autobiographical piece." When I ask during the interviews I conduct the following week, the students tell me it got their attention. As she was listening to Dr. Beilin talk about her own research, Rosalind felt curious to read what her professor had written. She had already known that her professor was a published writer, and that she loved studying women in history. Rosalind can definitely see why that would be interesting. She thinks Elaine's so funny: whenever they talk about a possible research idea Elaine's always saying, "Oooh, I could do that too. I guess I'll have to write it myself." Or, directing Rosalind in a kind of vicarious way: "Oh, you'll have to find this out, too." She thinks it's funny, too, that Elaine is talking about loving to work in the basement of the library, where everything is dusty, because Rosalind likes to do that, too. It's true. So many things in this world that you could look at get passed over, and it's so neat to make a discovery. Her professor doesn't "blow things out," but she does communicate very clearly how she works—reading, reading, reading, and then revising. Rosalind thinks Elaine Beilin is just like herself.

Francesca, too, would actually like to read some of what Professor Beilin has written. She likes that trait of following up on something you're curious about, so you don't have to keep wondering about it. Belinda, too, mentions becoming especially interested when Elaine told them something about her research into women authors. She knows from her Major British Writers I survey course this fall that there isn't a lot of literature from that period by or about women. She loves research, loves new things. So she was glad her professor brought in something of her own, because she still has the feeling that professors aren't real. She appreciates it when her teachers get personal. During their conference Professor Beilin told Belinda a similar story of having to do many revisions. In fact, to know that her teachers have a hard time writing, too—that it doesn't come easily to everyone—made Belinda feel better.

Andy's been feeling that his own writing has not been going well, and this has colored his whole feeling about the class. He started his research paper late and has had a lot of problems getting all his sources. He was glad to hear more people discussing and arguing about things, but when he heard everyone else's topic it just reminded him how far behind he was. As for Professor Beilin's story about doing all those drafts, he wished he could do that sort of thing, but, it seems, he can't.

He doesn't know where his concentration went. Motivation used to be his problem; now he's motivated, but he seems to be in a daze. Back in high school, when he was a "burnout," he used to be able, at least, to think and write. Now he can't do anything. His friends, the biggest burnouts in the world, used to be brilliant. They couldn't remember your name, but they still . . . oh, he doesn't know. Last night, he tells me, he wanted to revise one of his papers but he couldn't. He knew exactly what he wanted to do and he couldn't do it. His mind wasn't even somewhere else. All the work he'd had for the last few days had been connected with this class. He wanted to do that revision; he had to start his research. He didn't know, he was ready to do it, had it all planned out, had dinner, did laundry, it was time to start, and—he doesn't know. Writer's block is when he has no thoughts, but last night he knew exactly what he wanted to do and just couldn't revise. He wanted to change the whole introduction to his last paper. He was looking at it and he just kept feeling, I can't do this. The little critic wouldn't shut up. He needed the other little guy on his opposite shoulder to say, "It's good," but he just wouldn't. He has to talk to Ron Palmer, the tutor down at CASA—the Center for Academic Support and Advising—to set up an appointment to see Ron for a one-on-one, which he hasn't done.

As for Lee, she is feeling lucky to have been in class on the day Elaine talked about her work. Recently she was kicked out of the dorm for a week—because she was in possession of a cup, a blue cup. The girl she was walking with had a similar cup that had beer in it, but Lee hadn't filled hers yet. Her resident director told her that she could either plead guilty and get kicked out, or go to trial and then get kicked out. When her parents were at Assumption College, they were de-dormed for a day, not a week. Lee, who's an out-of-state student (which they didn't know, and obviously she's going to miss a few classes as a result of this), had to try to get in touch with her uncle, who lives in Framingham. But he'd gone to Australia. She left countless messages. So last week she'd decided to go home to New Jersey. She missed two classes. Her father even called the dean to challenge this rule. He told Lee he's not an idiot, he knows what goes on at college. "But," he said, "you're an idiot for getting caught." He has no problem with alcohol per se, since he knows that she hasn't been drinking that often (maybe five times since the start of the semester). It makes her mad to think that they send kids to Alcoholics Anonymous when they get caught. As Andy likes to point out, there are some real alcoholics here. Sending people like her to AA shows disrespect for real alcoholics, he thinks. There are people on her floor who will come in four nights a week so drunk that they are about to pass out. Nothing is done to help them. A girl who passed out many times in the bathroom got written up for loudness but nothing else. "I've had people, like, throw up on my floor," says Lee. "and they get nothing because they don't have anything in their hands."

And then all of this has been happening against the backdrop of her parents' maybe breaking up. "It's crunch time," as her dad would say, but she thinks she'll probably get everything done—or she'll drive herself insane.

As she filled out the question sheet about her topic, she reflected that it was good to be able to connect the work she was doing in her fashion class to her Essentials of Writing research project. She got some good feedback when she read her questions about her topic out loud, and she thinks that it will be OK to focus on issues of social class affecting eighteenth-century women's clothing. She's planning to get together with Marion to exchange books. It's not a topic that's easy to find things about. She's had to do a project for her fashion class, and at least she's become acquainted with the fashion library over in Hemenway Annex. She should be able to get enough information from that library, and from the book

Marion has. Once she finds the information, she'll also be able to find more pictures, which will help her out.

Marion felt reassured but also somewhat mystified by what Dr. Beilin said about her own research. On the one hand, she found it interesting to learn how her professor kept rewriting her introduction while her editor told her to change this and change that. "It's like when she reads my papers," Marion said. "It shows that that happens to the best of writers, that she's not perfect; even though she's a professor, she makes mistakes, too. Her editor grades her, just the way she grades the class."

In writing, Marion thinks, there's no such thing as perfect. One person may think it's really great, another may not. But what she wonders about is what impels her professor to do such hard, time-consuming research when she already has her teaching and her family. If she, Marion, had no free time, this extra project would be just something she'd put aside for later. Marion wonders what keeps Elaine Beilin going when she's tired.

I wonder about that, too, of course. As friends, my wife and I are invited the following weekend to the bat mitzvah of Rachel, Elaine's younger daughter. I don't dare to take my laptop, but I can't completely switch off my curiosity, either. Does having a strong, loving family add energy to Elaine's life, even as it subtracts time? It's a break for me, too, seeing Elaine shed the role of professor, and, for at least one day, give her thoughts entirely to family and friends. Especially family, since not only are her parents here from Ottawa, but her younger sister and her three children, ages seven to ten, are visiting from Australia, living in the third-floor apartment in Elaine and Bob's house. In fact, they'll be staying for the next three weeks.

That Saturday morning, November 2, is bright and windy. The weather has gone suddenly from Indian summer to pre-winter—and when we arrive we see Bob standing in his gray suit, without a topcoat or hat, outside the synagogue, greeting guests before they go inside the foyer to join clumps of Elaine's relatives,

Bob's relatives, their friends, and Rachel's eighth-grade schoolmates. Among the colleagues from Framingham State is Elaine's former teaching partner in women's literature, and now the provost and academic vice president, Helen Heineman. Helen is a devout Catholic but spent her summers when she was an undergraduate as the music counselor in an Orthodox Jewish camp in the Catskills. When the service starts, we can hear, in the midst of the congregation, Helen's beautiful, trained voice singing the Hebrew prayers.

Rachel reads and sings without a hitch, leading the entire service in English and Hebrew. At thirteen, she's at her full height, probably, a bit taller than Elaine, but still not quite a hundred pounds—wearing a green dress. Elaine is wearing a wool suit that's bright red, a color she hasn't worn to work yet this fall. Three angels have come to Abraham to promise him that Sarah will bear a son, Rachel explains about the Torah portion scheduled for this week, only Sarah is eighty at this point—no longer having her periods, Rachel explains—so she and Abraham merely laugh. They recall their skepticism later by naming their son *Yitzhak*, laughter. In today's passage from the prophets, too, Rachel notes more references to surprising reserves of energy and life, the widow whose oil jugs never run out of oil, and the mother whose son seems dead until the prophet Elisha gives him mouth-to-mouth resuscitation, stretching himself out on top of him.

Elaine, Bob, and Hannah join Rachel on the raised platform in front of the ark that holds the Torah scrolls. Elaine speaks first, describing how, while the "old Rachel" is still with them, there's lately been a new Rachel as well, a person concerned with world issues, eager to help others. She describes her daughter in a way that's both perceptive and objective. Not for her the fulsome praise some parents at this moment in the ceremony heap on their thirteen-year-old prodigies. Bob describes his daughter's "inability to pass a piano keyboard without playing whatever song happens to be on her mind" as "genetic," but tells us how proud they are of all she's accomplished on her own, especially these last few months when she was studying hard for this ceremony.

At the candle lighting during the luncheon which follows, Rachel reads some witty couplets to announce her various relatives, rhyming Hannah, for example, with "piana." All the Australian cousins come up together, two blond English-looking girls and one boy, in little sailor suits. Their friends from Elaine's time at Mount Holyoke, from their Jamaica Plain baby-sitting group, from Framingham State quiz each other about kids, jobs, projects. A tall young woman in a black dress, Elaine's former student, Hilary Hodgkins, walks from table to table, bouncing the baby in her arms as she chats with some of her former professors. Hilary is Elaine's all-time favorite student and is half-way through law school now. Her bad headache from earlier in the week totally gone, Elaine is feeling only joy—and, in the words of the Hebrew prayer they recited earlier, grateful to be given life, to be sustained, and to reach this occasion.

That night there is another party for Rachel's forty or fifty classmates. Sunday, the relatives and friends from out of town are still around. There isn't much time for marking papers or planning, that's for sure, and Monday's class doesn't go particularly well, Elaine feels. But Wednesday's does. By now, she feels that it's time to ask them to bring in drafts of their introductions. With luck, if their lives haven't got the best of them, they should be that far along. She also feels that by now they'll be comfortable reading the drafts aloud to the whole class and getting feedback. It's the day after the national election. Clinton has beaten Dole, so there's still a Democrat in the White House, but there's still a Republican congressional majority (less likely to be friendly to increasing federal aid to education, Elaine predicts). When she arrives at the classroom, the students are sitting in an almost dark room. Why do they do that sometimes? It's almost as though they're in a state of suspended animation until she comes in and turns on the lights.

Perhaps it's their circadian rhythms, and they're about to go into hibernation? She hopes not; there's too much for all of them to do.

They pass out copies of drafts of the first paragraphs of their research papers. "Is Rosalind's paper around the table?" Elaine asks. She distributes a sheet of suggestions for doing well on the research paper and asks the students to take a moment to jot down one "dumb" question—"anything we could possibly answer today—a loaded question about the research paper." Susie asks whether you can state an author's name right in the sentence, or do you just have to keep the name, title, and page in a parenthesis at the end of the sentence? May has a question about using journal articles from a CD in the library. Francesca wants to know how she can quote her grandmother in her paper. Phoebe wants to know how they're supposed to get this paper done in just another week.

"What's the particular problem?" asks Elaine Beilin.

"I don't know; just the fact that we're still drafting."

"Um hm, just remember, it's not a huge paper—1,500 words. You've already written at least two 750-word papers. But I've talked to some of you, and I know you're having difficulty getting sources. So I'm willing to give you some leeway." She tells them that by the due date she wants them to come to class with at least an initial draft. "We've got time in the schedule," she reassures them. "Then you can have a final draft in the following Monday. Does that seem reasonable?"

"I think the hardest part is—" says Andy. "I actually got some sources, but then you have to organize it."

Elaine Beilin nods. "Yes, I'm going to say something about that." Last night, in fact, when she was driving home she found herself wondering whether Andy ever got to finish checking *The Grove Dictionary.* Sometimes that's the way it happens—their faces floating to the surface of her mind.

"Is the introduction supposed to be investigating something no one knows, or can it be more general?" asks Phoebe. "Maybe come back to me."

"No, good question. Remember this is the sort of writing you've done all semester. Documented writing. Explaining. Arguing. Writing a substantive, explicit, clear thesis. The sources are more complicated because before you were using only one source. Now I'm saying expand this to three sources. But the skills you've been using all semester, you're going to use again."

Lee and Marion both have questions about using illustrations. Jeremy passes—no question. Belinda doesn't have a defined topic yet, she says. "Maybe we can help," says Elaine, "at nine o'clock, when our collective brain comes into gear."

"What if you want to quote something your teacher says in class?" asks Rosalind.

"What do you think?" Elaine asks them.

"I think it's OK," says May.

"That dialogue would come under the rubric of trying to catch the reader's attention," says Elaine. "If you'd actually interviewed the teacher, then it would be absolutely necessary for you to document with a works-cited citation, so you wouldn't be stealing the words. If you've invented them yourself, then you're simply writing dialogue."

"I want to quote something you said," says Rosalind. "That history texts are the worst source of factual information."

"I did?" says Elaine. "I deny it!"

Rosalind shakes her head.

"I didn't even say they are *often* the worst source?"

"No."

"Well," says Elaine, "the citation would follow the format for an interview, but it would say 'class session.'"

Now it's Lee's turn. "Who's the audience?" she asks. "Am I talking to you?"

"Who's going to be reading it next week?" Elaine asks.

"You?" says Lee.

"And?"

"The class?"

"Yes. We've had discussion over these past weeks, so you can build on a common body of knowledge. Assume, for example, you don't have to explain much about Paul Revere. You can assume, in this class, we know about him."

Jeremy has taken off not only his hat but also his glasses.

"George, do you have a question?"

"Can I use an actual videotape of actual conversations?"

She goes all the way around the table, answering this miscellany of questions—How to cite a videotape? An Internet source?—and then they start to discuss the drafts of the first paragraphs. They look at Phoebe's first. Phoebe began her research by intending to write about the eleven children's books she found about Paul Revere's ride, but ended up focusing on just one, Jean Fritz's *And Then What Happened, Paul Revere?*

"OK, so your question," says Elaine, "is why did Fritz want to present Paul Revere's ride to a young audience? The thesis then would be something explicit, substantive, and arguable about that. The advantage of focusing your question," she says to the class as a whole, "is that it saves you time by focusing your research."

"I think that's the problem I'm having," says Rosalind. "I don't think I can really answer the question I have. I just don't understand why it's common knowledge that history textbooks aren't a good source of factual information and yet people keep using them. And my brother, who's in an honors history class, is having to memorize from the textbook. But my real question is, why are history books presented the way they are?"

"Yes," says Elaine. "You'd really have to write a book. You've brought up a really good question, but for now you'll have to answer a little piece of that question. Let's boil your research down to something simpler. Here's what I'm hearing: Are history textbooks accurate? And what's your answer?"

"No."

"Well, there you are."

"I'm using one that's not," says Rosalind. "I'm not going to use ones that are."

"But no," says Elaine, "you don't have to exclude them. You

can't argue something that's always, always true. Then it's not an argument; it's a fact."

"I found one that said, 'The British are coming,' and then one that didn't mention that at all. So I suppose they are different."

"Well, you have to define accuracy. What are your standards? You may find you're starting to describe what a history text should be. Essentially what you're coming up with is, 'What should high school students be doing in a history class?' That's why you're going to have to write a book on this someday."

"Another thing I'm having a problem with," says Rosalind, "is that in 1,500 to 2,000 words you can only use a few examples, so that's not fair."

"But you're talking about something we've talked about before, the use of representative examples. So you want to define the scope, set that out." She turns to the rest of the class. "Rosalind's paper is shaping up to be argumentative. Does anyone want to volunteer to talk about how yours is shaping up to be something persuasive, not argumentative?"

"Is mine," asks Phoebe, "since I'm saying something positive about that book?"

"Well, when we turn to Phoebe's in a few minutes, let's see. I'd advise you to keep writing as you do your research. Then it doesn't become so overwhelming to write when you sit down finally."

"I think once you read a couple of things, you start to realize what you're going to talk about," says Rosalind.

"If you find that you strongly agree or disagree with something you read," says Elaine, "then it may be time to start shaping your thesis. When you find something you disagree with," she says, "that's when you know you have something to write. We've heard enough argument in this room to know that you're allowed to disagree, even with people with Ph.D.'s."

The sky is silver now, growing a little lighter, taking on a rippling texture. Jeremy's hat is back on. He's reading over the draft of his own paper in his lap, having finished reading Phoebe's without writing anything on it.

"Let's start with something Phoebe's done really well," says Elaine.

"She's said Fritz does a good job," says George. "That quote she uses, 'Watch out dogs, watch out chickens.' That's something pretty funny for children."

"OK, that's a vivid example, a very good example of how effectively you can use source materials in a text. A beautiful example. That's a wonderful sentence," says Elaine, "where she says Fritz is 'reeling her youthful audience into her pleasant historical world.'"

They go on to discuss the epigraph Phoebe has chosen from Emerson, because Lee says she doesn't understand how it goes with the rest of the paper.

"I don't think it has to," says Andy. "I mean, like in books you see an epigraph and you don't really understand it, but you can tell it's more important to the writer."

"But look at the end of it," says Elaine. "It's got one of those Emersonian zings at the end—'no kinsman of his *sin*.' I'm wondering if that's because you think a children's book should help a child be good, or rather that it should encourage a child's naughtiness? Think about it. If you love it, it should stay in. Take Andy's advice and don't explain it. Or put something in the first paragraph that picks up on the language of the epigraph that will show why it's appropriate to the paper."

Later, when Phoebe hands in the paper, that's exactly what she does:

Through Fritz' Charmingly Childish Eyes

> "Respect the child, respect him to the end, but also respect yourself. Be the companion of his thought, the friend of his friendship, the lover of his virtue—but no kinsman of his sin."
>
> —Ralph Waldo Emerson

A children's author has a great responsibility in writing a

> good children's book. American author, Jean Fritz, helps us better understand how and why children's books on Paul Revere and the period in which he lived have been written and successfully meets Emerson's goals for children's authors. Her book, *And Then What Happened, Paul Revere?*, respects children in two distinct ways: it presents Revere's story thoroughly and accurately and it uncovers his life appropriately for grade-school children, using comprehensible language along with humor, enthusiasm, and charming illustrations. Her writing tools prove effective, as her book stands out as a valuable and memorable reminiscence of Paul Revere, a positively intriguing story of a real historical figure, balancing his accomplishments and human foibles.

That day Mary, who so rarely volunteers, has no objection to reading her opening aloud. She reads rapidly and clearly, her voice easily audible:

> John Hancock: The Man Behind the Image
>
> The name John Hancock is well known yet very few people know the man behind the image. The real John Hancock hidden deep behind the public persona is a man greatly flawed. The history books have done much to protect the super hero image given to him because of his contributions to his country; yet in his own time Hancock was regarded with contempt by his fellow statesmen.

In commenting on the introduction, Elaine praises the way Mary has integrated supporting material.

"I thought you did well integrating quotes," says Rosalind. "Did you find any more information on him?"

"I have the only biography that's in print," says Mary, "but I don't know what was in the one that was impounded by Hancock's heirs."

There are voices in the hallway—another class has let out early—and, without being asked, Colleen gets up to close the door.

"This is good," says Lee. "You pretty much want to know why people would want to teach you that Hancock was a totally different way."

"Jeremy, you were nodding?" Elaine asks.

"The introduction really drives this," Jeremy says. "By the end of the first paragraph we really want to know more."

As usual, the sounds of Professor Ambacher lecturing in the next classroom are coming through the doorway that connects the two rooms. The door is open a few inches, and Andy, who's sitting near it, gets up to close it.

"We like the sense that there might be a cover-up," says Elaine.

"I like the way she says John Hancock is 'shrouded in mystery,'" says May. "She doesn't really run off; she keeps to the topic."

They discuss ways to make some of Mary's in-text citations less bulky, and how to pare the quotations down so that only the most important, most striking part is left. "I brought chalk with me today," says Elaine, going to the board to rework one of these sentences. "Mary, what do you think? Do you see anything that could be cut out?"

Mary's quotation reads: "Material was collected and read, when members of the family immediately offered the writer $1,000 to hand over the work and not make further investigations. The writer took the money, and the book was never published."

"I could probably summarize more," Mary says, "and just leave the important part of the quotation."

"What do you think the important part is?" asks Elaine, her hand poised at the board.

"The part about the thousand dollars," says Mary.

"Yah, that's definitely it. Do you want to comment a little more about that?"

They use the last few minutes to explore some of the details of Mary's text. And then, at twenty after the hour, they know they have to go or they might not get to their next classes on time. "I'd like to keep doing this next Wednesday. By that time you'll have more done. Anything else you'd like us to do?"

"If we could just spend more time doing what we've just been doing," says Rosalind.

At the end of that class, before they filed out, Elaine said to them, "Good luck, good hunting, and—" Here she paused, exactly the way the sergeant on *Hill Street Blues* always does before releasing his squad to the streets, "—be careful out there." In her office the following day, she tells me she's happy about this class. "I thought this session was pretty good because we were talking about the research papers at a very interesting level. Perhaps," she acknowledges, "it's taken some longer than others to see that they weren't writing the standard high school chore. And that it could be something they were connected to, that it could be something that had to do with themselves. Kate, Arthur, and Francesca are writing about family history. Kate wasn't in class, but she wrote me a note. That was very good. She wrote me on Tuesday explaining why she couldn't be there. She had to take her little brother to court."

Elaine thinks she sees some improvement in Kate's attitude. "She seems happier. She seems more involved in the class than fighting the class. Amelia seems to have disappeared, but I saw that coming. Amelia was so detached, missed so many classes. Even things that she handed in—she was deeply self-critical about them. When I mentioned something about them, her confidence seemed so low. Whatever her personal unhappiness is now, it's stopping her from committing. It's sad—she has the earmarks of someone who's talented. She could rescue herself by doing good work. Can she do the work, though, without working on her personal issues? And can she solve those issues without doing something to boost her confidence? I'll probably call her. I'll probably call Judy Klaas [the Dean of Students] and see if she's heard anything."

Greg has checked in briefly. "Because I didn't leave any of the materials in my out-box," she smiles. "He clearly hasn't got a clue about what to do about a research paper. He'll have to come and see me." But Lee, she notes, has made a "thorough re-entry." Lee is not quite caught up, but they're having a meeting tomorrow. "We're making plans." Lee has to catch up on at least one essay, but Elaine is optimistic about Lee's research project. "It connects with her grandmother, something she's putting herself into. She's decided she wants to do costume from the 1920s and 1930s. She saw things from her grandmother's closet that interested her." Lee is taking a fashion course in the Family and Consumer Science Department, so this project, Elaine believes, should dovetail with that. If it works out, it will combine her artistic ability and her interest in her grandmother and give her an opportunity to write about these things.

The thought of the fashion course reminds her of something about Marion, too. "It's funny—I called Becky Taylor [a professor in the family and consumer sciences department] and asked her if Marion could come over to speak with her. Marion was sitting right there. I tried to tell her Becky was friendly and approachable. But she did feel intimidated, I think. I might need to walk her over.

"Andy's writing needs work," she says. "And he works over at CASA," she adds, implying that he could so easily get help. "He's got the smarts. It's just that he's too busy to slow down, to do the revising. The field-trip paper was a rush. His girlfriend came, so he took her. He really doesn't like people to tell him that he isn't doing something well," she reflects. "But I think I'm going to lay it down a little more strongly," she says, as though coming to a decision. "He could do better if he'd take the time." She believes that Andy is "an underachiever" who can probably write up to a higher level but "needs a little more pushing to perform. He's just so genial," she says. "I was a little fooled by it. He's so agreeable, I thought 'He's actually going to do these revisions.'"

Though she's pleased with the way Mary's work is going, she has a different sort of concern here. "In that draft she turned in yesterday, everything was where she'd need it to blast away on that paper. But the sentences were these little short declarative sentences, five in a row. I really want to watch this. Is this how she writes to begin with, and then at some later point writes in some mature and sophisticated way, and then changes the sentence structure? They were very puerile sentences.

"Belinda I'm really pleased with," Elaine says. "She wrote a mediocre book review, and we had a wonderful conference. She went away and wrote a marvelous revision. She actually wrote all the things she wanted to say. The paper was focused, convincing, organized." Here, unlike Mary, she took chances with complex sentences but didn't master the commas and other punctuation. "So I said, 'Do it again, and work on that. Fix it.'" Looking over the latest draft from the top of a pile on her desk, she says "No question, that's an A paper. She was really happy." In Elaine's view, Belinda, like Rosalind, has benefited by being out of school for a while. "She's another person who took some time off—she worked in a dry cleaner's—and the effect on her was, 'Never again.'"

"Another person who did a great job of revision was May. May," she says, "really pulled it out, too. She went back, saw weaknesses, turned the whole essay around. The crucial thing with both of these two is to see if they can start from that new level with the research paper." She thinks a moment. "Francesca also did a revision. Did you read her first paragraph?" Elaine laughs. "Her first paragraph is a synopsis of World War II. She's writing about her grandmother, isn't she? But, actually, I could see where she's going. When my parents tell their stories about the war, they, too, always start with that overview: the ultimate fight against a monster. Then they'll tell a story connected to that. So," she considers, smiling still, "maybe it's a sort of overview from oral history."

As to why more people weren't in class yesterday, she believes it's because they've fallen behind and aren't prepared to bring in a draft. "But Jeremy will come in anyway," she says. "He comes to class—unprepared, but he comes. And he seems to get something out of it. He wrote me this heartrending self-assessment. 'Jeremy,' I said, 'come and talk to me.' He said he would. He seemed grateful. But he hasn't. If he finds a teacher who's teaching a subject that really gets to him, that will be a major difference. Partly, it's his own inertia. And I'm convinced there's some kind of writing or reading or learning disability of some kind. But he either doesn't know it or knows it and doesn't want it to be acknowledged. He was wearing his hat again," she shakes her head. "Retreating.

"Wednesday was great," she continues, "despite Monday's class." On Monday, as luck would have it, practically everyone was there, but she felt that the class wasn't good at all. "It was my fault. I couldn't follow my lesson plan. My body was there on Monday, but the teacher was sort of hanging out the window looking in. I can't remember a thing about the class. It was such a painful experience. I just eradicated it the moment I got out of there. All I remember was that I was suffering, and if I was suffering then probably the students were suffering, too."

I make no comment, except to say that I have days like that, too. I know the students probably can't tell the difference, but I feel the moves I'm making are clumsy, unsynchronized. "If it's of any help, I couldn't tell you were feeling that way."

From the look on her face I can tell this has helped a little, but not much. Whether she broods or not, I can't say, but it's clear to me that she doesn't allow herself to do it for long, and doesn't let it get in the way of her main task.

True, yesterday the students were getting up to close the doors, so it could be quieter in the room, while on Monday it was Elaine herself who asked Colleen to open the door a little for air. But then, too, on Monday I thought she'd given her most open explanation yet of what, in her view, the Fischer book really has to teach: "People make things happen," she'd explained. "This idea of the individual agent is absolutely important to Fischer's idea of history, but these individuals work within a network. History is not just great events, it's this network of people who all make choices and contribute to this tapestry." This idea coincides with my sense of the balance Elaine maintains between her own importance to the students in the classroom and the need for the students to feel that they are also making decisions that contribute to the weaving of the whole. Indeed, it's rare for her to wear her most crucial thoughts on her sleeve like that in class. Her very openness in articulating the life-lesson she hopes the students will learn from Fischer's book might, ironically, have been one result of her sense that she was "hanging out the window, looking in."

It had been Rosalind's question about history that triggered this wide-open response from Elaine. And today it's Rosalind that she's most interested in talking about. "She came to my office Monday, right after class, really revved up about her research project." Rosalind is indignant about the way her younger brother, now taking a supposed honors course in history in high school, is being taught: "He's experiencing the entire field as memorization. Memorize events and spew them out on Friday." Elaine suggested bringing him into the essay. She also wants Rosalind to reflect on the broader issues that form the basis for making her judgment, asking her whether what she's saying is wrong with history teaching isn't the same thing that's frequently wrong with English teaching as well.

"I got her to talk about the standard against which she was measuring her brother's class. Her complaint was not only that both the teacher and the book were inaccurate and biased, but that they both served an institution that says, 'Don't think about what I'm telling you, just tell me what the book said.'" And if students were taught this way, how could they avoid turning out to be ignorant and biased themselves? Elaine suggested, further, that Rosalind ought to read Jonathan Kozol, so she could see how a teacher addresses students in a way that is respectful towards the whole person, or even Paolo Freire, for a broader, more theoretical view, to see how pedagogy is related to social and political ideology. "Do we want passive students, obedient to authority, or do we want empowered, active thinking?"

Rosalind saw many of the implications of her own thinking, "which was great," says Elaine. "She says her mother saw an ad for a position that pays $71,000 a year. And Rosalind said, 'I could do that job, but I'd be so miserable in business.' So I said, 'Great, so you've chosen teaching, where you'll get paid half that amount but where you can fulfill your idealism. You have to hold on to that.' I told her to read the sign over at the McAuliffe Center." She means the quotation in big blue letters over the reception desk in the College's space-travel lab, which is named after Framingham alumna Christa McAuliffe: "I touch the future. I teach."

Elaine thinks Rosalind has what it takes to be an exceptional teacher. "She's so passionate." They got onto the subject of an event that happened recently in Foxboro involving some skinheads.

In Foxboro, a town near Dean College, where Rosalind's fiancé works, skinheads killed a young man who told them to leave a party. Dean College has a large population of foreign and black students, and Joey told her that the State Police were going to be at Dean for a few days, just in case, because one of the skinheads said they'd be coming to Dean. Rosalind worried. She knew that the chance of the skinheads showing up and anything bad happening was slim, especially since the State Police were there, and she kept telling herself that nothing really bad was going to happen. It was only that—when she started to think about it—it raised the whole issue of freedom for her. "All those escorts, police—it's a total infringement on people's freedom."

Rosalind told her she couldn't understand how people could hate each other because of religion or skin color. "She was practically in tears, and I said, 'That's what you have to hold on to. Be part of creating peaceful, tolerant human beings.'" Elaine believes that Rosalind will project those ideals.

As she's saying this I'm remembering what she's told me about Mr. Henderson, her teacher in thirteenth grade, or Mr. McDonald, in eighth grade, teaching her opera.

"The kids will see that," Elaine tells me. "They'll see that passion."

8. LOW COMPLIANCE

WHEN ROSALIND'S PAPER comes in the following week her brother's experience is now part of the introduction, and her paper also features an epigraph:

It's Written In A Text Book, So It Must Be True!

> Way up in some office building sit people—deciding all the issues of American History. . . . What shall we think of the Vietnam War? Of the American Revolution? What is the nature of American society and what are its values? The responsibility of these people seems awesome, for . . . the audiences are huge, impressionable, and captive. Children have to read textbooks.
>
> —Frances Fitzgerald on history textbooks.

"What are you doing," I inquired of my brother, noting the grim, bored look on his face. "Reading chapter four of my history book," he glumly replied and went on to tell me, "I have to take down every important event because we're having a test on Monday." This conversation with my younger brother stirred my curiosity. I remember being bored out of my mind studying American History not too long ago. I began to wonder why we are so bored studying history. The answer to this perplexing situation that has struck

> most high school students can be found within the methods used for teaching, the way the information is structured when it is presented to us, and the truthfulness and bias of the materials. In this paper, I am not attempting to answer all of the questions about why our school system is failing us. I am simply attempting to scrape the surface of the inaccuracies and biases contained in the materials that our generation is committing to memory; and to propose the possibility that history text books are taking away from the learning experience more than they are giving.

No mere mechanical exercise, this paper addresses at least a manageable piece of a problem Rosalind passionately cares about. Because of the course readings, Rosalind probably knows more about Paul Revere and his famous ride than the author of the history book she will critique. She can thus enter into an academic debate with the confidence that, for example, she has read all three versions of Revere's own written account. She knows, as the author of the textbook she has chosen to examine clearly does not, that Paul Revere never shouted "The British are coming!" (That's one of the textbook's chapter headings.) She knows that the primary source, Revere himself, never mentions shouting any such thing, and, as David Hackett Fischer, whom Rosalind refers to as "a trusted academic source," puts it: "Many New England express riders that night would speak of Regulars, Redcoats, and the King's men . . . but no messenger is known on good authority to have cried, 'The British are coming.'" As Rosalind goes on to say, "It is unrealistic to think that a colonist would shout the above, because the colonists believed they were British. They had not yet become Americans."

Confidence, though, is a double-edged term. As Herman Melville probed its implications in his unsettling novel, *The Confidence Man*, it stands for both faith and its opposite, the perception that all surfaces are deceiving, and that all that can be known about God or human beings is surface. According to Gregory

Colomb, an expert on teaching academic writing and on writing across the curriculum, a surface marred by errors is more than likely a reflection of incomplete understanding and still undeveloped thinking.[13] The writing in Rosalind's introductory paragraph above would please most teachers of undergraduates, since it not only detects a problem in an apparent consensus—that history should be taught using textbooks—but it also proposes a solution: if current history texts are "taking away from the learning experience more than they are giving," then different textbooks are needed, or an approach that would expose students to "trusted academic sources" or, indeed, to primary sources like the depositions Rosalind herself has read. These teachers would have to respect the spirited opening in which Rosalind gets the reader's attention, and the graceful way in which she pares down the subject. They (and most lay critics of contemporary higher education, too) would be gratified, as well, at the complex sentences, which are nearly error-free.

The clear thinking expressed in Rosalind's introduction is, then, of a piece with the mechanics of the sentences and paragraphs—as Colomb and many others would predict: Rosalind worked and reworked the logic of that paragraph, and, as she did so, corrected the numerous writing glitches. If the reader were to read on, however, she might find numerous errors in the body and conclusion of the piece. Elaine's final comment, after expressing her enthusiasm, cautions Rosalind on that very point: "You should note, however, that while the big picture is very sound, the details need work: You need to work on revising your final draft to look for sentence errors such as awkward constructions, punctuation errors, errors of reference and agreement, and spelling errors."

These very errors would tend to undermine most professors', and indeed most employers', confidence in this student. And how would one explain to the faculty of other departments, not to mention the college's trustees, why a professor would give an A- and much praise to a twenty-one-year-old freshman who refers to "depicting the event in a factual manor" or refers to a previously-pointed-out fallacy as "the proceeding inaccuracy"?

"If this is your A-student," one could imagine these critics saying, "I'd hate to see your B or C students!"

Elaine herself explains that she gave that grade assuming that Rosalind was going to correct all the errors. Had this been a student in whom she'd had less confidence, she'd have waited to make sure.

In one form or another, this debate over the teaching of writing has, as Paul Kameen has pointed out, been going on at least since Plato examined rhetoric in Socrates' dialogue with Gorgias. In this dialogue, Socrates asks "Is not the position of the rhetorician and of rhetoric . . . [that] it has no need to know the truth about things but merely to discover a technique of persuasion, so as to appear among the ignorant to have more knowledge than the expert?" And Gorgias, the teacher of rhetoric, replies: "But is this not a great comfort, Socrates, to be able without learning any other arts but this one to prove in no way inferior to the specialists?"

Kameen believes that this passage "brings into focus . . . the . . . competition between value- and performance-based . . . instruction . . . (between, that is, a rhetoric whose primary injunction is, following Socrates, 'know thyself' and another, whose primary injunction is, following Gorgias, 'know thy audience')."[14] Elaine Beilin, like most teachers of composition, belongs to neither the value camp nor the performance camp exclusively. Many times during the semester, she has referred to the importance of the writer's knowing her audience; yet at the very heart of her enterprise with these students is getting them to understand that academic writing is not some sort of marionette show to please a professor (then, later, an employer)—a kind of confidence game—but discovering real conviction and coming as close as possible to the truth as one's own learning and research can reveal it—that is, having the confidence to participate in the actual conversation of scholarship.

In this case, while not overlooking the rough edges of Rosalind's performance (and, in fact, offering her tangible, immediate help: "I'd be happy to go over these things with you," she writes at the end of her comment on Rosalind's paper, and "you should also check the relevant sections of *Writing Essentials* for help"), Elaine feels that Rosalind has hit the center of the target closely enough, and hit it hard, with personal conviction. She writes:

> Your dismay and disgust surface in words like "frightening" and "fluffy interpretation," and your evidence supports your reactions. The thesis that you finally hammered out at the end of the introduction is clear, explicit, and arguable—so that all that struggling with an unwieldy topic until you found your focus was worth the effort!

Of the many things that might be said of this student's effort, and of the teacher's response, one sure thing is that the product ought to be viewed as part of a *process* of instruction. No outside reader could know the ways in which this student has responded positively to her teacher's true teaching. As in any relationship, the enthusiasm of one person's response triggers enthusiasm in the other; and this mutually reinforcing pattern, which can be seen even early on in the relationship of these two women, is fully established by this point in the semester.

Yet all of this argues for a student having many teachers. The hard reality of other classrooms, where a paper with errors may blow up in the student's face (some professors still fail a student for committing too many errors), may teach Rosalind to care more about the small details of appearances. Yet none of these details would matter to an independent-minded student like Rosalind if she didn't understand that truth had to be at the heart of the enterprise. If she wanted to deal only with small details, without striving for larger meanings, she could stay on as night manager of the mail-order support-hose company, or take the job her mother found for her in the classifieds. As it is, Elaine hopes, something of her own teaching spark has been passed on to Rosalind. That message, "Find out the truth for yourself," and its wider implication for "creating peaceful, tolerant human beings," might, she hopes, get passed on to hundreds of Rosalind's students in the future—that is, if Rosalind can somehow find the money, and maintain the energy, to stay on and if she can resist the culture of her class, community, and family telling her that her upcoming marriage has to take priority, even over her education. Still, if she does stay on, after eight semesters' practice, rather than merely one, the small errors that betray her as unsteady on her feet will have burned off under the heat of her passion to do well—at least, so her teacher expects.

Some of the other papers—among those that have come in on time—show promise too. By the mid-November due date, Amelia, Susie, Jeremy, Arthur, and Kate haven't handed theirs in. Of those who have handed theirs in, George, Donna, Greg, and even Belinda have gotten D's. Belinda rewrites hers later for a B-grade; George, Donna, and Greg never do. All of these students have been passing up to this point, but the complexity of orchestrating even this short research project and writing it up has produced what seems like a disintegration of resolve. Of the twenty-one people who sat around the table and answered to their names when Elaine read the roll for the first time in September, only eleven can be said to be unequivocally passing the course at this point, two months later. This is worse than other years. But chance must enter into the make-up of any group of students. Whatever the case, Elaine is too experienced to panic at this point. A few of those who are late with their research papers or have done them poorly will be all right, Elaine Beilin is sure—Susie and Belinda, for example—though others, like George, Arthur, Jeremy, and Kate, may not be.

While Greg's paper has come in on time, it seems totally empty. Ominously, his title is merely "Paul Revere." Though the writing is fluid and confident—Greg wrote on his questionnaire the first day that he wants to be a writer—to Elaine's eye, it all has the appearance of a confidence game. In giving him the minimum passing grade, D-, she writes:

> Greg—Considering that your audience is a class that has

> spent weeks reading and discussing Fischer's book, I wonder why your essay simply recapitulates the basic facts of Revere's life and the thesis of Fischer's book—without once acknowledging Fischer as a source. In what sense is this a *research* paper? Your assignment sheet stipulated three primary or secondary sources, *excluding* encyclopedias. I see no evidence here that you have thought about the *issues* or *ideas* that Fischer raises or that you have pursued a line of thinking about Revere, his artworks, or his ride. You need a specific, concrete *thesis* about a particular aspect of Revere's life so that you can write a coherent, focused essay.

One quick tip-off that Greg hasn't done a true research project is his bibliography, which lists only Fischer's book and two encyclopedias. If he were a better confidence man, he'd certainly have listed more. But to Elaine's eye, this paper typifies the disconnect that Greg's silence, his very body language in class, has revealed. Even when placed in small groups, he sits back from the table, hardly saying anything. It's not that he doesn't come to class, but when he does come, is he really there? Greg received a minor warning at mid-semester—notice that his work, though passing, was at the D level. Though his second and third papers got B's, he missed or did very poorly on six of the ten shorter writing assignments. He seems to be almost deliberately hovering near the bottom, and as long as he doesn't totally fail, will probably continue at that level. It's Greg, not Jeremy, who's truly the "loose fish" of the class, the one eluding capture or examination.

"We're into the low-compliance time of the semester," Elaine concludes. It's not unusual, during these mid-November class sessions, to have as many as eight to ten students absent—or, like Jeremy, there, but without the book or assignment that's needed.

"I feel kind of desperate," Elaine tells me. They're about to move into the final phase of the course, where the students have been allowed to choose the readings. Most voted to read short stories, so Elaine has ordered a collection of stories about American families. But the thought of reading something with them that they'll find easier and more engaging than the Paul Revere text doesn't cheer her up, especially. For one thing, it introduces a whole new subject to the class—how to read literature—which is actually the focus of another course she teaches, Literary Study. What is she supposed to teach them in the remaining three weeks—just six more class sessions? "I always feel this way about teaching literature in Essentials," she says. "Always kind of desperate, not really clear about what they've learned about writing. Oh my God, I think, a few more classes, and there's so much more."

She feels bad that some of the students have simply slipped through the cracks. Greg seems to have eluded her entirely. And then there's Arthur. There's something so young about Arthur—the plump, cheerful boy's face, the green backwards baseball cap. She's not sure, but it seems as though he was brought up in a pretty strict working-class household and the freedom of dorm life has, in some way, overwhelmed him. "I read the riot act to Arthur," she tells me. "His roommate's in my Shakespeare class, and he's telling me Arthur-this, Arthur-that. I said Arthur should come and see me himself." Arthur ended up coming to class, but she wasn't sure why. He didn't have his book; he was two essays behind. She told him to make an appointment to come see her, and he didn't keep it, though he's scheduled to see her a little later today. "I said, 'Are you planning to fail this course?' and he said, 'Oop, well I've got to work, I've got to do this and that.' So I said, 'Fine, choose your priorities.'"

Though Amelia says she has two papers to turn in, she's been out for the last two weeks because of her grandmother's illness and death. Elaine has reminded Amelia that she needs to let all of her professors know, through the Dean's office, that there's been a death in the family. "You really have to get in touch," she tells her, or there will be no documentation for her absences. Amelia came to see her, though, and made an appointment for a conference—but then she called, saying she'd had a flat tire. Yesterday, she couldn't come to class because she had to replace the two tires. She also didn't have money to buy the short-story book they'll be using. Elaine offered to loan her the six dollars, but Amelia declined, saying she was getting paid today.

"She has a really great idea for a research paper," Elaine says. "She wants to write about some of the Historical Society houses and see if she can visit them. She's really interested in how they're constructed and in the function of the design." Elaine has told her that this could be interesting and might take the form of a process analysis. "But Amelia's still at stage one."

Kate, too, has hardly begun the research paper. She's abandoned her attempt to write about her grandmother's neighborhood in Dorchester. Now she wants to do a paper about a game involving vampires. Elaine has told Kate that she's very doubtful about this idea, because she doesn't think there will be anything substantial enough to study about the game. Kate's promised to bring in the game to show her. Kate has also told her that she has been working forty hours a week at her job again, but that she intends to get her hours cut so that she can do her work at the end of the semester. Elaine is afraid that unless she gets a lot more work done soon, she will drop out. "If she comes to see me, I'm going to have to tell her this is fish or cut bait time," says Elaine Beilin.

One person she felt was really engaged with the course, but who has not come to see her at all, is George. He seemed to be working hard during the first part of the semester—producing C papers but expressing willingness to try. Then he disappeared before the research project was due. His first attempt at the research paper on sports was unfocused, so Elaine suggested that he pick a single sport and focus on a question he wanted to answer. "That's such a good technique—getting them to ask what questions they have. But then they seem to revert to some ur-method of doing research, which gets them spread out all over the map again." She felt that George had made great progress, but now she thinks he has "reverted." She gets the feeling that he's under stress, that there's some pressure, some unhappiness that's "way beyond the pale of what I can deal with or help him with. He seems so withdrawn."

George will say very good things in class, but then, it seems to her, he'll recede.

"I tried to put the research paper where I thought people who tend to atrophy at the end of the semester would still have time to come for help and not implode." But she doesn't think she got it quite right. She should have put it one assignment ahead of where it was.

But there's still no easy explanation for why students like George, Arthur, Amelia, or Kate should be so much at risk. One possibility is a kind of poverty that might not register on economic charts. She cites a new study of seventh and eighth graders that found that their grades in math and science correlated with the amount of time they spent on homework, what kind of teaching they received, and what level classes they were put in, but, even more strongly with home environment. How many books were in the home? How many years of schooling had their parents had? These, more than other factors, determined how well they did. Of course, there are exceptions, like Greta, camped out in her mother's living room, begging rides to school—Greta's still doing well. And, unfortunately, there are exceptions the other way. Both of Lee's parents are college graduates, but something else is missing there—some solid sense that there will be a family to come back to.

Elaine thinks maybe that's why she's picked the story anthology she has. She has a sense that there are so many students in the class with divorced or estranged parents—Andy, Greta, Amelia, Lee (or so it's beginning to seem), May, Francesca, Susie, and maybe others, too—that she thinks these stories may reach them personally. And that personal response to the reading may give them the added energy they'll need to complete the final essays well. But one factor that continues to loom powerfully is class. Even Arthur, for example, who attended the best public high school in Boston but is the first in his family to attend college, seems to lack the previous experience most middle class kids have had in being away from home before coming to college. If he'd been away before, away from the restrictions of his home, perhaps he wouldn't have been thrown into such a tail spin by the relatively unrestricted life in the dorm?

More profoundly, there seems to be a sense of class alienation in many of the students at Framingham. The town itself has long been thought of as typical of the country. In fact, that's why in the 1950s it was selected as the site of the Framingham Heart Study, the longest running longitudinal study of heart disease, covering families over several generations, and still ongoing. But Framingham, like the heart of America itself, has changed. While the upper-income neighborhoods on the north side have made substantial gains in real income, the income of working-class families on the south side has stayed flat, at best. The twenty-one-dollar-an-hour jobs at the now-closed General Motors plant down there have been transferred to lower-wage workers in Canada and Mexico. Voting rates for those districts are down (while they're up in higher-income areas). And then there's the increase in the number of households headed by divorced women, who are usually poorer than they were when the marriage was intact. Beneath these students there's no safety net; in Framingham's current service economy, good jobs for young workers without college degrees are scarce.[15]

In some ways the students know this. Greta's mother, for example, regards her as the family's last hope to get someone through college. It's like that sad, terrible Raymond Carver story they're going to be reading: A father overloaded with pleas for help from his mother, his brother, his daughter, and his college student son, can't keep paying for all of them, and yet he feels he must—including the college son. "He was the first kid in the family, on either side of the family, to even *want* to go to college, so everybody thought it would be a good idea," says the narrator. "I thought so too," he says, "at first."[16] But without the grounding in the family, all too often these students arrive as freshmen and are at a loss about how to cope.

If these students are like immigrants to a new culture, they are often unwilling immigrants. They often have no discernable wanderlust, no determination to go far from home. In attempting to live lives much like their parents', they may find that a college degree is now necessary to enable them to earn enough to replicate their parents' level of comfort and security. But whether willing or not, these students are going to have to enter and cope with a new culture in order to succeed. Paolo Freire talks about the sense of alienation that students experience who are new to academic culture. "You don't feel connected, or that what you say really matters, and you feel excluded," Elaine explains. "So that removes the sense of 'Of course I should tell them if I'm not going to be there.' We have to figure out a way to reinvent the students' relationship toward the institution. Students should feel that their experience is really what's at issue, that what they think about doesn't have to fit into some kind of mold. Otherwise an endless circle is set up, and this has to do with self-esteem. The students feel inadequate to start, then they don't do the work, and then that proves it."

She sits in the November grayness of her office as though the magnitude of the problem, as she's just defined it, leaves her barely able to breathe.

When she thinks about the final three weeks she grabs her head in a comical mime of panic and despair. "I've had this feeling of paralysis in class at the thought of how much I want to do with these students. If they'll just do the reading, I really hope they'll connect with what they read. I want to try to get them to talk about their own reactions to the stories, because I really want the last two essays to say, 'This is how I'm feeling, thinking, seeing, but what I have to do is write analytically and say something that will interest my reader.' Again, it's figuring out how to connect one's feelings and thinking to the text. That's where I would start in Literary Study, too."

One change she might have suggested would have been to keep this group together another semester and let them take her Literary Study section. The main thing—the only essential thing—she needs to teach might not be conveyed in one semester, at least not to many of them. They have to learn that coming to college doesn't mean complying with a million assignments; it means finding an energy source within their own individual wills, a determination to *use* the instruction for their own purposes. But these purposes have to be channeled, within each course, into a particular discipline. This means understanding that one's own thinking has to take into account the entire tapestry of what others, too, have thought. Then it has to be presented, through one's own writing, in a way that others will respect.

Rosalind, for one, has already clearly tapped into her own internal energy source. Now, Elaine thinks, there's nothing in the entire department that Rosalind couldn't master. In fact, she's told Elaine she'd like to sign up for her advanced honors course, Poetry and Prose of the English Renaissance. Elaine is sure Rosalind can hold her own in that class, even with juniors and seniors.

But, in others, the critical mass of self-assertion hasn't been reached, and, thus, the energy isn't there. Many of them still think this is *her* work they're doing, not their own. In her own classroom, in her small corner of the institution, she wants more than anything to help them reshape their relationship with academic life.

She says a number of the students have tried to get into her section of Literary Study next semester, but it has already filled before most freshmen can register. She wants them to take the course, though, and she's been recommending that they try to get into Marilyn Harter's section— "though it would be good for them to keep working with me. I know their work, and the things we could really focus on. You have to spend so much time at the beginning of the semester getting them to realize that you're on their side. A lot of them trust me now. That would be a nice way to start."

9. KNOWLEDGE

IN JOHN UPDIKE's short story "Still of Some Use," a father returns to help his ex-wife and their two sons empty their former house. On the Monday before Thanksgiving, Elaine passes out copies of this story as a way of introducing this final phase of the course: writing about short stories that concern the family.

She begins by describing the anthology, *American Families*, and explaining why she chose it and how they will be using it to shape their discussions and writing for the remaining three weeks. The majority of the students, when she surveyed them, said they preferred reading short stories. Another reason she chose to assign fiction is that all semester they've been exploring the difference between fiction and history through Fischer's book on Paul Revere. "I wanted stories where we'd all know something about the reality, and this collection seemed to be the answer," she tells them. "We all have knowledge about families. We know about our own families; we know about other people's families. So I thought it would be interesting to look at a number of stories, and the ways that writers have taken on and shaped writing about the family." She goes on to say that the stories will allow the students to draw not only on their own knowledge and experience but also on the reading they've done before. "So what we'll be talking about is how we synthesize what we've known before with a new text."

Elaine knows that a course devoted entirely to reading history, or to reading fiction about the family, would have been more coherent—but in the real life of the classroom, coherence of this kind isn't the only desirable goal. Perhaps the coherence that matters more is keeping the class connected, or, in this case, trying to get them to connect better with the readings. Shifting gears is sometimes necessary for even the most experienced teacher. And knowing how to hold the class together can be more important, at times, than sticking doggedly to a single subject. Had she begun with short stories, it is easy to imagine a class of English majors remaining interested in the readings for the entire semester. Perhaps, if she could begin again, that's exactly what she would do. But in selecting readings, a professor makes the best guess she can, balancing her own enthusiasm for a topic—important to maintain—with the likelihood that the students will find her enthusiasm irresistibly contagious. If she's guessed wrong, the course can still be successful, provided she has the resiliency to modify the plan. Elaine's syllabus allowed for this too, initially keeping the terrain after Thanksgiving blank, but alluding to "Short Stories on American Families" to begin after the research papers were due. When she made up her syllabus over the summer, she anticipated that Paul Revere fatigue might have set in by this point. Now it's clear to her that any more work on Paul Revere would be a forced march, and that selecting readings that are short and that students will feel knowledgeable about may be the wisest move here. After all, the main goal for the course is for the students to write, not for them to master a certain body of history or literature.

Elaine explains that they will write two more essays. In the first, they'll compare two stories in the anthology. "And because these stories are all on a similar theme, it's not very hard to find stories to compare." Or another way they could write the paper is to bring something to bear from their own reading or experience. "Oh my gosh, that's just like the wedding I went to last year in my family," she says, by way of illustrating one possible response. "Or you might come across a character who reminds you of a favorite aunt, or, at least, a favorite cousin, or who might remind you of yourself."

The second essay she will assign will ask them to look at some important social issue that one of these stories treats—drug abuse, divorce, race relations, gender discrimination, the treatment of the elderly—and evaluate how this issue is portrayed. "Families are little hotbeds for all these social issues," she says. "And I'll ask you to argue that the writer wants the reader to think a certain way. Or that it makes a contribution to the public discussion of a particular issue. Or to say why you might recommend the story to someone to whom it might give solace or illumination."

The fourteen stories she has assigned, out of the twenty-eight in the book, are taken from lists the students submitted of stories in this anthology that looked interesting to them or which they'd already had time to read and had recommended. "The story I chose for today, though, isn't on anyone's list." She says she's picked the Updike story because it is the shortest story in the book, and thus can be read aloud right now.

She's divided the Xeroxed copies of the story into ten sections, she explains to those who will be reading it from their own books, and her goal is "to take manageable bites. I did try to follow the rhythm of the story." Each of the students will read a section aloud. Then they'll pause, underline, or make notes in the margin; that is, they'll "begin to work interactively with the text." At the end they'll write a one-sentence summary, just something that states who does what, when, where, and why. Only eleven students are here today, so that still leaves one student without a section to read. Instead of a section of the story, Amelia reads the blurb about the story in the introduction, how "a divorced father returns to help his former wife and their two sons clear out the house which they once shared as a family. Both the father and his younger son experience an unexpected sense of loss as they discard the possessions which once knitted them together" (xviii).

"OK, write any response to that," says Elaine. Susie uses a day-glow marker; Francesca makes some notes on lined paper; Rosalind writes directly in the book; Amelia works in her lap, her notebook out of sight, her face almost out of sight too, since her hair falls down both sides of her face; Mary just stares at the book and doesn't write anything. (Almost a year later, at our follow-up interview, she will tell me that the reading of this story will stand out in her mind as having moved her greatly. She had not allowed herself to think about how homesick she was feeling, separated from her large family. This story, about another sort of loss of family, awakened those feelings.)

After a few minutes, Belinda begins reading the story confidently, a little mechanically. She never quite hits a smooth rhythm, but catches once or twice during each sentence, like a nail snagging on cloth, then moves on. Everyone is writing after this first paragraph, including Elaine.

After a few more minutes, Greta continues the reading in a soft voice, subtly acting out the dialog. *"What shall we do with all these games?" Foster shouted, in a kind of agony, to his scattered family as they moved up and down the attic stairs.*

"Trash 'em," his younger son, a strapping nineteen, urged.

Rosalind takes over after another pause, her reading loud, confident. *It was a game of sorts to hit the truck bed with objects dropped from the height of the house.*

Marion, who reads smoothly, can't read the dialogue as if people were actually speaking. *"What's the matter?"*

"Nothing. These games weren't used much."

"I know. It happens fast. You better stop now; it's making you too sad."

May, with her bright, intrepid voice, like a child who is confident in her reading, seems to have no sense of Foster's point of view, his sadness. She also makes no attempt to do Ted's voice—the ex-wife's boyfriend—as Foster would probably render it.

Phoebe, though, gets some sadness into her reading: *Ted's big hand was cupped under Mrs. Foster's chin while his thumb rubbed away a smudge of dirt along her jaw which Foster hadn't noticed.* But then she reads, *Foster saw them suddenly as a touching, aging couple, and this perception seemed permission to go,* and her voice is flat, adult sadness filtered through youthful imperviousness.

Mary reads distinctly, easily: *Foster tossed the tokens into the truck; they rattled to rest on the metal. "This depress you?"*

"Naa." The boy amended, "Kind of."

When done reading the story they are to write a one-sentence summary, but Elaine interrupts them. "Before that," she says, "let's talk about some of the things you found yourself connecting with, things that seemed familiar—things that seemed too familiar. Things that you thought brought new life to describing this situation, or things you thought might be clichéd."

One of the advantages of talking personally in literature classes is that the class always has the safety hatch of criticism. They can always safely retreat to a discussion of "effectiveness" and "technique."

Amelia says, "I went through the same thing last semester when my parents got divorced and sold their house." Her eyes tear up.

"My mom and I just moved and had a tag sale, and I saw things I hadn't used in a long time," says Francesca. "But I felt I shouldn't sell those things because they were mine." She pauses, almost as if recalling that there's a story they're supposed to be talking about. "That's what I was reminded of when Foster was sitting there thinking about all those games."

"So you were thinking sympathetically about the father?" asks Elaine.

"My father also has a lot of junk," says Andy. "My father also has ridiculous answers when you ask him why he keeps things. I think it's a kind of cowardice, or inertia."

"That's an interesting answer," says Elaine. "Cowardice, inertia, clinging to the past. Did those words strike anyone as an interesting way to answer the question about how Foster is feeling? Are those things all the same?"

"He doesn't want to move on," Andy says. "Moving on, he has to start all over again."

"I related to going through old stuff and knowing you have to get rid of it, have to move on," says May. "Before I came here I went through old stuff thinking, maybe I'll keep this, maybe I'll keep that. I didn't want to throw much out," she says, "I didn't want to let go."

"Why is it so hard to let go?"

"Well, I have My Little Ponies," says May.

The class laughs.

"True confession," says Elaine.

"No, I'm really attached to them. But sometimes you want something to remember," says May.

"Any place where you have the sense Foster feels that way?" Elaine asks the class.

"Yeah, 'Foster saw . . . in his melancholy: he had not played enough with these games,'" says Andy. "If he lets go of games, he lets go of his own life."

"He didn't do enough," says Greta. "He played and lost everything."

It cannot escape Elaine's attention that so far every student who has spoken—Amelia, Francesca, May, Andy, and Greta—is the son or daughter of a divorced couple. It seems remarkable how much adult anguish these students have already witnessed when they're hardly adults themselves.

"His whole marriage," says Phoebe, "is like a game, and he didn't want to stop playing."

"I get the impression he didn't really pay attention to his ex-wife," says Marion. "That sentence about rubbing the smudge of dirt away—I got the impression he got so wrapped up in work he didn't notice her."

"I know what you're saying," says Rosalind. "But when I read that, I thought he was probably one of those people who doesn't notice things. He never thought there was a problem, but then suddenly she says 'I'm sick of you.'"

"And she's the one who says at the end, 'Pay attention to the younger son,'" says Elaine. "Did anyone write anything about the relationship with the son?"

"It made me mad," said Greta, "that he wasn't going to go to the dump with this son. As though he didn't learn anything." Perhaps Greta, who hasn't spoken to her father since she was eleven, knows all too much about men who don't learn? "But then he did go, as though he did learn something."

"So this is a kind of realization story?" says Elaine.

"The son is described as still having a trace of baby fat, despite the beer glass," says Amelia. "So Foster could see his son still needed him."

"He realizes," says Belinda, "no matter how old you are, you still need parents, and that security."

"'This protective gesture made her face look small, pouty, and frail,'" Rosalind reads from the text. "At the end he says to his son, 'I'll protect you.' So that's the issue: he didn't protect his wife, but he'll protect his son."

"He's still needed somewhere," says Amelia, "and that makes me feel mad at him."

"Does this story cast some light on the situation?" asks Elaine, looking around. "Anything interesting?" she asks again, then stops to think a bit. "Anything useful?" And then, "Would you recommend the story? Mary, would you?"

"It's not a bad story," says Mary. "It gives you a sense of how he still feels useful. At the end, he finds those pieces of the games, as though he finds that one more piece that makes him feel useful again."

"I'd recommend it to my friend who went through his parents' divorce last year," says Susie. "He's the kind of person who can accept change and move on."

"So one way to read this is that there is hope in a situation which is devoid of hope," says Elaine.

"Normally I like morbid things," says Phoebe. "I do, I really do. I don't know, though. This story drags on me."

"Can you put things more precisely?" Elaine asks her.

"I'm just looking at words," says Phoebe wearily, in a way that sounds a little like Hamlet's "Words, words, words."

"Well, sometimes a story seems more interesting when you

reread it," says Elaine, but she concedes that "it's also important to go with that first reaction."

"It's important to connect with that aspect of life," says Andy. As a child of a divorced couple, is he speaking to the students who aren't? "If you don't connect, you might not like it."

"So you're saying that to enjoy it," Elaine asks, "you have to connect the story with your own life?"

"Not really," Andy answers, as though reluctant to be cornered.

"It's about sadness and loss. And most of us know something about that," says Elaine Beilin, "because we know something."

During the week before Thanksgiving, the weather is cool and sunny. Some stubborn brown leaves cling to the enormous maple in front of Dwight, but the younger maple on the north side of the building still has nearly all its foliage, dull brown leaves mixed with green ones. On Monday morning there's frost on the windshield, but the classroom seems overheated. Elaine opens the window only to shut it again because a leaf blower on the lawn below is whining like a motorboat approaching on a lake. Then, on Wednesday, there's a light dusting of snow, leaden skies, bumper-to-bumper traffic on the Mass Pike, a dreary cortege of headlights. Still, the campus has another kind of beauty, an outline of snow on every cornice and chimney top, as though the school is about to be transformed into an engraving. Then, with the sky lightening, silvering, and the snow stopping, a flock of about twenty birds in two parallel lines rises near the school's power plant.

Some students who have missed class for several weeks come back, as though hoping that they can make up for the impression of absence by last-minute attendance. George shows up in the very same Atlanta Braves cap and blue Fila jacket he was wearing weeks ago, as though it's his mandatory uniform, and Max shows up, too, his hair shaved so close he seems like a stranger, a new student, a visitor, though he still has the little reddish chin beard, only that's shaved much closer now, too

The discussion of stories about the family continues for the second week—depressing stories, though somehow the classes are not. There's a sense of seeing the end in sight, a little lift. But something in the quality of discussion has changed, too. Some students seem to have more to say. Once Elaine has to call a brief pause because several people are speaking at the same time. The students often seem to perform a "reality check," measuring the truth of the story against their own experience—of divorce or alcoholism or depression or parent-child conflict. In one of the stories, a neglectful father uses the phrase "home, sweet home," and Elaine asks what phrase might be more apt.

"Home, dysfunctional home?" Rosalind suggests with a laugh.

Elaine doesn't like "dysfunctional"—too faddish, she explains. Instead, she suggests "depressing."

Greta suggests "lonely."

"Other suggestions?" Elaine asks. "Home, lonely home," she repeats, with a kind of ghostly sigh on the word "lonely." She asks them to think of some other adjectives.

"Why are you looking at me?" Phoebe asks her. But then she comes up with "bitter."

"That might make a good title for a paper. Home, bitter home," Elaine says, trying it out.

In the story they're reading now, "The Sorrows of Gin" by John Cheever, they get a young girl's perception of her alcoholic upper-middle-class parents. Rosalind says, "I don't feel bad for the father. But it's a disease. Mr. Lawton is an alcoholic, and that has its own big set of problems. But," she says, reflecting on the ending, how things may go with this family, "when you see someone who's an alcoholic, and then you see them later when they've stopped drinking, you see a completely different person."

More than any of the other students, Rosalind makes her presence felt continuously, as though even just a few additional years of growth and experience have given her some strong reaction to, and some piece of personal knowledge about, these characters and their issues.

Story after story of "home, bitter home" seems to be wearing

Elaine down more than the students, who seem up to date on the reading and eager to discuss it. "I begin to long for a story in which a child is loved and appreciated," says Elaine, "but I guess it wouldn't make it into this anthology."

Then in the class right before Thanksgiving, they get to a story that moves her even more than the others, Tillie Olsen's masterpiece, "I Stand Here Ironing."

"I haven't read this story in twenty-three years," she tells them. "But it really got to me. I read it before I had kids." Of this story, where a mother reviews her relationship with her oldest daughter because a note has come from the high-school guidance counselor, Elaine tells them that she feels like the mother in the story. She reads to them:

> The old man living in the back once said in his gentle way:
> "You should smile at Emily more when you look at her."
> What *was* in my face when I looked at her?

"That's one of the lines that got to me," she says. "I'm stressed out, I've got to get those one hundred and two papers graded, and I wonder what's in my face when I look at my daughters. I could feel this story knifing its way in." She tells them this is one of those works that grew on her in rereading because of her life experience. "Did the story seem to you to have that kind of ability," she asks them, "to get at what goes on between parents and children?"

May is the first one to answer. "This just occurred to me now," she says. "The same thing happened to me. My mother was twenty-five when she divorced my father. She found out he was cheating on her before I was three months old. She did the opposite of the woman in the story, I guess. She pawned rings so she could buy me Christmas presents." She reflects for a moment. "I'm thinking how sad this story is."

"That could make you empathize even more," says Elaine, "with this mother who was overwhelmed."

"I'm thinking how my father walked out on us when we were

young," says Greta. "Four kids, two in diapers. Wow, this is what it might have been like."

The students have been assigned stories to report on in class. Marion reads aloud from the section of Olsen's story where the daughter, Emily, invents a word to mean comforting: "shoogily."

As Emily gets older, Marion points out, she assumes more and more responsibility as the oldest of four children in a house with no father.

"What's your sense of the role Emily plays?" Elaine asks the class.

"She's not like a daughter," says Amelia. "She's more like a maid, helping to get the kids to school, surrogate mother, housekeeper, helping with shopping."

"That's like my oldest brother," says Greta, "and my sister, who's six years older. She always had to take care of us, and I never had to do anything, since I was the youngest."

Claudia, too, who seems to come from a stable home, sensitive to her own needs, feels affected by the story. The plight of Emily in the story reminds her of her own life now. Barely seventeen, she misses the attention she once had as a child. "My mother had another baby, and she's six now," Claudia says. "She tells my brother and me, 'We gave you all this attention, too, when you were smaller.' Still, sometimes I miss her. It's not her fault," she says. "But my mother has to go with my father and my younger sister a lot."

"Good," says Elaine, meaning the comment. "So does this help you to understand what happens to Emily—a lost childhood?"

"She must feel really rejected," says Claudia.

But then Elaine asks the class how Emily managed "to forge herself out of what seems to be a deprived childhood. How did she do it?"

"Puts on an act?" suggests Claudia. "She acts."

"This is what you always hear," says Greta. "The people who are hurt the most are the funniest."

Rosalind points out that Emily never directly protests or rebels.

"People tell us that's what first children try to do," says Elaine, who is a first child herself, "to be good for the parent. Something younger children aren't burdened with. Is that something connected to her thrill at having entertained people?"

"I can agree with that," says Amelia. "There are people who the only way they can find joy is to make people happy."

"After a life of being deprived of smiles and happiness, making people laugh, hearing applause gives her a kind of acceptance or reward. But I'm still not sure," says Elaine, "if we've completely seen how the comedy comes out of the sorrow and the loss. I think Greta is right. We often hear that all the greatest comics had terrible lives."

"Before, the only time she got her mother's attention was when she could tell her a story," Rosalind points out.

"I remember having conversations long, long ago about whether creative artists have to know suffering to do what they do, even if that creativity comes out in something like comedy. Does that make sense to anyone," Elaine asks, "that to be comic you'd have to know more than just happy?" She pauses to see whether anyone will respond. "It's kind of a big question," she says, without giving more of her own theory on the subject.

"Single mother, five kids, no time for others—the mother's life didn't turn out the way it might have, either," says Amelia.

"In a sense, that's true," says Elaine. "This could be read as the story of the mother's life. Part of this is being a victim of the Depression, of fear, of war? Francesca, is that the sense you get of the story?"

"Maybe without her knowing it, she might have made her daughter feel that way," says Francesca.

"So her own sense of non-expectation transferred itself to her oldest child. How many of you think the mother's sympathetic?"

"I'm not sure why," says Claudia, "but I just do. It's reality. It's hard. That's why I can sympathize. If I were in this situation, I'd stress out."

"If you have trouble taking care of one kid, why produce four more?" asks Amelia.

"That was their mentality," says Claudia. "Women had kids then."

The students seem so acute in getting at these issues, almost as though not only life experience, but TV talk-show experience, has a made a nation of young people who can all talk sympathetically about emotions.

For the first time in the semester, I raise my hand, too. I once heard Tillie Olsen read this story to a class. "She told us that the daughter who is Emily is now a mother herself and an activist, setting up a group of cooperative day-care centers in California." There's silence then in the room, as everyone seems to be considering this.

"What tells you this is real?" Elaine asks the class.

"I thought 'shoogily' had to be real," says Rosalind.

"Yes, that's the first thing you'll want to ask Emily if you meet her," says Elaine. "Did she really say 'shoogily?'"

"The whole story is real," says Greta. "It's imaginative, but real."

"I agree," says Elaine. "It's at that hard-to-define meeting place between fact and reality. But it's a very carefully shaped story."

The discussion goes further than that to consider formal and aesthetic issues. They discuss the motif of the ironing board, the use of the word "tormented." What the students don't bring up—an issue that would have mattered to Tillie Olsen—is the effect of poverty and the lack of help (or the grotesque charity) given to this mother by the social system.

The students' knowledge really seems to fail in discerning the imprint of race and class in what they read. While students on some campuses are accused of being almost uniformly "politically correct," these students don't even seem to notice the lower case in "negroes" when discussing Kate Chopin's "Regret"—or even worse, the caricatured way in which black people are described in that story: "There was a pleasant odor of pinks in the air, and the sound of negroes' laughter was coming across the flowering cotton field" (3).

After Susie reads the paragraph with that sentence aloud, Elaine asks, "What impression does this give you of this world?"

"It was prospering," says Rosalind. "Also it seems like it wasn't a bad place to be—because of the 'negroes' laughter.' Chopin doesn't show Mamzelle yelling at them."

Elaine asks what particular words tell us that Chopin wants us to see this as a happy world. The class answers with various images. "What image does sunlight on white boards give you? What kind of house? What does she achieve by calling it 'white sunlight?'"

Greta says this suggests a place that's peaceful, happy.

"I bet it's hot," says Elaine. "But that's not what she's emphasizing. Here it adds to the sense of harmoniousness. She's not emphasizing backbreaking labor, but that they're laughing. There's a whole political history hidden away here. This description of a kind of Edenic environment is a very loaded description, one that tries to shape your response to the story." She hesitates, as though waiting for comments from them. It's rare for her to state her own interpretation openly. But in this all-white class, in a college that—like the state itself—is at least 90% white, perhaps she can't trust the students to be willing to acknowledge the social (including the racial) implications in this story.

"Now if you were writing about this story, one question would be what is the connection between the way Chopin creates this world, the well-ordered, smoothly working farm that Mamzelle has organized, and the action that takes place in the story with the arrival of the four children?"

In "Regret," a woman of fifty who has never been married—and has never felt that she regretted this—is asked to care for a neighbor's children for a few weeks. When the children leave: "She gave one slow glance through the room, into which the evening shadows were creeping and deepening around her solitary figure. She let her head fall down upon her bended arm, and began to cry. Oh, but she cried! Not softly, as women often do. She cried like a man, with sobs that seemed to tear her very soul" (5).

"It's interesting, too," says Elaine, "that when Chopin says she regretted not being a mother, she would say that she cried like a man."

"She didn't get to have a baby grow inside her," says Claudia. "She wasn't like a woman in that way."

"When men cry, it's scary," says Rosalind. "I've seen my father cry just once. When his grandfather died, he was just, like, beyond upset. His grandfather raised him. That's the way she's crying, a very deep crying."

"If she'd never had that experience of taking care of the children," says Phoebe, "she'd have gone through life without any regrets."

"So you're talking about a universal theme, that word 'regret,'" says Elaine. "But I'd like you to look at this story in a more localized way, the way it's planted within a very specific time and place."

It remains to be seen if the students, even with her encouragement, will be able to read through the story to the author's—and her culture's—assumptions. Though all the students in this class would identify themselves as white, it isn't likely that they'd consider whiteness as anything other than "normal American" or reflect about whether, by virtue of being white in a society that still favors whiteness, they'd consider themselves privileged. Indeed, though some, like Rosalind, are genuinely appalled by racism, they don't seem to think of themselves as "white Americans" who therefore could have a role in changing the way things are.[17] (Life will teach some of them lessons about this, though. During the following summer, May will spend several months in Alaska with her boyfriend's family, and will vow never to go back: "Eighty percent of the island population are native Klinkuts," May will explain to me at our interview the following year. "They take care of their own. . . . His tribe is a rich, rich tribe. But I just could not handle it. No one was rude to me, but I never felt like such an outsider. . . . I never felt so white.")

This blindness to their own whiteness is tested when the class moves on to a story they seem greatly to admire, "The Sky Is Gray" by Ernest J. Gaines. Depicting an eight-year-old's struggle not to reveal that he has a toothache (not because he's afraid of the dentist, but because he knows that the cost of the bus trip, the dentist's fee, and the half-day his mother will have to take off from her work in the fields will be a hardship on his family), and then the difficult day they have in town when they go to the dentist, the story asks its readers to look hard at the consequences of economic hardship compounded by racism. As Francesca wrote in her paper on this story:

> One of the parts that struck me hard was when the boy and his mama were in the dentist's office waiting room and the nurse comes out to say, "The doctor is treating his last patient now." The mother replies, "My little boy's sick. Right now his tooth almost killing him." After the nurse told her that she'd have to wait until this evening, another lady spoke. She says, "Don't feel 'jected, honey . . . I been round them a long time—they take you when they want to. If you was white, that's something else; but we the wrong color" (126). I felt very frustrated when I read this part for I can't believe how the black were treated, whether on the bus or in the dentist's office. If someone needs help, what they look like or the color of their skin should not matter.

Later in the story, a white woman invites mother and son to warm up in her house and feeds them. To save their pride, she pretends she needs her garbage cans moved to the front of the house, a job the boy can do (though he knows very well the cans are empty and that this is a gesture to disguise an act of charity). Francesca took this woman to be a symbol "that not all 'white' people discriminated against 'colored' people." Yet poor as this white woman happens to be herself, she is also privileged by her whiteness. It seems natural to everyone—the lady herself, the boy's mama, and perhaps even to Francesca, a white reader—that a phone call by this lady to the white nurse has the power to ensure that the boy will be seen by the dentist immediately. As Francesca concludes,

> I admired the mama in the story for she had a lot of pride that sometimes we don't see a lot of in such horrible situations. Even though she didn't have a lot of money, she still wanted the exact amount of meat that equaled the money that she had when the kind "white" lady tried to give her a little more. I respect her for her actions throughout the story and for the courage she displayed. She shows that in a tough world you have to be tough. You have to be strong and carry on through the coldness of the world, because some day things will get better.

For Francesca, the kind woman's whiteness is an almost arbitrary, imaginary quality, to be set off in quotation marks. When I read this paper I think of Francesca telling me in one of our interviews about her own mother; she recently had to leave their home because of a divorce. Certainly Francesca wouldn't consider herself or her family privileged, nor, I speculate, would she be likely to think of the kind "white" lady as privileged; but, clearly, until this consciousness of white privilege extends to whites, what hope is there that "some day things will get better?"

In class, Elaine tries to suggest that the portrait of the kind white lady might be double-edged.

"The dentist can have lunch at his own convenience because he's not working with white people," says Greta.

"And if you look further at the story, what is it going to take for James and his mother to get noticed?" Elaine asks.

Someone mentions the phone call.

"Yes," says Elaine, "the white lady has to intercede."

"The role the white woman is playing is that not every white person is bad," says Greta. "She tried to give them more meat than the mother had paid for, trying to show that even though society is cold, not everyone is like that."

"I agree with you," says Elaine, "but I don't think Gaines lets us have that so simply, either."

In this class there also seems to be a presumption that everyone is Christian. Andy, the only Jew in class, tells me in an interview that he doesn't feel he's in any way different, or treated differently:

> I'm not religious. Of course you can tell I'm not Hasidic. But I was bar mitzvahed, and I'd sometimes go to temple. My mother didn't want me to go where there was a school with no Jewish population. My mother went to Quinnipiac, and her roommate had never seen a Jewish person and looked behind her to see if she had a tail. No one's ever said to me, 'What religion are you?' If I say I'm Jewish, no one's ever said, like, 'Wow.' A couple of kids have come up to me to ask questions about being Jewish. Like, the last name's Stein, so I guess they figured out I was Jewish. But it's not a huge issue to me. I'd like it if school were closed for the holidays. Essentials was canceled, and in my other classes I told them I was going home for the holidays, and they understood. I was stuck in a bus stop for three hours on Friday night. I couldn't get home. My bus never came. The hardest part was getting home.

Indeed, with his stylishly short haircut and his single earring, perhaps Andy doesn't look much different from anyone else. Though his speech is New-York-flavored, he doesn't seem to feel that he stands out as one of only a few Jewish students on campus, under 2% of the total.

When the class discusses Roberta Silman's "Wedding Day," a story about a young Jewish woman on the eve of her marriage, neither Andy nor Elaine offers to explain to the others terms like *chupa, ketubah,* or *minyan.*[18] And the question of whether this is a story about a wedding—anyone's, more or less—or a Jewish wedding doesn't get asked, not by the Jews in the room nor by anyone in the Christian majority. Yet—perhaps for this reason?—the discussion seems less enthusiastic than that about other stories, as though in some way this story has bewildered the class. Colleen says the story is "kind of annoying to read. I was getting bored."

"Sooo," Elaine responds, "Did anyone share this sense of why doesn't this character get up and do something?" She waits a moment. "It's not a story that depends a lot on action. The scope is very small."

The only time I have ever raised my hand to say anything in this class was to tell them about Tillie Olsen's daughter. Here, though, I find myself impatient with the discussion. Still, recalling the silence that greeted my first attempt all semester to interject a comment, I remain quiet. It seems to me the story could be read as being about the assimilation (still incomplete for this family) of Jews into the majority culture through life in suburbia. Where once a religion and its customs held together a community, it is now hard to know even how to plan a wedding where the grandfather is an Orthodox rabbi and scholar, the bride a thoroughly Americanized agnostic, and her father and mother the generation caught in the middle. The small wedding described in the story is actually nearly conflated with a funeral, since a close friend has died and the officiating rabbi is trying to spend as much time as possible with the widow. The class discusses the pivotal symbol of the story, a spider's web that the mother unaccountably (despite her frequent cleaning frenzies and her employment of a cleaning woman) has let survive. Some see the web as symbolic of family connection, something fragile but somehow surviving, at least for the moment. But no one in the class asks why a family this well-established (and financially well-off) should be represented by a fragile web, one from which the creating spider is missing. Perhaps the missing spider stands for the bride herself, who will be leaving home (much to her loving father's dismay) but in whose life the fragile web of family love will be replaced by the love of husband and wife. The light shining in the web, Amelia notices, connects with the light in the groom's eyes at the end. "There ought to be some connection there," she says, "but I don't know how to put it into words."

"Well, what does the hug at the end suggest—where the father and mother make a sandwich with their daughter in the middle?" asks Elaine. "Luh . . . luh . . . love?" she prompts.

"The guy's eyes were clear and full of love," says Amelia, "and so the bride's kind of starting over."

Yet (I think but do not say) no one suggests that the spider, the web's missing creator, could be God.

> My mother sits there [following the news of the friend's death], stunned, and I wonder what her faith tells her now. She believes unequivocally in God which is more than my father and sisters and I do. I start to say, "If there's a God, why . . ." but she turns to me, her face gray.
>
> "Not today, darling, please, not today." Then she cries tearlessly. I bring her a damp washcloth which she puts across her forehead as she lies down on the bed. . . .
>
> My parents' friends are making weddings, watching over the births of grandchildren, and dying. I remember an old record player in my other grandmother's house; it had an enormous handle, and if we were good we could crank it. Round and round we turned and the music happened on our ears. Who cranks that bigger handle, I wonder. (201)

Amelia sums this up as "a loss of traditional values."

"You could compare the bride saying they should have gone to a justice of the peace," says Elaine, "to the grandparents, who come in waving a little handkerchief knotted at all four corners, which represents the world. The bride's reaction is, 'Superstitious.' There's an abyss between the grandparents and grandchildren."

"The bride doesn't care if the meal's kosher," Greta says, "but the grandparents have to have that."

"And even so, the grandmother won't eat," says Elaine. "The wedding plays up this huge shift between these generations, with the parents sort of wobbling between the two."

But what no one says is that the story raises the question of whether these suburbanized Jews can remain Jewish at all in a majority-Gentile culture without their traditional (quite different) religious beliefs. No one sees this as a specifically Jewish problem (or story), but rather, as Amelia puts it, a sort of generic case, "the loss of traditional values," which could affect anyone.[19]

The truth is that moving in any way from the psychological to the social represents a challenge for these students. Social issues such as divorce, alcoholism, child neglect, estrangement between parent and child, the alienation of the elderly, the silence (or silencing?) of women, appear in these stories, but will the students simply look into them with the bromidic assumptions they have already gleaned from their television sets, or will they use the knowledge that's come out in class discussion, the knowledge they have from their own lives so far, including their consciousness of themselves as members of an American white, Christian majority?

Professors at elite colleges may find, in fact, that the students' personal relationship with a story gives way all too readily to just this sort of social awareness. Suddenly they seem willing to put aside the pleasure and pain they register as "naive" readers and instead begin to categorize the elements of the story as elements in a social allegory.[20]

These Framingham students, however, seem more stubborn in resisting categories, almost as though unwilling to see where such categorization might place them. It is to their advantage, if they are to thrive, to disbelieve in class-based determinism, or what would become of their own aspirations? Like many Americans who are not by many measures in fact middle class, they need to believe that they are. Or perhaps, more profoundly, these students, with their extensive work experience and with their experience of family instability and upheavals, already know too much about the fluidities and complexities of social class and even of race in America to fall back on any theory.

Though the students don't analyze these stories within the frame of race and class, they do find ways to understand the stories from their own experience, and, as well, find ways to understand their experience via these stories. Some turn in papers that are exceptionally good examples of the way this can happen.

Claudia writes a paper about a friend, Tracy,[21] who was raped by her own boyfriend. "For Tracy, whose family is composed of rigorous Mormons, rape by a boyfriend is unthinkable. She was not even supposed to be dating, or 'kissing boys.'" Tracy never tells her parents. It's only when reading the Mary Gordon story, "Violation," that Claudia fully understands Tracy's determination to keep her rape a secret:

> The narrator in "Violation" suffers the same trauma Tracy does. She has been sexually assaulted by her Uncle William, a trusted family member. Even though her parents are entitled to know about the incident, she does not reveal it to them. I can understand her feelings after the assault to my friend Tracy's, "My great fear was that I would betray, by some lapse of warmth or interest in the morning, my uncle's drunken act" (Gordon 362). I felt outraged reading this sentence. The narrator found excuses for the assaulter, just as Tracy found reasons not to express to the world her sadness. Above all, I found this story enlightening to me because of the narrator's words: "I was stronger. I was filled with a clean, painful love for them, which strikes me now each time I see them. They are gallant; they are innocent, and I must keep them so" (363). Tracy thought the same way. She finally said to me after a long breakfast, answering my frustration at her maintaining her rape a secret, "My parents are naive, they don't know what I am up to all day. In their eyes, I am a good 'Mormon girl'. How could I in one day reveal to them that I'm really not their little angel, just with one confession?" I never forgot her words, and I never told anyone what happened.

Claudia sees her friend's parents all the time, but feels forced to keep her friend's secret. "The narrator," in "Violation," she concludes, "has kept silence for about twenty years. It is my conclusion that Tracy will too. I cannot help thinking I could have done better to help her, but unless I could have prevented the rape, I could not have done anything at all."

It's not as though Mary Gordon's story gives Claudia any further impetus to action, but a deeper sense of the tragic impossibility of her having been able to do anything other than what she did. Certain to approach any future encounter such as this with humility, she might nevertheless be able to suggest that talking this over with someone other than herself—and perhaps even with family—might be the better course. But whatever the case, the knowledge that has flowed from the story has clarified Claudia's understanding of Claudia. She knows now the full scope of what she was up against when every day she had to keep this secret from Tracy's parents.

One of the approaches to freshman writing is to encourage a great deal of personal writing. In this way students are supposed to be learning that writing is a form of working out what the writer honestly thinks. Claudia's piece was outstanding from that point of view. Approaching freshman composition as a course in personal writing can, however, often lead to a certain unspoken uniformity of self-revelation; students confessing that they have done wrong or acted foolishly may be rewarded for pseudo-insights (or even true ones) that lead the professor to think they have become more moral or more wise.[22] Claudia, by contrast, sees more, but does not pretend to be equipped by virtue of this insight to act any differently. Another quality that sets this essay apart from the kinds of narratives freshmen often write when writing from experience is that Claudia has more than a story to tell—she has an idea about a work of literature to illustrate. Her friend's story, Claudia argues, "is quite similar to Mary Gordon's 'Violation.' The narrator of the story is too overwhelmed by the idea of a perfect family to reveal her secrets of sexual assault." Just as Elaine has been urging them to all semester, Claudia has written an essay with an explicit, substantive, and arguable thesis, and has provided specific evidence from her own life and the text, never losing sight of the parallel she is seeking to argue exists between this text and her life experience.

Elaine's response to this essay shows that she was not only impressed by it, but also moved:

> That incredible protectiveness of the parents in each case seems unbearable, yet each person bears it. I'm reminded of the mother's words in "I Stand Here Ironing"—"What in me demanded that goodness in her? And what was the cost, the cost to her of such goodness?" (71).

Clearly, literature here provides both student and professor with a metaphoric, allusive language to understand each other better, and themselves. The writing seems so interesting, in fact, that it makes me wonder whether Elaine shouldn't simply have focused the course around literature about the family, rather than a work of history. Still, had Elaine reversed the order of the course, beginning with these stories and then moving on to academic writing, it isn't clear the students would have written about the stories the way they did—seeking to prove a clear idea, and balancing personal references so well with references to the text.

For Amelia, literature and life moved into an almost perfect juxtaposition when she was listening to the class reading "Still of Some Use." She writes about this story almost as though it actually happened to her, but, because it is told from the point of view of the father, her understanding of herself and her own experience widens, as does her understanding of others. The knowledge flows from the text to Amelia's understanding of her own life, and back the other way. Though Elaine has never been drawn to Updike's men, and certainly did not much like Foster, Amelia's paper has changed her reading. "You've improved the story for me," she writes in her comment. "Since reading your essay, I feel much more sympathy for his unhappiness."

Elaine's comment on this paper is one of the shortest she has written this semester. And Amelia gets the highest grade she has gotten, an A-. In fact, Kate reports that Amelia is going around showing the last page of the paper to her friends, gloating. For a talented story teller like Amelia, this assignment—asking the students to draw on personal experience—is a fat pitch over the plate. As for Elaine, she seems so moved that she forgets to put in any suggestions for improvement other than the usual dozen or so proofreading comments per page. If the story Amelia heard read aloud in class that day enabled her to "look back" on her life and "understand what had actually happened," it also deepened her understanding of herself and of her father. They are mirrors for each other—both seeking to put distance between themselves and Amelia's mother, and both grieving for lost love.

Though Amelia's father lives elsewhere, Amelia has always remained in touch. Indirectly, she depends on him for financial support. "My mother's job doesn't pay a lot, but Dad pays her a lot," she says. She stresses that she could never ask him directly for money. "I don't get money directly from anyone," she tells me. "It's never been a question in my family, and I'm too scared to ask. That way, I stay clear of control. I've had to be independent and support myself where I could. In fact," she adds, "if I could find a way to move out, I probably would. Just to get that much more away from Mom." Since her mother receives money from her father and, in turn, pays the part of Amelia's tuition not covered by financial aid, Amelia still depends upon her father. Perhaps, in some ways, she wishes to. Though she earns $400 a month at Boston Market, even now, in late November, she is still waiting for her father to buy a printer for her laptop.

On the other hand, Amelia has always tried to put as much space as she can between herself and her mother, with whom she lives when she is not at school. Her mother, according to Amelia, "still lives an upper middle class life." Though she always asks Amelia if she has enough money, Amelia complains that "it's like pulling teeth from that woman to get half a tank of gas." This leaves Amelia never wanting to ask her mother for money and paying for repairs on her own car, not to mention spending about $20 a week for her pack-a-day cigarette habit. For now, her car has to be left at home because Amelia can't afford to pay for the insurance. So her father, who lives in nearby Southboro, will often pick her up at school at the end of the week and give her a lift. "Every once in a while, we get together for dinner," she tells me, "or go shopping."

Embedded in Amelia's essay is the near-realization of how much she still needs her parents in her life, despite the "independence kick" she's been on since high school (and since their divorce). Her own experience has made her an acute reader of this story.

Moving Day

> Fiction and life often have parallels, and some of these parallels can be almost shocking. We often are so moved by the things we read that we are then able to look back upon past events in our lives and able to see and understand what has actually happened. This was the case when I read "Still of Some Use" by John Updike. I was moved to tears when I read his words and could see the events playing out as he described them. The story he tells is a poignant reminder to me of the day we moved out of the house my family had once lived in together before the divorce.
>
> It was late November of 1995 when our house went up for sale and sold within a week. It was a sharp blow to both my father and me, for both of us were expecting it to be a while before it sold. It was only too soon when it was time to clean out the house and move. My father came to help with the cleanup efforts, and I think he, like Foster, realized this was the end of his old life. As I helped him clean the attic and the basement cupboards, where our old toys and games were, I was astonished by his ability not to show any emotion. I was fighting tears back the whole time, as I also realized that I had to start a new life. The games and toys had been untouched for years and were missing pieces, but

it still hurt me to throw them away. I felt as though a part of my childhood was going with them, and I think my father saw that his little girl was almost grown. When the house was cleaned out, and we were leaving, my father said he just wanted to double check to make sure we did not leave anything behind. I followed him a little later and found him in the playroom. The playroom was a special room for him because he had done most of the woodwork as well as most of the parenting in this room. His back was turned and he did not hear me come in, but then I heard the sound of muffled crying coming from him. He had not noticed me to that point, so I slipped away without him knowing I was there. It was then that I realized he was in pain as well, and how scared he was.

We had a lot of useless items stowed away in various places, little pieces of a history that was insignificant, yet these things were never thrown away. They were kept as precious relics from a life we once knew, the way Foster and his family had not thrown away the games, but merely stowed them away. Then the question enters why we still had many things; Foster and his family are wondering much the same thing. Foster thinks and realizes, "Cowardice, the answer was. Inertia. Clinging to the past" (401). The case was the same with my family; all of us were fearful of change, and we wanted to stay suspended in a time that we all knew, when we were happy. Games and toys brought back memories of birthday parties and the few days after when the novelty had yet to wear away, much as they did with Foster.

"Foster saw in the depth of downward space the cause of his melancholy: he had not played enough with these games. Now no one wanted to play" (402). This line makes me think of seeing my father in the playroom crying alone and thinking that no one knew. We spent much of our time with him in his room, but he worked a lot and was rarely around for more than an hour before bedtime. That line makes me think that he could have been feeling the same thing as Foster. He had not spent as much time with us as I am sure he wanted, and now we were not small children anymore and did not need him in the way we had. We did not want to play anymore either. When Foster picked up the lantern and followed his wife out of the attic I remembered things I saw the day I moved. Foster placed the lamp on a bookshelf that he had once built and admired his handiwork. This scene reminded me of the way I saw my father in the playroom looking at his work and crying. I also saw my father running his hands over the polished railings that he had made himself. These were both things he was proud of, like Foster's bookshelf.

With the cleaning done, it was time for us to leave. We were soon on our way to the new condo. I, much like Foster's younger son, was really scared and sad, and I also kept this hidden. In my car we had put many of the things that were to go to the Salvation Army and I was to drive down there by myself. As I was about the leave, my father came out to say good-bye. I had trouble hiding my pain, but I tried anyway, and my father was walking away with his head bowed and his shoulders hunched, before I realized how much I still needed him. I asked if he would join me, but he declined, saying he had to go. He walked a few steps further, and then turned, and he must have seen the pain in my eyes because he asked if I was okay. I said yes, although I really was not. I told him I would not take long and that my invitation was still open and this time he agreed to join me. It was at this moment that it seems he realized that I needed him as a part of my life. This parallels the way that Foster seems to realize that his son still needs him.

Fiction and reality are so alike that it is often hard to see which is which. In this story, Foster's story almost aped mine. As I read through the story I had trouble telling if I was reading about Foster or about me. Fiction can also give

> us some priceless insights into life that are so often overlooked in haste. I got lucky this time, however, because I got a second chance to see the things I missed the first time.

In the Austrian writer Peter Handke's account of the final years of his mother's life before her suicide, *A Sorrow Beyond Dreams*, he describes the way his mother, after years of scrimping and relentless house cleaning (to nullify the disgrace of poverty), finally has a chance to read. In her reading she has no measure for assessing the characters other than her own character. "I'm like that," she might say. Or "I'm not like that." Too late, apparently, for the knowledge to flow the other way, for her to say, as she reads, "Ah, so that's what I'm like." Perhaps, indeed, her suicidal hopelessness originates from the fixed, ossified view she has of her own character.

The young read differently. Children may read to prepare themselves for experiences they have not yet had. But in this class, some of these students—barely, or perhaps incompletely out of adolescence—read to understand themselves and the unsettling experiences they have already had.

In the next assignment, the last official essay before the final, Elaine will ask them to extrapolate from a work of fiction the author's ideas about social and political reality. But for this one moment in the semester all that the students already know confronts what the text knows on more-or-less equal footing.

"It's a story about sadness and loss," Elaine said. "And most of us know something about that," she added, "because we know something." Isn't this precisely the reason she wishes to push them beyond the personal? They have so much to gain in addressing the world with a wider frame of reference, and in a more professional voice.

Still, I think, the students must be grateful for the warm interest she takes in their personal writing during this interval when she's encouraged the class to do it. Some of us, it seems, can't give up our belief that personal stories provide the best knowledge. But personal knowledge has to be widened to encompass the experience of others. Elaine has managed to get Claudia and Amelia and many others to weave into their personal stories the knowledge they've gained from reading, until, in some ways, reading, too—the acquisition of new knowledge—has become their personal story. In this way they have joined the young woman Elaine was, years ago, so excited to be conveying even part of her joy and awe in encountering *Hamlet*.

10. THE LAST CLASS

ON THE LAST day of classes Elaine Beilin has to drop off her daughter Rachel at school, so she doesn't arrive at the college till after eight. Kate's already sitting on the steps of May Hall, sipping her large coffee-to-go (undoubtedly cold by now, since she's brought it all the way from the Gourmet Panda, in Foxboro). She has a napkin, spotted with blood, wrapped around her hand. "I fell in the parking lot," she says.

Of course she has a lit cigarette; there's a Marlboro pack and a blue Bic lighter on the steps beside her. Generally, Elaine glares at her when she sees her smoking, so Kate's certainly aware of her teacher's feelings. Once when Elaine gave the class one of her famous one-minute breaks (in the middle of a two-hour class) Kate said to her, "You've never smoked, have you Doctor Beilin? It's hard to go outside"—smoking is forbidden in all campus buildings—"light up and smoke a cigarette in one minute."

"Ready to go on?" Elaine asked the class. "Should I open the window?" It was about forty degrees outside.

She and Kate have struck a deal about the research paper. Kate's collected some reputable sources on vampirism, so it seems that's going to be her topic. But to avoid a failing grade, she's going to have to get the work in by the end of exam week. Kate told her she'd gotten about eight pages of material already. "Am I going to pass the course?" she asked.

"You've got to get that paper in," Elaine said.

"Dr. Beilin," said Kate. "I want to thank you for your patience with me."

"You're very welcome, Kate. Just pay me back by doing well," said Elaine, determined, as she told me later, "that butter would not melt."

The room is full once again, though not as full as it was at the beginning of the semester, seventeen present out of twenty-one. Lee is missing—not a good sign—but Arthur is back, and, surprisingly, so is Greg. Elaine guesses that's because otherwise Greg can't find out the topic for the final. George hasn't surfaced much since the mid-term, and she's not surprised that he isn't here now. After trying to so hard, he seems to have given up. The one time recently he was present—still in his Atlanta Braves cap and Fila jacket—he was vehement about a character in a Malamud story who was depressed about being drafted during the Vietnam War. "Fifty-six thousand died," George said, "but more than that came back alive. He's a coward; he's not facing life; he's dead already. I don't know if war is the only problem. This kid doesn't want to face anything." What then, Elaine wonders, has happened to George? He never handed in the fifth or the sixth essay. Now he's not here, so will he even turn in the final? He told her he was going back to UMass Boston, and maybe once he made that decision he decided simply to let himself fail and start again next semester over there? Well, it makes no sense, but she can't talk to him if he's not around, and, anyway, he's missing so much work that it may already be too late. This kid, she tells herself, doesn't want to face anything.

For a while she thought Lee was going to make it, but now it seems that she, too, may not. She's tried finding out about Lee by calling her, even by asking Andy. According to him, "she's not adjusting well." He was sure she'd at least show up to get the assignment for the final, but she hasn't. "If something happens in her personal life—something not that big, but big to her—she's going to let it ruin the rest of her week," Andy told her. "It could be a fight with her boyfriend. The distance is hard. She had a fight with him the night before last, so now for a whole week she won't function correctly."

Hearing this, Elaine even dropped off some of the assignments, and some of Lee's graded papers, at the dorm where Lee lives. But if Lee hasn't shown up today, she probably won't show up at the final either. So that will make four essays and the final she'll be missing. There's no way Elaine can justify giving her even an Incomplete. Clearly there's a lot going on. Lee wrote Elaine a note about all her stress; then, too, she's had to go home to New Jersey every week because her parents are battling.

Elaine's still chasing other students too, but she feels guardedly optimistic about catching them. Amelia's here—but still hasn't handed in her field-trip essay. Her research paper on the history of American house architecture starts off fine, but then skips two centuries, as though to say, "I'm desperate. Maybe she won't notice that I've skipped a couple of centuries." An even worse interpretation is that she doesn't realize she's skipped two centuries, but Elaine thinks Amelia is too bright not to know. She ran out of steam. It's probably a paper she did in one draft. She's probably done that before too—written a paper at one go and handed that in—but that rarely works with a research paper. So that paper was a disappointment. Her shorter papers were great, though. The one on "Still of Some Use" was lovely. It was a moving paper. That's what Elaine hopes they'll learn—that good criticism will happen when they feel something and they learn how to connect analysis with feeling.

As Elaine makes her way to her seat this morning, she can do a quick shoe-check on Jeremy: a soaking in winter slush has darkened Jeremy's red Converse high-top sneakers to a plum color, and the holes on the outsides have grown enough for much of his (undoubtedly wet) socks to be visible. She hopes he's wearing these as some sort of statement, not because he can't afford any others. Either way, the shoes demonstrate his tenacity. Jeremy, whose attendance has been good, has hung on in this course as well.

With Elaine's help, he's made some intelligent adaptations.

He veered away from history, switched his research topic to a band he admires, Rodan, and found his métier. His writing about music has more energy than his writing about history or literature; and he also brings to it an informed vocabulary. He still has all the faults he's had all semester—in fact, Elaine is still convinced he's got some sort of learning or reading difficulty—but he's really doing a great job of analyzing that band, arguing that Rodan, now split up, influenced many others. The technical mishaps of Jeremy's writing are balanced by some evidence of genuine thinking, which, Elaine thinks with some gratitude, is better any day than an essay that's technically correct but vapid and boring.

Jeremy's given her a Rodan tape along with the paper, and she's listened to it. And she has to admit that what he wrote in the paper was helpful in illuminating the music. Jeremy seems happy writing about music. It resonates deeply within him. It's all about who he is. He says this band criticizes society for being "Roman-like," by which he means materialistic, and he does a good job of showing how their form and content are related. When she heard the music, the first thing that came to her mind was rage. She wonders if he would agree that the attack quality of the music comes from rage and frustration—and powerlessness and disenfranchisement—all things she believes say a lot about where Jeremy lives.

As she surveys the many students still here, she thinks about how the course has gone according to plan for so few. After all these years, she still has the greatest insecurity about what she has actually done for any of these students. What, exactly, has she done? For people like Rosalind or Phoebe, she's just set up a situation where they will do what's expected, and succeed. Still, it seems hard to gauge how helpful she has been. Because they're so tuned in to doing what's expected, maybe she's just kept them preoccupied with fulfilling assignments. The good students think so much about how to fulfill requirements that they find all the little trip wires and possible ambiguities or the different ways of doing the work, that the student who just sits there and says "Oh" doesn't discover.

They'll both be in her Literary Study class next semester, which she's looking forward to, and Rosalind's even going to attempt her upper-level honors course, Prose and Poetry of the English Renaissance. But Rosalind has some specific difficulties that Phoebe doesn't have. Rosalind either never really had a strong background in the mechanics of punctuation, or she's rusty: comma splices, the use of apostrophes—she's pretty haphazard about that sort of thing. Rosalind needs to develop a set of procedures for proofing her own writing, perhaps even to develop a checklist. Phoebe's got a lot of those procedures in place already, and her corrections of her own rough drafts show it. Today, in fact, when Elaine calls people to the board to rewrite some problem sentences in their earlier drafts, she's going to call on Rosalind.

While some students go to the board to write out their "before" and "after" examples, she glances out the window. The young sweet gum tree has only a couple of dozen leaves clinging here and there; otherwise it's a vein system. The sky is streaked with blurred high clouds. The scream of the goose on the roof of the lab building across the way sounds like the opening of a heavy, rusty door.

"OK," she says, "let's look at Rosalind's example of a dangling modifier." Taken from her field-trip paper about Strawberry Banke, Rosalind's original sentence was: "Upon questioning her on the design of the house, she was knowledgeable in the way the house was centered around the chimney." Typical, really, of the way Rosalind could still sometimes tie her sentences in knots. "Here's the word you always have to look for," she tells them, "the word ending with i-n-g, the participial phrase, the one you're most likely to leave dangling out there. So Rosalind's question is, who is doing the questioning? It seems as if 'she' is doing the questioning, but as you see from Rosalind's correction, it's Rosalind who's doing the questioning."

Rosalind is nodding as Elaine is speaking. Beneath the first sentence she has written, "When I questioned her about the design of the house, she was knowledgeable about the way the house was centered around the chimney."

Someday, Rosalind will catch these things herself. Soon, Elaine hopes, since Rosalind can't continue writing with such tangles and bloopers much longer.

"Watch out for that in your final essay. Make sure every time you see a participle that you've actually got the thing it refers to."

How many times will she find herself back in this very room—wearing this same long gray-green cardigan (impervious to chalk dust), gray skirt, black stockings, and black shoes with one-inch heels—saying these very words to students? Yet without these reminders, Rosalind might get cut to pieces in one of her other classes by a professor who's not going to see the truly searching mind beneath the sometimes contorted surface of her inexpert writing. All semester, too, Rosalind has watched her professor with such intensity, as though she's decided to take every word Elaine Beilin speaks into her deepest memory. Now they're discussing the relative merits of a semi-colon versus a full stop in two sentences Francesca has put on the board. "You could put a period," Rosalind is suggesting.

"Yes, but you have to weigh the meaning you want to suggest." Elaine's arms are in front of her, and she raises her palms in an alternating motion.

Something largely non-verbal is being transferred here—maybe it's related to that passion that Elaine spoke about weeks ago when she was imagining Rosalind becoming a teacher someday—something each senses in the face, voice, body language of the other, a kind of learning chemistry. It's not something students or teachers necessarily want to acknowledge, since it can look so much like a crush or, at the very least, as Elaine prefers to describe it, the feeling of connecting with a teammate in the playoffs.

A couple of days ago, the two of them were having their final conference. Elaine sat in her swivel chair reading over Rosalind's written self-assessment:

> I am disappointed that the semester is over. Now I have to go and work full-time until school starts again!! Yuck!!! This is not the only reason why I am disappointed however, I feel like I did not get as much out of my classes as I had hoped. I am finding that my intellect is sharper than it has been in years, but I feel as though I missed something.
>
> I am disappointed in myself also for not taking the time early in the semester to revise my own writing. When I started doing this about a week ago, I was amazed at how I am now able to word things and think critically about them. I feel that I pretty much got as much out of the class room experience as I could, it is the homework and essays that I could have gotten more out of.

Elaine told me that when she finished reading this, she was reminded of Bob's grandfather saying, "You should always get up hungry from the table." He had all these aphorisms. "It's not a bad idea to leave a course still hungry. Otherwise, what's left? This is only your first semester. I'm more pleased that you feel that way than the other way. The feast will continue next semester. And you need a break."

"To clean up my car," said Rosalind.

"You might even like going back to the support-hose company, as comic relief." A silence settled momentarily. "Even after having written a paper on which you got a good grade you're still asking yourself, How can I do this better? That's a good way to be."

"Yeah, well, things were jumping out at me."

Elaine suggested that Rosalind work in a more organized way, like devoting one whole revision of the paper to look at every single sentence with something like comma splices in mind. She reached for one of Rosalind's papers and looked at it a moment. "Basic literacy," she said, "is knowing what to do with apostrophes. So go through just for that. You'll probably hate the process so much that you'll probably write them correctly the first time."

Rosalind grinned and nodded.

"I think what's happening is that you have a lot to say and you're overloading the sentences, trying to bottle everything up in one." They went through some specific sentences together. "Any others where the structure got kind of held up?"

"This one," said Rosalind laughing. Elaine grinned, too. No one watching them would have thought they were going over grammar errors.

"OK, I see the logic here," Elaine was saying. "But instead of taking a whole sentence just for that, you've crammed it in here in a kind of code." She raised her hand. "Alarm system!"

Again Rosalind broke into laughter.

"So you see, you need a system. Try reading out loud. If your tongue gets stuck, the sentence needs to be fixed. Some of your sentences, though, are wonderful, as if you're in process. That first paragraph," she said, indicating the research paper. "And I remember the kind of work it took." And then, after not saying anything for a moment, Elaine simply grinned.

Rosalind raised her eyebrows.

"I love what you said. You feel as though you're sharper."

"In real life—sorry, in my other life," said Rosalind, meaning her life outside of college, "my brain's been kind of sleeping." At work she would name some characters in a short story, and her co-workers wouldn't know how to respond. "And I'll say, 'No, it's a great short story.' As though they would ever read it."

The conference over, they chatted a few more minutes about Rosalind's other classes. Rosalind thought that Excel and Access were neat. "My computer professor taught us to average and scale."

"My husband taught me that," said Elaine. "I was thinking, why did it take me so long to do this?"

But both women seemed too conscious of managing time to chat long. "Are you going to have the papers by tomorrow?" Rosalind asked, standing up.

"I hope so," said Elaine. "I started at five-thirty this morning, so it already feels like midnight."

"I'm not going to be here tomorrow," said Rosalind, somewhat disappointed.

"What time are you leaving today?"

"Two-thirty."

"I might have some done at two-thirty. Stop by."

With the rewrite exercises done at the board, Elaine shifts the focus to the Raymond Carver story they're going to be writing about on the take-home part of their final. Amelia is particularly looking forward to hearing what people say about this story. This, like the other stories they've read about divorced men, is making her father more understandable to her. These stories tell her he isn't the only one—maybe he's one of millions—who's had to go through such ordeals. The main character in "Elephant" is struggling to support his mother, his daughter and her kids (and maybe even her boyfriend), his deadbeat brother, and his son, who goes to a private college in New England and wants to spend a year in Europe. Amelia knows her own father has to pay her mother $600 a week, and that's why she's embarrassed to ask him for any money for herself. Not that she sees much of this money, if any. But she doesn't want to be like this guy's son. He says if his father doesn't give him money, he'll have to sell drugs. And then, even more desperate, he calls again to say he's found he's allergic to cocaine—so he can't be a drug dealer. Truly lame! Now his dad will have to send him money or he'll kill himself. She wonders, too, if her father ever feels like freaking out, the way this character does, standing by the roadside with both arms straight out, then taking off with a buddy from work on a wild joy ride toward the mountains. Or if her father misses his own father taking care of him, the way this man remembers being carried as a child on his father's shoulders while they pretended he was on an elephant ride.

Elaine asks them to take a few moments to jot some notes about Mary's report on the story. Her report takes maybe a minute, at most. At one of our interviews, Amelia has asked me how Mary can say so little in class when she always seems to have her work done, and seems pretty smart, too.

Amelia is eager to speak about this story. She directs everyone's attention to a passage where the son is talking about how it's a completely materialistic society. "Ironic," she says, "that he and the others in his family can't hold a conversation without mentioning money, and that his purpose here, as usual, is to ask for money."

Claudia agrees with her. "The son says nobody talks to him, except about money. But that's all *he* talks about. That's the only reason he calls his father."

Amelia doesn't ever want to seem like that. That's partly why she's tried, ever since high school, ever since the divorce, to be as independent as she could. It wasn't even legal for them to hire her at the riding school that young, but they paid her under the table.

"We can see the irony, but do you think the father sees?" asks Elaine. "Does he see that this is a kind of emotional blackmail?"

Greta and Arthur both have their hands up.

"I think he does," says Greta, "but he pretends not to."

"The father is real gullible," says Arthur.

"OK, so one interpretation is that the father is dumb, gullible," says Elaine. "Do Arthur's words work?"

"I think gullible would work," Amelia says. "I don't know about dumb."

"He'd rather owe the bank a thousand dollars than to have something bad happen to some relative of his," says Rosalind.

"I agree with Rosalind," Claudia is saying. "I don't think he's dumb or gullible, but he doesn't want to feel guilt."

What Claudia and Rosalind are saying makes sense to Amelia, but in her opinion it's wrong. Before she knows it, Amelia starts to tell the whole class what it's like for this guy—that, in fact, it's a matter of conditioning, as though he gets cast in a certain role and he doesn't know how to play any other—only Claudia's not finished either, and Doctor Beilin has put her arms up like a referee.

"Wait, wait, wait," she's saying. "One person talk at a time."

"I think he just got walked over early," says Amelia.

Now Belinda has her hand up. Her nails today are forest green. That means: Hang on, the semester is almost over, things are hopeful. Soon she can give her mother a check for Christmas. "I don't think he's gullible at all," Belinda is saying. "He knows what he's doing and that he shouldn't, but he's caught in a Catch-22 situation."

Belinda tells them to look on page 413. "They had me and they knew it," she reads to them. "He knows," says Belinda. "He's not that gullible, but when it comes to his family he just wants to be a provider. This connects to that memory he has about his father playing elephant, holding on to him so he won't fall. He wants to be that strong person."

"I agree," May says. "In the Malamud story, the father says it's better to worry about oneself than someone else. I guess that's why the man in 'Elephant' ran off with the car at the end."

"Yes, no one has mentioned how the ending affects how we understand what the father does, and who he is," says Elaine. She has them read the ending aloud, one paragraph per person. Phoebe starts, then Francesca. Then Francesca hands her book to May—they own one between them. Then Claudia reads, then Greta. They've skipped Jeremy, who's in back, away from the table. And Greg, of course, who doesn't even have a book. Then the goose on the lab roof lets out another cry. Elaine reminds herself that the biology department denied the rumor that the goose screams whenever they draw its blood. No, it just screams when it feels like screaming. And then Belinda reads the last two paragraphs, ending with, "We streaked down the road in a big unpaid-for car."

Now Elaine wants them to take some time to think about this story, to write down their reactions. Jeremy stares out the window. He has his long-sleeve shirt under his T-shirt. Greg is leaning back from the table, looking sheepish, casting quick glances half-way up or to the side. Susie, a new blond streak in her hair, is wearing stylish brown corduroy overalls I haven't seen before; she's not moving her lips when she writes, the way she used to.

"How does the ending shed light on the main character?" Elaine asks. "Does this give you a clearer—or a muddier—sense about him?"

"It almost seems like he's making a clean break," says Arthur. "Kind of thinking for himself now."

Elaine's sitting at the corner of the table today, and light from the sun is striking her from the side when she speaks. Phoebe has told me that she notices it has a strange effect on her when Doctor Beilin changes places in the room. Everyone else generally sits in the same area. But when Doctor Beilin shifts her seat, it feels odd, and Phoebe feels it changes the way she learns, though she can't quite explain why. She'll have to get used to this new seating arrangement, at least for today. "I think his getting in the car seems like an escape," she says. "It's funny—the man driving the car was just another leech, just the same kind of person his children were."

"You know that because—" says Elaine.

"Oh, his final thought."

"And Arthur's told us they're taking off. Where does that come from?"

"They're going towards the mountains," says Amelia.

"I think it's good that he's using someone else for something," says Greta.

"I was struck by how he puts down his lunch pail and raises his arms to his shoulders," says Elaine. "That seems to be some kind of transition moment when he stops in front of the café and raises his arms to his shoulders. What does he look like? Does someone want to demonstrate that?—"

"A cross," says Greta.

"OK, is that something that's going on here?" Truthfully, she'd been thinking more of a scarecrow, but, yes, a cross! "What are the implications?" she asks them, ready to take the ball they've pitched to her and run with it.

"A man sacrificing himself for his family," says Phoebe, matter-of-factly, as though slightly embarrassed to deliver to Elaine the answer she has clearly wanted. "I think he's more like a bird, ready to fly away."

"It reminds me of when he was riding on the shoulders of his own father," says Andy, "and he tried to keep his balance. Look at page 414, about half-way down." He reads, "I kept them out like that for balance." Then Andy continues: "He wanted to be with his father. He wanted that safety. The burden was getting to him. He hadn't thought about his father for a long time, but then he had a dream, and woke up content. He realized he's going to keep giving all his relatives money. He can't do anything about that. But this moment, at the end, is his moment to be free. Just to ride in that car going faster and faster."

"When he was up on his dad's shoulders," Jeremy says, "he felt free, unencumbered, like he could do anything."

"That image Andy mentions must articulate something vital, because Carver uses it in the title," says Elaine.

"The father's larger than life," Rosalind explains. "If you were riding on an elephant, you couldn't hurt it. You wouldn't be a burden on its shoulders."

"It was only when his father assured him," Elaine says, "that he was able to let go like that, tah dah! He could just ride without clinging for dear life. Even though before his father had him firmly by the ankles. So can you attach that idea to the elephant?"

"Maybe if he gives his family a sense of security," says Rosalind, "they'll feel strong enough to do things on their own."

"So what's the state of his mind at the end?"

"He's hopeful," says Rosalind. "Just more hopeful. It's not a burden to him anymore. He understands why he's supporting them, and understands that there's nothing else he can do."

Elaine can't think of anything to add to this.

Later when she shifts the discussion to the social class of Carver's character, it's clear to her that, for most of this group, as for most Americans, ideas of class are fluid and vague. And alcohol probably plays a pretty large role in their family lives, too, she can easily guess, judging by how many of them wrote so authoritatively about alcoholism as a social issue addressed in these stories. Many seem to know all about its effects on the life of an alcoholic's family.

As they explore the gulf in class between the son in the story, who goes to a private college, and the father, who carries a lunch pail, Rosalind says, "The son could definitely work. He just doesn't *want* to work. It's totally not necessary for him to spend a semester in Germany. The son's got a college education now; he could get a job. He's just, like, pushing it." For Rosalind, Europe is associated with her father's Portuguese-speaking relatives down in Fall River, the ones she had to spend time with recently when he implored her to go with him to a family wake, not with a place to supplement an education.

"I'm puzzled by the daughter," says Elaine. "Part of me is sympathetic," she tilts her head, and then tilts it the other way, "and part of me is saying, 'Oh, c'mon.'"

"Why should they do anything for themselves," says Amelia, "if they don't have to?"

"That's an interesting way to look at it," says Elaine. "As though he enables some kind of addiction."

"I was just reading something about him drinking whiskey," says Marion. "He says, 'Drinking whiskey, that was the worst thing I could have done.'" She looks around. "So he might be an alcoholic."

"If that's so," says Rosalind, "that could explain why he's this way: he's trying to make up for times when he wasn't there for his family."

"Like the time when he smashed the window. He feels guilty trying to make up for his mistakes."

When Elaine looks around the room to identify the soft but articulate voice, she notices that it is Mary. Mary, volunteering a comment for the first time without being asked, on the last day of class.

"So what we're decoding," says Elaine, "is a history of violence. And to use the buzzword 'dysfunctional family,' do you correlate this with the way Carver depicts the environment? Susie, can you connect this to the ending?"

Susie says no, and Elaine waves her hand as though to erase the question. "Anyone working on this?" she asks.

"This story sickened me," says Amelia. "It was disgusting to look and see the college part of this. I'm, like, 'Ugh, the son in college didn't want to work.'"

Elaine nods emphatically. "I was bristling about that. It's a kind of stereotype, isn't it? Those college students live off the fat of the land. But then they're working thirty-five hours a week!" She makes an attempt not to look at Kate, but the truth is that almost three-quarters of these students are working just about as many hours as Kate is. "But it's not an unfamiliar thing that I've heard, older people complaining about students who take advantage of the system. So I feel uneasy with that aspect of the story. Anyone feel sympathetic with the portraits here?"

"I feel sympathetic with the daughter," says Greta, "trying to go to work. But the rest of them, I don't. Like living off welfare or living off dad—it's all the same."

"But," says Rosalind. "They might not have been given any strength from him. When he describes that scene of a father who reassures his child, it's not himself who's the father there; it's his own father reassuring him. It could be his kids didn't get any strength from him, so that's why they're having such trouble with their lives."

"So if you juxtapose those two images—his father carrying him, and him kicking in his son's car window—that could explain it," says Elaine. She notices that she's said this almost as a question, looking at Rosalind.

Yet a few moments later, when Elaine is assigning the topic for the take-home final—essentially a repeat of essay five, she's decided, an essay of comparison—Rosalind seems panicky.

"I have a question about comparison. On this essay, can we use something from real life?"

It's one of those moments when, the professor having given

something out in writing, and having explained it orally in detail, a student asks a question that makes it seem as though she's just woken up from a deep sleep. "Well, I set it up so you'll be doing a literary comparison," says Elaine, wondering what Rosalind is getting at.

"I guess I don't really understand comparison," says Rosalind, her face troubled, like someone who just begins to realize she's in deep water and may drown. "What are you trying to say?"

Trying?, Elaine thinks. How many ways can she say it? But instead she says: "Let me turn this into a question for you, Rosalind. When you wrote a composition about Sue Miller's story 'Appropriate Affect,' and compared it to your grandmother's life, what were you trying to do?" That, in Elaine's view, had been a straight-A piece of work, a moving essay explaining so honestly and forthrightly how Rosalind connected with the story that Elaine found herself imagining the experience Rosalind described as if it had happened to herself. Rosalind's *memère,* who was well loved by everyone, like the grandmother in Miller's story, tried to commit suicide by overdosing on her prescription drugs. Rosalind wrote: "As Grandma Frannie muttered, 'The. Nasty. Man.' (Miller 370), my *memère* muttered, 'the bastard was supposed to be dead ten years ago.' Needless to say, I can sympathize with Charlotte in the story. I was completely mortified by *memère's* statement of contempt towards my *pepère.*" For Elaine, Rosalind's essay peeled back some of the layers of the story. She analyzed so perceptively the need of the children—and grandchildren—to fix the grandmother as happy, loving, sweet, and contented. So why now did she seem not to understand how to write what would just be another example of a comparison essay, only this one comparing two short stories rather than one short story with a story from real life, as Rosalind had done so well just a couple of weeks before?

"I guess I was trying to learn something," Rosalind answered.

"Comparison is really a technique to stimulate critical thinking," Elaine explains. "For example, what about the roles of the fathers in these stories? Let's say Carver is showing you something about fatherhood. So comparing one story to another helps you articulate something about fatherhood that was floating around there." Somehow, Rosalind's expression of distress and anxiety brings out a corresponding feeling of anxiety in Elaine. Usually Rosalind seems to take things in with a rapt look, embedding them, it seems, in the very core of her brain. Now, though, Elaine is reading only a blank fearful look of incomprehension, as though suddenly Elaine had stopped speaking English. "All right," says Elaine, as though making up her mind not to let herself panic, too. "Let's take something very simple," she says, "like two pieces of fruit. A green Delicious apple and a Macintosh apple. Perhaps you're really going to define the essence of that green and red apple by talking about how they're both part of the category apple. 'Oh, yes, this is what apples are all about.' But you didn't put your finger on what's different until you took into account taste, or how far it would spurt if you bit into it. This comparison would show how it's part of a category, but also how it's unique."

Rosalind's face is still unsettled. "So basically, take one character and compare him or her to someone else?"

Elaine doesn't know exactly how to answer. She almost feels that if she says anything more, Rosalind will become more rather than less confused.

"I mean do you have to, like, learn something from this?" Now Rosalind seems to be passing from distress to outright anger. "Or just compare?"

"I'm not sure how you can differentiate," says Elaine. She looks like she wants to shake her by the shoulders, wake her up and tell her she's only having a bad dream. "Rosalind, the essay you wrote was a good model for this."

There's no response. Rosalind seems now to have damped down her anxiety and put on a blank face as though saying to herself, "Enough, drop it."

"I suppose you could talk about the metaphysics of comparison," says Elaine, wondering what she herself is getting at, and knowing for sure she's only making a bad moment worse. She decides to break the evil spell by handing out the form students will use to evaluate their class participation for the semester. When things are falling apart, she tells herself, throw a concrete task at them. Maybe the anxiety of trying to figure out how much they contributed to the class will distract them from the anxiety of how to write the final, a form of completion anxiety. Students at Framingham often visit the department chair's office in their senior year asking that their list of courses be re-checked, sure that they skipped something, as though their own academic success is hard for them to believe.

Who is to say why Rosalind suffered this momentary crisis of confidence in a class in which she has clearly been one of the stand-outs? "It could be his kids didn't get any strength from him, so that's why they're having such trouble with their lives." That's what she said just moments before this last exchange about the final. Could it be that she, too, feels she *didn't get any strength* and therefore doubts herself? Or is it that comparisons do lead to learning and conclusions that Rosalind, dauntless in other ways, doesn't want to face? What would occur to her if she compared this father to a father in another story, without being able to control or define just how her conclusions might apply to her own life? These students so often seem like buildings attacked by termites: so solid in some areas, and unpredictably shaky in others. Just where their vulnerabilities lie, the issues that trigger their panic, is hard to know or predict, even in such a motivated, seemingly self-sufficient student as Rosalind.

Elaine is never sure how to end this course. On the revised syllabus she handed out before Thanksgiving, she left this day blank. "We'll figure out what to do when we're closer to the end," she said. She's decided each of them will pick a passage from something they've written for this class and read it. Let them hear how their writing voices sound now.

As they read, one after another, what she can hear—and she hopes they hear it—is a tone of conviction. Listening to them, she seems frozen, her right hand holding the bottom of her face, the anthology of stories open in her left hand. She could be concealing a smile at times. After following along with a long quotation from one of the short stories in the anthology, she puts down the anthology, and its pages wing out on both sides of her blue pen.

Around the table they go, taking turns. When it's Kate's turn, she says she couldn't find anything. Amelia reads a paragraph, but it's her shortest! Susie reads well, growing louder as she seems to forget herself in her own line of reasoning. Phoebe reads an impressive paragraph, loud and clear:

> A sad but realistic element of the story is that alcoholism becomes normal to Amy, something that even creeps up on her playtime. While many young children incorporate things they know and learn from their parents into games like "house" by doing things like nurturing a doll, Amy incorporates more troubling examples from her parents into hers. Staggering around on her lawn she cries, "I'm drunk! I'm a drunken man!" (61) in a more serious game of imitation. Children pick up a great deal from their parents, consciously as well as unconsciously, and a great many do bring what they have learned into their own lives. They imitate and mimic and often role-play how their parents appear in their eyes, as Amy showed on her lawn. In an unfortunate situation like Amy's, Amy's parents' role is a negative and distorted one, where staggering about drunkenly is normal. Perhaps the most unfortunate aspect of alcoholism is that while at a young age children often make games out of their parents' behavior, they may later turn it into their own behavior as adults.

A controlled and confident voice, Elaine is thinking, perhaps rather clinical, yet clearly and convincingly articulating her view of the social context of the story de-romanticizing gin and the high life. As she listens, all of this feels like a kind of harvest. Even though it's an incredible amount of work, there's a moment when you get a stack of student essays and you have this hope that you're going to read something wonderful. And sometimes you do. Strangely, one of the other really strong finishers has been Marion. Steady, consistent, playing it safe and aiming for a B each time or else rewriting the paper, Marion, quiet and shy through high school, seems to have spent her first semester discovering that she's actually smart and can do much better than average work. She's in the same seat she always sits in, across the table, down toward the door—in fact, she hasn't been absent once the whole semester. Perhaps, after getting A's on her last two essays, she's making the mildest little statement of triumph today by wearing her straight shoulder-length brown hair pinned back on one side. Marion is reading a paragraph from her paper on social class in E. L. Doctorow's "The Writer in the Family," about a young man who's asked to fake letters from his dead father to his grandmother to "protect" her by making her think her son is still alive. The young man's domineering, wealthy relatives try to control even his father's death, and insist that it be put off until the grandmother herself is dead:

> The difference in economic classes in this story imitates what is often depicted in many other stories as well as in movies. Ruth, Jonathan, and Harold worked hard for their money and cherished the smaller things in life. Even something as simple as Harold's girlfriend coming over for dinner is enough to create excitement and a strong sense of warmth in their three-room apartment. Frances and her family, however, are extremely materialistic and self-centered. They were very comfortable financially but continued to let greed control them. They valued only the most expensive things and did not seem to have a strong sense of family unity. She had to have the most elegant clothes and the biggest car. Her sons had to be educated at a prestigious and expensive school. Frances would never have thought of having her own sons

> or even herself write the letter because she did not want to be bothered with it. Perhaps someone like Frances, with so much money, should have more manners and class, but it is obvious that she does not possess them. Her fancy clothes, expensive car, and luxurious environment only stand for the fact that money is wasted on the wrong people. Ruth and her children may not have had the money or social standing, but they have more class than Frances will ever have.

Elaine's heard that tone often before, that pride in not being too impressed by the possessions or opportunities of the rich or spoiled. The way, for example, Marion doesn't deign to mention Amherst College (where Bob went to school) but merely consigns it to the category of "prestigious and expensive." What pleases Elaine most about this essay is the way Marion supplies the evidence but also seems to be standing up for the poor branch of the family, like a lawyer walloping a jury with a summation. Marion has connected feelings with analysis, so the writing here is wonderful: clear, focused, and fluent.

Students at Framingham State don't often applaud at the end of the last class session. It's hard to say why there's no school tradition for this form of thanks. One might be tempted to guess that it's all part of professors seeming to be a species apart—much like the kindergarten teacher Belinda didn't think went home at night—or, at any rate, a reflection of the students' shyness. Younger college students are still in the habit of regarding school as a kind of imposition, or, at the very least, an examination process to deem them worthy of professional and managerial jobs. It's hard for them to feel generous when they're not feeling confident that they'll survive. Others might not want to appear to be "brown-nosing" by showing gratitude to their professor in public. Then, too, students in interactive classes may not consider the professor's role a performance. The custom of applause may have started at colleges with star professors, famous for their inspiring lectures, and have spread as a courtesy to their less inspiring colleagues. Whatever the reason, Elaine doesn't expect a round of applause in a few minutes, when they will have all-too-soon run out of time. True, she'll see them again for the final—but only the way people see ghosts, *seeing* them but not able to talk with them since the room has to stay quiet till the last student hands in her paper—and that will be even more of an anticlimax.

Her colleague, Helen Heineman, says that the only loving relationship that can end without bitterness is the one between a teacher and a student. Does Elaine love this class? She has memories of some things she was really happy with—like the session where they debated about whether Longfellow's poem should be required reading for tenth graders. She likes to hear students arguing, thinking about how to make a case. They rose to the challenge, and it was interesting to hear what they came up with. And today's discussion? That couldn't have happened back in September. Still, she remembers some difficult classes, too. Twenty years of teaching, and still it's a struggle sometimes. She's not sure she handled particularly well the classes where the students didn't do the reading or where they were tired or didn't feel like talking.

This makes her think of a movie she and Bob saw recently, *A Mid-Winter's Tale,* about a director who's putting on a production of *Hamlet* to save a church. He auditions a bunch of actors, and the auditions are so funny! The things people do—nobody could invent stuff like that. The cast is made up of totally mismatched failures and has-beens. The director, who has a barbed wit, is going to play the title role. For days after seeing the film, Elaine and Bob went around imitating the director's one-liners. Somehow, preparing to perform this play makes the whole cast into real actors. But there's one moment—the designer doesn't have a design the day before the performance—when the director explodes, he has so much anger. "You're all useless," he tells them. "Why am I an actor? I may as well be dead."

They're all crushed. They realize that this performance means everything to them. So of course they get it all back together. It's a love story about acting. The woman playing Ophelia has been married, but her husband, a fighter pilot, had crashed when he was thirty-three. A young widow, she's acting to find some meaning in what's happened. When she does Ophelia's mad scene—the one where in her madness she's singing little scraps of songs, *he's dead and gone, he will never come again*—she's working through her husband's death. She's so completely connected to Ophelia at that moment that everyone is stunned. It turns out that she's the one who really responds to the director's outburst. She lets him know how much they depend on the confidence of the director.

These students, too, may be more fragile than she can ever grasp. Once when she was teaching at Boston University, she came to class and no one had done the reading. She was really mad, so mad that she said: "You didn't do the reading? Fine, I'm not going to teach the class. Go away." It was the sort of thing a teacher can risk doing to a class only once. After that, they did the reading a lot more, they were so stunned. But she didn't really feel good. She should have talked to them. Instead she avoided dealing with what was going on.

When students don't respond, her way is too often to think: Oh, I guess you're not really interested. OK, let's go on to the next thing. She knows she ought to open up more and talk to them. That's something she'll need to think about—but nothing she can do anything about now. It's something a teacher has to establish from the very beginning of the course.

Or something that's embedded in one's personality. When she tells me all this later, it makes me wonder whether we all carry a cross of regret about ourselves, no matter how well we have done—like the woman in Kate Chopin's story.

It's winter now for real. Gray skies, the campus covered with snow. Even the flag in front of Dwight is hanging straight down, as though frozen. All semester Elaine's had to expose herself to my scrutiny, my tap-tapping on my laptop, even when she's been ashamed, and it's only amplified her constant sense of exposure to her own high, unremitting expectations, and, now I see, even her desire to be somewhat other than she is.

Her expectations are no less high for the students, of course. If the students have most of the work in, but not all, she'll give them an Incomplete—a mercy grade of sorts, since it allows the students till the fourth week of the following semester to complete the assignments. But she's merciless in another way, since if they do not hand in the missing work, the Incomplete is converted automatically to a failing grade. She will not just lower their grades a little and forget about the missing work; she will collect it, whether the semester is over or not.

If this is love, it can be tough. To these students, many of them barely out of adolescence, Elaine is someone who assigns hard work, someone who insists on a seemingly unreachable level of competence, someone who's always going to remind them if they should falter and fail to hand something in. Her demands—not unlike the demands of a parent—can cause friction, though the students were more likely to vent their hostility against the Fischer text than against her: Phoebe joked that this semester has taught her more than she ever wanted to know about Paul Revere. But the students also appreciated these demands. Though many reported that this course took as much as four times as much time as any of their others, these same students cited it as their favorite. Still, their approval won't reach that layer of Elaine where she takes herself to task.

What should she say now, this final moment that doesn't at all feel final? She looks around. The same big square table as in September, but smaller. The same faces, but each one a volume of writings, of struggle, of mystery, of triumph—of the wish, anyway, not to be beaten down. "There're a couple of things I want to remind you about." She recommends the on-campus performance of Puccini's *La Boheme.* "I've been going to these opera performances all semester. They're really amazing events. The phrase I heard one student use was, 'I'm blown away.' I saw students weeping. I went through at least three Kleenexes.

"The *one last* thing I wanted to remind you of was your technique of summary. You'll be needing to write a summary on the exam you take here. Does everyone feel confident about that? Would anyone like to remind us of what you're trying to achieve when you write a summary?"

"Main point," says Kate.

"Who they were, what they did," says Andy.

"No examples," she says to them. "Go for the jugular, without all the frills and furbelows."

OK, now, she tells herself, this is it. "I just want to tell you how much I enjoyed meeting you," she says, her voice clipped, business-like, as though she won't take the time to say more. "I know I'll be seeing some of you next semester. I'm always happy to talk to you, whether you're my advisees or not."

And that's it. They're shuffling to their feet, leaving. Amelia has a question about the field-trip paper she owes. Rosalind needs a paper clip. A little line forms to hand in papers.

"Did you say we can pick up this last essay before the weekend?" Phoebe asks.

"Yes, yes, I'm going to get this done before the weekend."

But Phoebe lingers. "So the folder comes in by the sixteenth?"

"Yes, I want to see what revisions you've done."

"Oh," Phoebe says, "have you seen a little British shop, going west, right off Route 9, you know, where Domino's Pizza is? They have these little jams and cookies—"

"And tea?" says Elaine. "Huh! I'm desperate to get good tea, and every time I see a British shop I look for PG Tips. That's the working man's tea in England, so you can buy a quarter pound for fifty pence. It's more expensive here, of course, if they even carry it. It's really good, not the sweepings from some factory floor. But I don't want to tell you what they charge."

"They probably have it," says Phoebe. "I was thinking of you."

"Well, thank you," says Elaine. "That sounds like not only a good place for me, but a good place for me to send members of my family to buy things for me."

"I'm going home Wednesday," says May. "Could I have my folder back by Wednesday?"

"Sure," says Elaine. "They're saying Saturday to Monday we're going to have a snow of epic proportions. So I'll just burrow in and read folders."

"Snow, huh?" says May.

"Well, we'll have to see," says Elaine. "Yep. That's what we say in New England."

Francesca is packing her books and notebook into her book bag. She and May are the last students to leave.

"I think it should be illegal to give tests before the holidays," Francesca says.

Elaine notices a woolen hat, still on the table. "Is that your hat?" she asks them.

"Maybe it's Jeremy's," says May.

When they're all gone, Elaine stares at the empty room a moment, then switches off the lights.

EPILOGUE: WOMEN AND MEN

THE BEILIN-BROWNS usually take a family vacation in Wellfleet on Cape Cod near where our family has a cottage. (This summer even their daughters are too busy to take more time off than one week, with Rachel going to arts camp and Hannah holding down her first job in a grocery store.) As Bob and I are sailing south out of Blackfish Creek on my twin-keeled sloop, *Willy*, close hauled against a gusty, rainy wind, Bob tells me he isn't the sort to make decisions based on some bookkeeping system, that he works more by instinct.

He's talking about the offer made to him this past June to move to New York City to chair Columbia's neurology department. The offer, which included a post for Elaine at Columbia's Institute for Gender Studies, free tuition for Hannah at Barnard, and a vastly higher salary for him, gave him pause for a week or two, but he didn't delay too much in turning it down. He could see his time at Columbia spent almost entirely on administration, just when there seems to be hope of making some real headway against a disease he's been fighting his whole professional life.

"I had this dream," he tells me. "I died, and one by one I saw the face of every ALS patient and felt responsible for their deaths."

Later, my hat blows off. We put *Willy* into the wind and come up on the hat close enough for Bob to get the boat hook under it.

But I haven't slowed the boat enough, and the hat slips off the end of the hook. Bob sees the hat floating now perhaps a hundred yards away in the gray, white-capped water, and he tells me he's going to dive in and get it. He's beginning to strip off his sweatshirt.

"What makes you think I can get you back on board," I ask him, "if the two of us couldn't even get the hat?"

He says a person would be easier. He could wave his arms, so he'd be more visible than the hat.

Courageous? Self-sacrificing? Foolhardy? "I'm not letting you do it," I say.

He seems doubtful, but he stays on board.

During our follow-up interview in the fall, I ask Elaine how she feels coming back to Framingham State when she nearly had a research job at Columbia, teaching only two courses a year for the same salary she gets at Framingham to teach six, just when James Carlin, owner of an insurance agency, the new head of the Massachusetts higher education system, has called for an end to "meaningless research" by state college faculty, who, he says, ought to be in the classroom more.

"I couldn't survive here," she tells me, "if I had to teach four, rather than three courses a semester. I already work sixty-five hours a week. It's ironic. We're doing a good job with our teaching by paying a lot of attention. If we had to teach more, it would make us less able to work one-on-one."

Bob, too, might have reason to regret turning down the Columbia offer. Shortly after our sail together, one of the three major grants he depends on was discontinued, taking with it a third of his pay. He and Elaine both, it's my impression, seem ineluctably drawn to what they do. As she praises this semester's classes, this semester's good students—and even when she frets over the ones she's disappointed with—I somehow want to believe that, much the way the faces of Bob's patients would haunt him, the faces of these students would haunt her if she were to leave.

Last February, Amelia Goudreault's car struck a boy as he was crossing a busy highway in front of a McDonald's. Amelia and I are sitting where we usually do when I interview students, in a corner of my office, out of sight of the window on my door, a little table with wheels between us where I put my laptop. The tears are starting to well up in her eyes. I cross the office to my desk to get the box of tissues I keep there. It's early fall again, months after the accident, and Amelia can't talk about it without breaking down.

"It's hard for me to know that I have to live the rest of my life knowing he's dead," Amelia says. She tells me about the horrible night of the accident and its aftermath. "Twisted as it is, this has brought our family more together. My dad's always been supportive, and my mother never has been. But she really came around." The writing class Amelia was taking last spring also proved to be a major source of support. In the story Amelia wrote for that class, she makes clear how none of the friends and adults rallying to her side could really touch the grief and shock inside her.

He Was Only Fifteen

The phone rings again for about the fifth time in one hour. Again it is my mother for about the fourth time that day.

"How are you, are you doing okay?"

"Fine, mother, I'm fine."

"Do you want your sister to come stay with you?"

I realized that I did. It was my first day alone and I will admit that it was hard to be alone at a time like this. So I told her yes I would like that. All this time I was fighting back tears which had again welled up in my eyes.

I hung up the phone, knowing full well that it will ring in about another ten minutes. A few minutes later as if on cue the phone rings once again.

"Hello, may I please speak to Anne, um, Goudreault?"

"No, she's at work right now." 'click'

I again placed the receiver back into its cradle, hoping for a few minutes of silence so I could collect my thoughts,

> and bring my emotions back into check. Yet, before I had even taken my hand from the receiver it sprang to life ringing wildly again.
>
> "Hi, tiger, how are you feeling?"
>
> It was my father calling for his second time of the day. He, like my mother, just wanted to check to see how I was "coping."

As I reflect on what Amelia has told me, and read the story she wrote for Bernard Horn's spring Prose Writing class, I can't help thinking of a passage in Deuteronomy that speaks of setting aside three cities of refuge for people who have accidentally killed. "Now this is the case of the manslayer who may flee there and live: One who has killed another unwittingly, without having been his enemy in the past. For instance a man goes with his neighbor into a grove to cut wood; as his hand swings the ax to cut down a tree, the axhead flies off the handle and strikes the other so that he dies. That man shall flee to one of these cities and live" (Deut. 19, 4-5). Amelia's "support system" is in full gear—her parents combining for once in their sympathy, her best friend (who sounds in Amelia's story more like a mother than a friend) trying to remind her that she's not really a killer. But Amelia, at her young age, knows what they do not: that the killing, however inadvertent, will forever be part of her.

Indeed, in a gloss on this passage in the Talmud, the "manslayer" must acknowledge this identity no matter what other honors others may wish to bestow. He "must say to them, 'I am a manslayer.' If then they said to him, 'Even so,' he may accept [the honor] from them."[23] Amelia may believe that no one can love or honor her until she first tells them what she has done. Nor can she forget that death can strike anyone, no matter how young—even someone much younger than she.

"I've had to grow up a lot," she tells me. "I wasn't focused on school. Now I'm focused on school, big time. You don't realize how precious every little thing is." Somehow, realizing that she, too, could die at any time, produced not a nihilism, but the reverse. "I really have a much stronger desire to do well in school, to finish school. I want to be a teacher, a high school teacher." I remember Amelia, wearing her Boston College cap, leaning her chair back against the wall of the classroom *à la* Kate, and saying how she'd taken over her high school class for two days and how it wasn't too bad; you just had to keep it interesting. But then there was the time she'd been in tears right in class because she'd done the wrong assignment. Hard for me to imagine Amelia, who had to take an Incomplete because otherwise she would have gotten a D+, becoming a teacher. Still, I hoped it would happen. "I've been this way since second grade, but now I feel much more of a desire," she tells me. "Last fall I was more into everything social. Rather flighty, I guess you could say. I feel like I've come really far. Just the improvement in my grades will show you that."

When I check everyone's grades, I discover that it wasn't only Amelia who needed improvement. Out of twenty-one students enrolled in Elaine Beilin's Essentials class last fall, only Mary, Phoebe, May, and Francesca actually completed the "standard" eight courses during their freshman year. Many failed or dropped out of courses. Rosalind and Claudia, however, decided that a three-course load was as much as they could do well with and got very high grades.

Claudia's average amazes me when I check it. If she continues to do this well, she'll graduate *magna* or perhaps even *summa cum laude.* "I was very confused for a while," she says when she comes to see me a few weeks later. "About school, majors, what I wanted to be. I sat one Sunday for five hours, brainstormed, looked at the catalog, every single class, thinking what I was going to get out of it. Before school started, I came to see Dr. Beilin. I was telling her about how I knew I wanted to stay an English major so I could write, speak, express anything effectively, and easily get into a graduate program in the future. She was very positive about it, very glad. She pointed out that since I was raised in Brazil, and

English is not my first language, the better my English is, the better I will do in the future in anything."

Claudia has continued working at the same company where her father is an executive, and though only part-time, she is given the responsibility of arranging the copy and illustrations for the company's catalogs and ads. With Chris, her boss, whom she admires, she virtually runs the whole marketing department. "Chris can speak perfectly and writes amazing letters. That helps his job, and his job, you would think, has nothing to do with language." Comfortable now with her major, Claudia also has many friends on campus, many people, including professors, she feels close to, many organizations she wants to work with. For her, the combination of staying with her well-educated, close-knit family, working at a responsible job where people know her, and taking a reduced load of courses has proved to be an ideal way to adjust to college life. She still plans to transfer to a private college or university for her final two years and will undoubtedly get a scholarship based on merit.

Those who would measure the success of a college like Framingham by citing its mere 50% rate of student retention (that is, only half the freshmen will go on to earn Framingham State degrees) ought to bear in mind that not all successful adjustments to college mean that the student will stay. In some cases, success might mean successfully transferring. Andy, for example, has returned to New York to live at home and attend Brooklyn College. Perhaps Andy's mother, who is a New York City teacher, encouraged him to separate from his high school friends and to attend a smaller school than one of the city colleges, at least for his first year. As a New Yorker—even as a Jew—Andy was unusual at Framingham. When I interviewed him in early October of his freshman year, he was well aware of how rare Jewish students are at Framingham, but he was inclined to deny that for him this was any big deal. Now that he's back in Brooklyn, however, he gives a somewhat different account of his feelings. In fact, he's absorbed some of his mother's narrative about her first year at Quinnipiac College: "I met some people in Framingham—I was probably the first Jewish person they ever met."

He sounds happy to be back in New York's multi-ethnic environment. "There's Asians, and other ethnics, all different ethnics, cultures coming together. Just a whole different feeling to it. It's not like knowing everyone. At Framingham, everyone you'd pass walking to class you'd recognize. Here there's different faces every day. I was used to a mixture in high school. In New York City, that's how it is. Since I want to do film, I feel like being with all different cultures, all different social settings, will be a better experience. Brooklyn College has a lot of Hasidics. Park on the right side of school, it's the most Hasidic area you'll see. On the left-hand side of the college, you're in the black ghetto, in the projects. Brooklyn College is like the boundary."

There are things Andy genuinely misses about Framingham. For one thing, "it's not the same friendly relationship with the professor," he says. Some of his classes have ninety students. Andy's year at Framingham brought him into the academic world in a way his high school years never did. As someone who had mainly hung out with his friends in high school, an underachiever, Andy found the confidence at Framingham to go on to a larger, more impersonal college.

When he thinks of the Essentials class now, he thinks of Rosalind: "I remember no matter if no one else had something to say, she would. And if I had something to say, and it was half-decent, she would always say, 'I agree.' I once saw her after class. She said, 'That point you made was really good.'"

Many of the students remember Rosalind. Last spring she signed up for an honors course Elaine Beilin was offering, Poetry and Prose of the English Renaissance, a course enrolling mainly juniors and seniors, and she got an A.

But her all-important honeymoon has been scheduled for the middle of the fall semester. Couldn't she marry and take her honeymoon some other time, Elaine and I both wonder. Elaine feels saddened that Rosalind is responding to working-class (or is it Old World?) attitudes that put a woman's honeymoon ahead of her college courses.

Rosalind stops by my office late one afternoon on her way to a "hair rehearsal" for the wedding. She's been working full time for Dean College (where Joey works) as a financial aid officer, but she thinks it will be a while before she has enough money to resume studying. All in all, she doesn't seem to like it any better than the mail-order support-hose company. Again, though, she seems to be assuming more responsibility than someone of her age and education generally would.

She explains that she's helping students and their families figure out how to afford college—an irony that makes us both smile faintly, since for now she herself can't afford to continue—and she's discovered it's a touchy subject. Some parents have screamed at her, though others have thanked her. "Still," Rosalind says, "I'm not reaching people the way I want to reach them."

Rosalind would prefer to come back to Framingham at some point and prepare to be a teacher. "I'll talk to my adviser here," she says. "Get a few general education courses out of the way at Dean. Then, watch, I'll end up with four Beilin courses [by which she means tough courses] in one semester."

She's not planning to have children right away. "Once I have children, I'm no longer Rosalind. I'm a mom. At least I'll have my degree under my belt." She seems to look to Elaine Beilin as a model. "She just seems to be able to balance family and work—being a very good professor—and I don't doubt that she's an excellent parent. She's extremely intelligent and appears to have order to her life." For now, though, Rosalind's key objective is to have enough money so that she and Joey can afford to set up house together.

Jeremy is looking less like a street person than he did a year ago. He's exchanged his wool watch cap for a tan United Parcel hat, probably to honor the successful strike the workers in that company waged over the summer, and he's replaced his red high-tops with leather workboots. Besides that, he looks healthier—his cheeks ruddy, his skin clearer. His clothes seem cleaner, too, and he seems to smile more. "At the end of fall semester," he says, "I had misgivings about school, but my parents convinced me to stay on. I knew that I really have to go to college, and I do want to complete school, but I didn't know if I wanted to go full time."

In the spring, Jeremy took only one course, Prose Writing, with Bernard Horn, a course and teacher Elaine recommended for him. Elaine's thinking was that if Jeremy could keep even the slenderest contact with the college, take only a course he was likely to enjoy and succeed with, he might build up in the future to taking a fuller program. Professor Horn, she knew, combined a bright and empathic mind with a flexible, almost customized approach to his writing students. Jeremy, who clearly had an issue with authority, was least likely to be turned off by such a course.

The referral worked. "I really enjoyed Dr. Horn as a teacher, and enjoyed the class," Jeremy says. "It was quite contrary to our Essentials class, not as focused, or as constricting, and you could write about whatever you wanted to, and Dr. Horn would tell you what to improve on and how to make it better. He's a nice guy." Jeremy wrote three three-to-six page essays in that course, and at the end was told to revise the one he'd liked best. "This was a lot like when Dr. Beilin let me do my research paper on Rodan," he says, referring to his favorite rock group. Having a free choice of what to write about made things much easier for him, and writing about music, something he loves, gave the writing more life.

"It didn't seem as though Dr. Beilin and I got along," he tells me. "She wrote something on my paper that I really took offense to—something about my choice of words, and how I worded things, something about it being—cluttered? That comment just didn't need to be there. It seemed like she wanted to change the way I wrote. As though she was saying, 'You're wrong, do it this way.' That's not what I have in my head about a college curriculum. It should point you in the right direction, but it shouldn't make a mold for you—especially an English teacher. I still did most of my work. But I didn't change—that was for sure. I wasn't going to change. I think it would have been difficult for me to change. I'm not saying I'm never going to change, but it's going to take a while. I know I have a lot of problems, grammatical things, and I'm going to have to do something about that, but if I think a word should go there, it's going to go there. And if I think that's the way I want to explain something, that's the way it's going to get done. Basically, she told me that's how she felt, and I said I don't see myself changing in the near future."

In my poetry-writing class this fall semester, Jeremy has been holding to the same position, that the words he chooses are the ones he wants, even if they might seem unidiomatic, or, in some cases, portmanteau words that he seems (unwittingly?) to have created himself. I find that I'm beginning somehow to associate his use of language with his clothes, which also might seem stubbornly unchanging, as though if he put something else on, and someone happened to tell him it looked good, he'd be irritated at the implied criticism.

But Jeremy seems less hurt by criticism from some teachers than others: "I had to do some short essays for Dr. Desmond McCarthy. In his Ethnic Literature class, I wrote about motifs of mechanization in Ralph Ellison's *Invisible Man,* and how the Invisible Man was becoming a robot, just following what he was taught in college, and how this was connected to Booker T. Washington's theory of non-resistance: Do whatever you're told; you'll get some rights, but won't achieve freedom. I was told it was really good. Then I wrote an essay on *Huckleberry Finn* in his American Writers II class, and it wasn't good. But he gave me a great compliment. He said, 'You're a writer; you can do this.' In his class I was feeling more confident. Desmond's a really nice guy, and he was trying to push me to do more things. He asks how you're doing, not just 'Did you get the paper done?'"

This semester, Jeremy is taking three courses, and is liking—

and passing—them all. More interesting still, he's developing a taste for news-writing, one of the strictest genres of writing. (Only a year later, in fact, he will begin to publish articles, impeccably correct, on the front page of the college paper.) "For me, though, to do well," he tells me in the fall of his second year, "I won't be able to take a full course load," he acknowledges. "My parents are fine with this. Three courses is full-time, so we've gotten financial aid from the school." His parents have accepted, apparently, that Jeremy's progress toward a degree will take longer than four years, but they're satisfied that he's still making some progress. As for Jeremy, he seems happier with himself and his life than a year ago. He's still working at Newbury Comics, and, in fact, just got a raise. His job pays the bills, just barely, but he enjoys dealing with music: "My band is going well. We played our first show a month ago, and we're going to play at the same club again." Jeremy plays guitar and bass, and he writes the songs—both music and lyrics—for the group. When I ask him what the music is like he tells me: "It's similar to Rodan—abrasive, yet having melody under the abrasion. It's really hard music, but has a caring voice, a nice melody of words. That," he says, "is one thing in my life I can really get behind and enjoy, no matter what is happening."

Most students I've interviewed this fall have positive feelings about their first writing class, though, in truth, the whole experience has begun to fade into the general swirl of memories from their freshman year. Many took away from the class permission to begin to think of themselves as full-fledged citizens of a learning community, however little they might recall the specifics. Amelia received the highest grade on the mid-term in her literature class in the spring, despite the accident. "I was incredibly proud of myself," she tells me later. "I went in thinking I wasn't all that prepared, but luckily I knew what I wanted to say. This gave me an inkling that I could be really good. It proves to me, if I try I could do that well, or better. Professor Beilin's papers last fall probably helped because we had to do several on the Paul Revere book, and even though I know mine weren't the greatest, I knew I had to know those quotes, I had to be able to analyze them with some background in order to make the paper decent. Professor Beilin is a great teacher," Amelia reflects, "but I really didn't give her course the effort I could have to make it a good class. That's why I was glad when she told me if I needed a class, just to ask her, because I'd like to take another class with her; I really would."

When I ask Amelia if she would have changed anything about the class, other than her own level of effort, she says she wouldn't: "We had some really good class discussions, I thought. A lot of people in there who had motivation, who wanted to be in school, who were in the English major for a reason, people who went to class, who did their work—the class was good. I remember that older girl, Rosalind, I believe. She definitely had her head on straight. And that other one who liked to argue—Kate—I enjoyed arguing with her. Kate was great."

As for Claudia, who came to college a year ago thinking of herself as young—though not too young to make a start—the freshman writing class was only one more in a series of transitions and adjustments in her life. "I've learned through so many things," she tells me. "I'm still only eighteen, but I've moved so many times; I've changed schools. There's only so much my parents can do, and after that I'm on my own. The first day of school here last year, I was on my own. That writing class eased me into college, and that was the writing class from which I've learned the most. Professor Beilin's approach made me want to write more." And Andy, too, from the vantage of Brooklyn College, asserts how helpful the course was for him. "I had taken writing in high school, but this was the first time a group of people could sit down together and talk about everything and compare, putting their minds together and debating and working in a collaborative manner. I definitely had to adjust my writing at the beginning of the class, which was frustrating, but it definitely helped me at the end."

Greta is even more emphatic. "Beilin's class was the only real college class that I had. I loved that class because I actually learned something." She considers a moment. "My whole Approaches to Literature class was oral; you had to read things out loud. That was easy, but you learned something. I knew if I participated in class I'd get a good grade. In Beilin's class, I was forced to be more organized. I couldn't just slip through, but that felt good. Hey, I'd feel, I learned something about Paul Revere. This is how a college class is supposed to be. I wasn't pushed; I wanted to work hard. I liked her syllabus. It rocked—so concise; you always knew what you had to do. I hate not getting a syllabus! Now I have something to contrast my other classes with," she tells me.

Greta has never had a problem with confidence. Even so, she identifies her freshman writing course with Elaine Beilin as an important milestone for her. "I've always had a pretty high level of confidence. That's my favorite thing about myself. I used to be a little timid, but now I'm willing to tell you what I think. Now I don't care if you like my ideas. That's been happening for a few years, really. But getting a B in her class—I know I worked for it, so I could see that I could do what I set my mind to. This was the only B I ever worked for. My speaking up in class increased. I wouldn't raise my hand unless I was sure I was one-hundred-percent right. Now I feel, 'Oh, so I'm wrong; so what.' In Beilin's class the response would be, 'You brought up an interesting idea.' I learned that it was OK to be wrong sometimes. Like, sometimes, if you said something wrong, it started a new conversation."

Here, Greta has hit on a theme I have heard again and again in interviewing the students. If they've taken the trouble to learn something and to think about it, they want the opportunity to have their opinions taken seriously.

As Marion told me: "In Beilin's class, it's not like if I came out with the wrong idea, I'd be made fun of or laughed at, but I need to go through more before I begin spurting out ideas. In Beilin's class, a lot of people came up with ideas that were off base, but she would say, 'You're on the right track,' and she'd help us see things in different ways. In her class, I basically learned that it's enjoyable to discuss literature and points of view. It's different from high school, where you have to be there and don't have a choice. The students there could care less. And people would laugh at you, chastise you. In our class last fall, ideas were welcome. We were invited to look at each other's point of view, and in high school I never used to think of school that way."

It interests me that, from the very first, conversation—speaking up and being heard, as well as hearing what others have to say—has seemed so important in what is, after all, a course in writing. Phoebe tells me: "I think what I got out of the course was more social than English issues. I was already comfortable and good with grammar and research and all those things that we did pay a lot of attention to. If I'd done things the way I was supposed to in high school, I suppose I could have waived the course—I don't think I needed it. But I learned a lot about other freshmen and about Professor Beilin. She's great. I would take ten more courses with her. Though I learned to put more examples in my writing—when I tutor people now, I'm stressing using examples, supporting your idea with evidence, using all the same words Professor Beilin did—I found the social aspect of the course more interesting. It was interesting to see where other people were coming from. They were also freshmen. I think about Greta, for example. I'm a real people-watcher, and she fascinated me. And Jeremy—he's interesting. I see him at Newbury Comics. It was interesting to see how people were in the same boat, how we all dealt with coming to school differently. Some people were quiet and shy; others were outgoing. And I've watched people change from last year. Francesca is a lot more open, trying a lot harder to speak up."

"Francesca," I tell her, "has switched her boyfriend, I think." It's as if, of all the students, Phoebe has taken on the role of studying the class with me. Still, I have to restrain myself from sharing all the information I know: Francesca met her new boyfriend over the Internet. They E-mail poetry back and forth. May also dumped last year's boyfriend, the one who took her to Alaska and wanted her to move there and work in the store on the reservation. Marion has also broken off with her freshman-year boyfriend, who wanted to be a chef, and she's going out with an actor, a film afficinado. And when Marion took her father to his first choral concert—Beethoven's Ninth—her father made her promise to tell him the next time she goes; he'd like to come along again. "Someday, if you become a sociologist or something," I say to Phoebe, "you could do a study of how young women, once they begin to become more educated, upgrade their boyfriends—and, in some cases, help educate their own parents."

"Sure," says Phoebe, who grins at me indulgently. "Maybe that should be *your* next book."

Just as Rosalind has, Phoebe has found in Professor Beilin a woman she would like to think of as a model for herself. "She's very down to earth, very knowledgeable, and she just has such enthusiasm for what she's doing—that's her key to making her classes enjoyable. She's very organized and hands out everything she wants done, which is very helpful to me. She's always open to questions and differing opinions, she's open-minded—" Phoebe shrugs. "She's great. I can't think of anything I don't like about her. I've thought that at her age I want to be somewhat like her. With age, a lot of people forget how it was to be a college-age student, or they just block it out. She's in touch with everyone. I've seen her meet with other professors, and she can communicate with everyone. She's very approachable. I want to be that way, too—I don't want there to be a wall between me and anybody else. You can really talk about anything with her. I took Poetry and Prose of the English Renaissance with her. People take so many things from what they read. Nothing shocks her, embarrasses her, or turns her off. We were talking about orgies—really, anything, anything goes. She'll stop and think about it. She's a real thinker."

I ask her if she thinks that having a woman professor was especially helpful to her. I'm thinking of Rosalind's remark about how she was sure Elaine was both a good mother and a good teacher, and that her ability to organize her life so she could have both her family and her profession also served as a model. "I don't think it really matters, when it comes to professors, whether it's a man or woman. You and Dr. Beilin are both awesome," she smiles at me. "But," she adds, "I can't grow up to be a great man."

As for Kate, she, too, seems to be growing up, becoming more capable as a student—or at least she's trying. Kate herself says she realizes how important it is to try to keep going. "I got hit really hard over the summer with what my life would be like if I didn't get an education," she tells me. "Three-and-a-half years of waiting tables, and I just don't want to do it anymore. It was because I was pulling fifty hours a week that I realized it. It's just that I'd never worked full-time. The daytime shift is so much harder, and there's so much more to put up with. Customers are evil. I got yelled at last week because I didn't bring a guy's chocolate milk fast enough."

Kate's hair seems wavier, perhaps lightened. Her face seems even younger than last year, perhaps because she's wearing less make-up, and still there's something about her—perhaps it's her full cheeks and large eyes, or simply her vehement sincerity and her sardonic self-deprecation—that makes me sympathize with her. Possibly it's because she seems so impoverished, not only by a chronic shortage of money (she's always about to cave in under the expense of maintaining her gas-guzzling, ancient Ford Fairlane), but by a dearth of sheer savvy and sophistication. Only when I asked her last year why she drives so far did she find out that her home town is miles closer to Bridgewater State than it is to us. Her fixation on our college—for her, that college on a hill—began when she was just starting high school and her friend Leslie's older sister graduated from Framingham and told Kate about it, possibly gave her a ride to see it. Even now, as we talk, I discover that she doesn't know that she can do anything other than teach if she stays an English major.

"Oh, that's good," she tells me when I list other possibilities, because she's having trouble with the World Literature survey, one of the courses she's required to take for teaching certification. "*The Iliad,*" she says, as if that sums up her problems. "It's the way the professor is teaching it; I'm not understanding it. This is the first book I've ever had to buy the Cliff Notes for. This woman flies all over the place."

Academically, Kate's been hanging by a thread ever since she got here a year ago, though she assures me that this semester will be different. She thinks she's going to pass her remedial math course this time around, and has never had any difficulty with Spanish. Her fourth course is Shakespeare, with Elaine Beilin. "If I could just take her for the rest of my career here," Kate says, "I'd be happy. She's constantly at me, 'Kate you can do better than this.' This semester I got a B from her on my first paper. I was so happy! If you sit and read the Shakespeare long enough, you can figure it out," she reassures me. "And Dr. Beilin will explain something till it's in your head."

I ask her if she'll bring me one of the papers she's done in Shakespeare, so I can see how her writing is developing.

"Sure," she looks at me quizzically, as though I'd just asked her to bring me two glasses of water.

She's certainly less lonely here than she was a year ago. "I see more people, like Greta—we sit in the commuter caf, and we talk. I'm friends with Winnie Lang. We had some interesting conversations."

I know Winnie . She's a thoughtful, intense, highly literary person—another bookworm, to use the phrase Kate once used to describe herself a year ago. One might take her for a young boy, with her very short hair, her jeans, and her motorcycle jacket. Winnie writes poems, some of them outspoken on the ups and down of her love life as a lesbian. I notice that Winnie, who is perhaps eight years older than Kate, and who is a first-rate student, has taken Kate under her wing, trying to help her get through World Literature, and when things don't go well for Kate (she fails the mid-term), it's Winnie who shepherds Kate to my office to complain, to ask advice. I tell her—looking over at Winnie almost as though I'm speaking to a mom who's come in with her daughter—maybe she'd better bail out. I know this professor works best with strong students.

Later I wonder if I haven't given Kate bad advice. Kate just increases her hours at her job and gets in trouble in some of her other courses, even Shakespeare, where she had been doing well. Elaine has to have a talk with her, and so do I. I'm Kate's official advisor, but, more to the point, she has the habit now, since our "interviewing" days last year, of coming to see me if she has problems, just as several of the students from last fall's class do. I tell Kate to let her boss know she'll need to take extra time off during the weeks before mid-terms and finals. "He wants to see you succeed, he'll understand," I tell her, though, of course, I've never made it down to the Gourmet Panda, so how do I know?

"No, that's true," says Kate. "He will."

For now, it's still up and down with Kate. "My first semester I didn't care, I just wanted to get through it and get it over with. In the back of my head, I wanted to be here, but when I was actually sitting here, I just wanted to go home, go to bed. It was a waste of my time, I kept thinking, when I could be home making money instead of paying people money with me not wanting to be here. When I got a letter from the dean saying if I didn't pick my grades up, I couldn't come back, I burst into tears. I didn't know what to do. I quit my job at Honey Dew Donuts and put more time into my school work. It makes me mad when I do lousy. I knew I could do better; I just wasn't doing as well as I could. Spring was decent, and I pulled myself off probation. But this is another trial semester. I was pretty sure I was off probation, but I lost financial aid because of low grades. I have no idea how much money I lost—about eight hundred dollars for this semester."

Since Kate is still smoking, I see her standing, often with Winnie and some of the poets from my class, even in the coldest weather, on the sunny side of May Hall, trying to stay warm while having a cigarette. One day, she actually brings me a short paper from her Shakespeare class, as promised. Other than to take more time with her papers, Kate never figured out the key to success last fall. And even throwing more time at a project didn't always help her. "One paper I worked really hard on," she recalls. "That field-trip one, and I got a C. I cried the whole way home. I don't remember what was wrong with it; I only remember I spent a lot of time on it. My mother and I spent a whole day in Lexington, a weekend day; I took a whole day off work, so it was a lot of money. I was mad at myself. I decided to get another person to proofread for me—my friend Leslie. She's evil. She'll tell you what she thinks, whether you like it or not. She's a little twisted, but she's a good writer. When we were in high school, she wrote a children's story where the hero ended up popping someone's eye out with a dull spoon. Anyway, our schedules are different now, so I don't go to Leslie."

When I read over the paper, at least two things amaze me. One is that Kate (through the vagaries of the search-and-replace feature of her word processor) has somehow managed frequently to misspell the word "the" and the other is that emerging from the chaos of this young woman's ill-organized and difficult life is the voice of someone who is beginning to defend well-founded ideas. Kate, in Elaine's words, has learned to use the "because" clause—however much she still seems to need "evil" Leslie (or someone) to proof her work.

For Kate, as for all of us, an education will come in many small increments, as will maturity. Perhaps someday she will no more think of handing in misspelled work with her name on it than she would coming to work with her blouse stained with ketchup. But that day hasn't come yet.

In the meantime, Elaine Beilin, her teacher, will be patiently listening to her, has heard her make a well-argued distinction between a movie Henry V and the Shakespeare original, whether we might agree with her interpretation or not. Yet it's still too soon to take for granted that Kate, the daughter of a waitress who writes poetry but never was able to go to college, will succeed in getting her degree and not have to spend her life on her feet.

It's December again, a year after the class I am writing about ended. While I've been working on this book, Elaine has taught yet another semester of classes. Hannah has completed her first semester away from home as a freshman at Barnard. Elaine seems more confident about Hannah's adjustment than she was last spring when the imminence of Hannah's going away was making everyone nervous. "She had to go through a real adjustment in time management," Elaine tells me. "She's playing rugby, of all things. But she's thrown herself into her course work a lot, and she's been pulling all-nighters. She read her latest E-mail from me at one-thirty in the morning. But she's doing well. I've been reading her essays, and I'd be very pleased if my freshmen wrote like that.

"Actually, Hannah didn't go into her English course expecting to like it that much. It's a course in women's literature, very eclectic: *Antigone, As You Like It*, all over the map—Carol Gilligan, Nancy Chodorow, theoretical stuff. She had a ten-page paper where she had to connect two or three of the texts. That really stretched her. But for the first time, she's actually beginning to realize what I do. She even asked if during break she could sit in on one of my classes."

Elaine has met Hannah's friends from Barnard, even some of their parents. She's grateful for Hannah's roommate. "Hannah lives in a maelstrom of mess, and Megan never says a word about it. Anyway, she loves New York City. She's been helping a first grade or second grade teacher at P.S. 163. The other night she called and told me, 'Mom, it isn't Needham.' They're mostly Hispanic kids, and the kids she's working with have learning disabilities. Just their stories give you pause."

"And how's Rachel?" I ask. "Does she miss Hannah?"

"Rachel's been flying. She made freshman basketball at Needham High. She's doing very well in her courses, and particularly loves Latin and French. Yes," Elaine nods and smiles, "she misses Hannah. They E-mail each other, real-time messages sometimes. But Rachel came home the other day and said, 'I have to talk to Hannah.' I suggested she E-mail. 'No, I have to talk to Hannah right now.' And then I hear her on the phone: 'Hannah, when you get a rebound, are you supposed to hold it over your head, or down near your stomach?'"

The semester is almost over by now, and it's been a grueling one for Elaine. She's taught a senior seminar, a seminar for sophomores called Literary Study, and her Shakespeare class. "The Shakespeare class is huge, and they write short assignments all the time. But I've had such wonderful students, the best students, the most I've ever had here. Literary Study was superb; the senior seminar wonderful. There's only one student there I may kill. But she is the exception," says Elaine. "The class is full of bright, committed students. Or take _______ ," and here she mentions a student I don't know. "Not the brightest spark in the world, but she tries, she tries. She just might bring it off out of sheer stick-to-it-iveness. During the last class they read a few pages of their papers, and they were nice to each other. They offered each other good criticism, but they weren't cruel either. Basically, in the last two classes I said very little. And at the conclusion of the last class I said: 'I just want to point out that you ran these classes. That's the mark of a good seminar.'"

"Do you see many of the students from our class?" I say, meaning last fall's Essentials.

To Elaine's surprise and pleasure, Arthur MacGregor, who failed her Essentials class and had to retake it in the spring, is also in Shakespeare and doing well. "He turned in a very good paper, arguing that *Othello* is a play without a hero, and he adopted this breezily cynical voice. He basically bashed each character in turn and had a great time doing it. So I told him, 'Keep that verve, but you've got to be more accurate, and don't leave yourself so easily open to disagreement by ignoring parts of the play.' But he's very, very talented. His attendance has been better, too—he's probably missed a class every other week. Sometimes he'd pay attention; sometimes he'd sit way back in the corner with a couple of kids he was friendly with, and I'd have to take a stroll down the aisle.

"Kate is in my Shakespeare, of course. She looked like she was heading for a crisis, working too many hours again, clearly exhausted in class, looking catatonic. She handed in her second essay on *Othello,* and it was essentially a plot summary with some quotations, so I gave her the word. And of course she was in my office in a flash and knew exactly what I was talking about.

"She'd written the paper in the wee small hours, without much attention. She was interested in Iago, and it only took maybe half-a-dozen Socratic questions to get her back on track knowing what she wanted to say. I got her to write down adjectives to describe Iago in her view, but she clearly had something else going on that she was fascinated by and rather admired him for what he was able to do. She worked out a thesis about Iago being evil but fascinating and attractive. She will re-do the paper. She wants to do well; no question. When I compare it to the inferior stuff she was doing in Essentials—she didn't want to fail, but she wasn't going to make a major effort. Remember? She was doing that Dracula stuff. Now she's light years away from what she was dealing with then. She's reading complicated material and has something to say about it. Hanging around with Winnie Lang doesn't hurt, either. But I had to say to her, 'Try to cut your work hours down to twenty-five from forty.'"

I hear Kate has a new boyfriend. In May, a few months after I conclude my final interviews, I see Kate coming down the steps of the Student Union. When we greet each other, I try not to look down at her waist. "The baby's due September," she tells me with excitement, obviating my need to ask. "But we're not getting married till October, so I can stay on my parents' health insurance."

I congratulate her warmly, of course, while in my heart I have a sinking feeling. So this, I think, is how she's relieving her academic troubles.

When I think of Kate dropping out, I feel sad. But then I remember her first college essay: "Although a tinderbox is inflammable, there is always a way to set fire." Do we know that even Kate, who is still so young, may not be back? I think of one of the past editors-in-chief of our student paper who was a young mother—single, in fact—and of our college's excellent day-care center. I think how the average age of Framingham graduates is now twenty-four, and many are "returning" students or "adults returning to college." If Kate does return, I think, she may come back stronger because of the courses that, with such pain, she was able to complete. Some of these sparks do catch.

But then I hear that Kate is coming back, at least to study in the evening. The baby, born a month early, died in the hospital after six days. She leaves a message on my voice mail while I'm away for the summer. She needs to talk to me about trying to get into courses. She knows it's probably too late—although it's not, and Elaine and I will help her. I think of how much she has gone through, how different her college years will be from the idyllic images presented in college recruitment viewbooks. I think of Hannah playing rugby in Riverside Park.

Now it's the fall of 1998, and some of the students in Elaine's freshman writing class have actually become juniors. "Well," Elaine says, after I've asked her to read over the manuscript of this book, "You've described what you set out to describe."

"But?" I ask.

"But," she says. "I wonder if anyone else will be as interested in them as we are?"

"I don't know," I say. Her worry could have so many dimensions. Will people care as much as they should about the future of such students? Will the faculty who come to Framingham after we retire care about them? And when people read about these students, what will they think?

Uncharacteristically—since she's always in a hurry—she lingers at the doorway to my office before leaving. "I was just wondering."

"What?"

"Maybe I should give Rosalind a call. To see if she's considering coming back."

"Why not?"

"Yes," she nods to herself. "I will."

From time to time I still see them on campus. Phoebe wins a special scholarship; she speaks, without notes, to a large audience. Jeremy continues writing lead articles for the college newspaper, flawlessly. His journalism instructor says he's learning to catch his own errors. Marion and her boyfriend show up for an evening screening of a difficult film by Angelopoulos, a Greek director—they own a video of one of this director's other films. I see Amelia on the staircase in May Hall, ask her how she's doing, and her eyes tear up. "Come and see me, if you want. You know I'm always good for some free advice."

"I know," she says, hurrying away.

From time to time I check up on them, the ones who are still with us. I log on to the college's database, type in a student's ID, and a list of her completed courses fills the screen.

UPDATE

Francesca Bartlett, May O'Neill, Marion Parabicoli, Phoebe Schottenhamel, Greta Weed, and *Mary Zubrowka* graduated from Framingham State College, May, 2000.

Susie Benson completed her requirements for graduation and will graduate May, 2001; *Arthur MacGregor* is scheduled to complete his requirements during the summer of 2001.

Donna Monahan, transferred to University of Massachusetts, Boston; *Claudia Santos* to Boston College; *Andy Stein* to Brooklyn College. All were expected to graduate in 2001.

Rosalind Prevost, a budget analyst for a college in the Boston area, now a junior, is continuing to study there part-time; *Lee Davis* is enrolled in a degree program in fashion merchandizing at a school in Philadelphia.

Belinda Carr is working for an insurance company and thinking of beginning courses in American Sign Language; *Kate Velasquez* is married and has a child. She is still working part-time at the Gourmet Panda, and thinking about taking courses at the local community college.

Greg Dumont, Colleen Ingram, and *Max Lelievre,* have withdrawn from Framingham State without immediate plans to return to college.

George Coverdale, Amelia Goudreault, and *Jeremy Moles* have withdrawn from Framingham State; their plans are not known at this time.

ELAINE BEILIN received the Distinguished Faculty Award at Framingham's 1999 Commencement.

COURSE SYLLABUS

21.102E Essentials of Writing
Dr. Elaine Beilin
Fall 1996

Office: May Hall 104
Phone: 508-626-4837
Office Hours: W 10:30, R 1:30, F 9:30

e-mail: ebeilin@frc.mass.edu

Course Description

Essentials of Writing introduces students to some fundamental aspects of college writing: analytic reading, critical thinking, writing for specific readers, and research. By participating in discussions, group work, library sessions, and conferences; and by doing oral reports, short assignments, and a series of expository and persuasive essays, students in this section will practice the skills essential for creating thoughtful, interesting, lucidly written essays.

Our main text is David Hackett Fischer's *Paul Revere's Ride,* a narrative account of a defining moment in American history. We will explore the text by writing about it in a number of different ways: describing the experience of reading it; responding critically to the narrative; studying Fischer's strategies and techniques as a writer; evaluating his use of evidence and the success of his argument; using the text as a resource for research and as a catalyst for thinking—and arguing about—ideas and issues; comparing this historical narrative to other versions of Paul Revere's ride, including Revere's own accounts. Students will continually be engaged in documented writing and will design individual research projects suggested by a particular aspect of the text that interests them.

As English majors, you will be concerned with many different kinds of texts. "Text" comes from a Latin word that means literally "that which is woven." As readers you will be studying how different writers "weave" their texts; as writers, you will be the "weavers" of words. Ideally, the insights you gain into the process of writing this semester will initiate your continuing development as readers and writers of texts over the next four years.

Required Texts

David Hackett Fischer, *Paul Revere's Ride,* Oxford University Press, 1994.

Paul Revere's Three Accounts of his Famous Ride, Massachusetts Historical Society, 3rd ed., 1976.

Dawn Rodrigues & Myron C. Tuman, *Writing Essentials,* Norton, 1996.

English Department, *The Source Paper: A Guide to Method and Style, 1991.*

[added later: Barbara H. Solomon, ed., *American Families: 28 Short Stories,* Mentor,1989.]

Objectives

1. To develop reading, thinking, and research skills essential for effective expository and persuasive writing.
2. To write for specific readers by effectively deploying the language and conventions of the essay.

3. To improve effective communication by developing speaking and listening skills.
4. To develop a writing community which provides a supportive, informative, and collaborative environment for the individual writer.

Requirements

Reading. Your reading consists of assignments from the primary texts and the handbook. You will have longer assignments between the Wednesday class and the Monday class, so please plan accordingly. Adopt the practices of active reading: underline what you think are key points and make marginal notes reacting positively or negatively to words, sentences, or ideas. You will have formal writing to do for all reading assignments.

Short Assignments. These written assignments help you to develop basic skills such as paraphrase and summary and prepare you to write analysis and argument.

Short assignments will be graded on a scale from 1-10: 10 (Couldn't Be Better); 9 (Very Fine Response); 8 (Very Good: Could be More Detailed/More Thoughtful); 7 (O.K.; Needs significantly more thought/Details); 6 (Weak; Check the Instructions/Reread the Text); 5 or lower (Not Acceptable). Assignments must be handed in by each due date to receive full credit. One point per day, up to two days, will be deducted from your grade for unavoidably late work. After two days, the assignment will receive a failing grade.

Essays. You will write six 500-word essays and one 1500-2000 word research essay. You will find the requirements for each essay and the criteria for grading on the assignment sheets. Because we're working on a very full schedule, essays must be handed in by the due date. If problems arise, you should notify me as quickly as possible by phone, email, or note, and I will work something out with you. Ordinarily, if you haven't made a specific arrangement with me about a late paper, I will deduct five percentage points per calendar day from your grade; essays more than five days late will receive a failing grade.

Oral Reports. During each class, a team of two to three students will give a five-minute oral report commenting on specific aspects of the assigned reading. The rest of us will be listening closely, ready with questions and responses. See Guide to Oral Reports.

Group Work. Frequently, you will be divided into three groups to discuss the texts, to share your work with one another, and to complete cooperative assignments. Group members may wish to use email to communicate outside of class.

Library Sessions. Attendance is required at these sessions which will introduce you to the Reference collection and online research resources. Each session will conclude with a workshop assignment.

Portfolios. Each student will maintain a portfolio, an orderly, labeled, dated collection of all the writing done for this class. It will include in-class writing and drafts of essays as well as final drafts and revisions. It will also include two written self-assessments, each completed before your conferences with me. Your portfolio should demonstrate the efforts you make to improve your writing by revising, correcting, and polishing your work.

Conferences. Each student will have at least two individual conferences with me. We will look at your portfolio together, discuss current work, and review your self-assessment. You may, of course, make additional appointments for conferences as needed, and I may ask you to come for a conference about a specific essay.

Class Attendance and Participation. Class attendance is required and will be recorded. Our class meetings will always include discussions which depend on the contributions of each member of the class. Your reactions to your reading, research, and writing assignments will all prepare you for class discussion. See Guidelines for Class Participation Grade.

Lateness. Class will start promptly at 8:30. You are expected to come to class on time. If you are unavoidably late, please come in quietly and sit near the door so that you do not disrupt the class. If you are habitually late, I will issue a warning. If you continue to be late, I will mark you absent each time and your grade will be lowered accordingly.

Make-Up Policy. To make up work, you must have a letter signed by a doctor or by Dr. Judy Klaas, the Dean of Undergraduate Education. Dr. Klaas' office assists students with documenting emergencies, particularly confidential matters.

Emergencies or special difficulties will always be taken into consideration.

Writing support. In addition to receiving support from your fellow students and me, you may work with a tutor at CASA. Drop-in help is available, or you may make an appointment with a particular tutor.

Academic Honesty. Your work must comply with the College Policy Regarding Academic Honesty stated in the College catalogue. Plagiarism, the use of someone else's words or ideas as if they were your own, is a serious offence. Consult the College catalogue or the English Department Source Paper Guide (pp. 3 & 10) for definitions of plagiarism and examples of correct ways to document the work of others in your essays. The penalties for plagiarism vary according to the extent of the offence. A completely plagiarized essay will result in an "E" for the whole course.

Grade

Short Written & Oral Assignments		10
Essays 1 & 2	2 x 5	10
Essays 3 & 4	2 x 10	20
Research Essay		20
Essays 5 & 6	2 x 7.5	15
Class Attendance & Participation		10
Final Examination		15
		100

Schedule of Assignments

Week/date Assignment

1	W 9/4	Introduction; in-class writing: Assignment 1; revised Assignment 1 due 9/6.
2	M 9/9	Due: *Paul Revere's Ride*, Introduction & pp. 3-43; Writing: Assignments 2 & 3. W 9/11 Due: *PRR*, 44-64; Writing: Assignment 4.
3	M 9/16	Due: *PRR*, 65-112; Writing: Essay 1. W 9/18 Due: *PRR*, 113-128; Writing: Assignment 5; Preparation for Library Session 1.
4	M 9/23	No Class. W 9/25 Due: *PRR*, 129-173; Writing: Assignment 6.
5	M 9/30	Due: *PRR*, 174-232; Writing: Essay 2. W 10/2 Due: *PRR*, 233-260.
6	M 10/7	Due: *PRR*, 261-295. Writing: Assignment 7. W 10/9 Due: Essay 3, a book review of *Paul Revere's Ride*.
7	M 10/14	No Class. W 10/16 Due: *Paul Revere's Three Accounts*; Writing: Assignment 8.
8	M 10/21	Due: Longfellow, "Paul Revere's Ride"; Writing: Assignment 9. W 10/23 Due: Essay 4, based on Field Trip.

9 M 10/28	Writing: Assignment 10, Library Session 2. W 10/30 Research Workshop.
10 M 11/4	Research Workshop. W 11/6 Research Workshop. 11 M 11/11 No Class. W 11/13 Research Workshop.
	[revised section of syllabus]
12 M 11/18	Due: Research Essay; Intro: *American Families: 28 Short Stories*; "Still of Some Use" (read aloud in class). W 11/20 "The Sorrows of Gin."
13 M 11/25	Comparison: "My Coney Island Uncle," "Wedding Day"; Review *Writing Essentials*, Chapter 13, Effective Sentences. W 11/27 "I Stand Here Ironing" (Rosalind, Colleen); "My Son the Murderer" (Phoebe, Arthur); Review *Writing Essentials*, Chapter 14, Errors in Sentence Wording; Due: Essay 5, Comparison.
14 M 12/2	"Simple and Cousin F. D. Roosevelt Brown" (Susie, Greta, George); "The Writer in the Family" (Andy, Marion); Review *Writing Essentials*, Chapter 15, Errors in Punctuating Sentences. W 12/ 4 "Regret" (Francesca, Claudia)

	"The Sky is Gray" (Max, Jeremy, May); Review *Writing Essentials*, Chapter 24, The Comma.
15 M 12/9	"Violation," (Kate, Donna, Lee) "Elephant" (Melissa, Amelia, Mary); Review *Writing Essentials*, Chapters 25, 26; Due: Essay 6, Persuasive Essay on a Social Issue in a Short Story. W 12/11 Conclusion. M 12/16 1 PM—Final Examination

The students whose names appear after the title of the story are responsible for starting class discussion of that story on that day. Since Essay 6 will focus on the author's handling of a social issue in one of the stories, discussion should include, where relevant, such issues as the treatment of the elderly, child abuse, gender roles, divorce, racism, the effects of war, cultural reactions to death . . . Each of the designated students will read a One-Sentence Summary expanded into three or four sentences; or a Word Journal of three or four sentences; or a Double Entry Journal with three or four sentences in the right column. The rest of the class will listen attentively and jot down agreements, disagreements, modifications, or developments, particularly as they relate to a relevant social issue.

ENDNOTES

[1]The survey used by the admissions office at Framingham State College is conducted by the American Council on Education and the University of California at Los Angeles Cooperative Institutional Research Program. The statistics about our students in this paragraph, and the next, are drawn from the Freshman Surveys for 1995 and 2000.

[2]For a discussion of how being a first-generation college student affects "persistence" at college, see Janet Mancini Billson and Margaret Brooks Terry, "In Search of the Silken Purse: Factors in Attrition among First-Generation Students," *College and University*, Fall, 1982. Other research has also shown that parents who have not gone to college tend to treat teachers the way most people treat surgeons, with blind trust, while parents with college degrees tend to address teachers as equals. On this basis it would be safe to assume that second- and third-generation college students have had stronger advocates throughout their schooling than first-generation students. See Annette Lareau, *Home Advantage: Social Class and Parental Involvement in Schooling* (Philadelphia: The Falmer Press, 1989; reprinted 1993). This advantage seems to carry through to college. Second-generation college students were more likely to report that their efforts to pursue higher education were supported by their families than were first-generation students.

See Dollean C. York-Anderson and Sharon L. Bowman in "Assessing the College Knowledge of First-Generation and Second-Generation College Students," *Journal of College Student Development* 32 (1991).

[3] I was inspired by David Denby's account of several Humanities and Contemporary Civilization sections he attended at Columbia College in New York City. He focuses, however, on his own recent responses to the material he (and I) read back in the 1960s when we were freshmen, not on the dynamics within one classroom over an entire semester. See *Great Books: My Adventures with Homer, Rousseau, Woolf, and Other Indestructible Writers of the Western World* (New York: Simon & Schuster, 1996).

[4] The U.S. Department of Education, National Center for Education Statistics, available at http://nces.ed.gov/pubs2000/digest99/tables/PDF/Table249.pdf. About 95% of colleges required all arts and sciences students to take at least one composition course in 1991-92, and another 4% required some students to take a composition course, according to Bettina J. Huber, "Undergraduate English Programs: Findings from an MLA Survey of the 1991-92 Academic Year," *ADE Bulletin* 115 (Winter 1996) : 35.

[5] See Wendy Bishop, "Places To Stand: The Reflective Writer-Teacher-Writer in Composition," *CCC* 51, no. 1 (September 1999) : 9-31.

[6] Jeffrey Selingo, "Facing New Missions and Rivals, State Colleges Seek a Makeover," *Chronicle of Higher Education*, 17 November, 2000, A40-42.

[7] Nell Ann Pickett, "The Two-Year College as Democracy in Action," *CCC* 49, no. 1 (February 1998) : 90-98.

[8] *The Digest of Education Statistics 1999*, available at nces.edu.gov/pubs 2000/digest99 reports that—in 1996—4,020,201 students , or about 28% of the nationwide total, attended institutions of higher education which enrolled fewer than 5,000 students. According to the *Digest*, 592,285 students, or 4.08% of the higher education total, attended 204 public four-year colleges of this size. These statistics don't take into account large institutions broken into smaller local campuses, however, so there are, in effect, more than 204 small-scale state-sponsored campuses like Framingham's. Most schools on this scale, however, are private; the vast majority of students in public higher education attend large research universities, community colleges, and large-scale state colleges.

[9] See the Boyer Commision's 1998 report, *Reinventing Undergraduate Education: A Blueprint for America's Research Universities*, available at notes.cc.sunysb.edu/Pres/boyer.nsf.

[10] David Hackett Fischer, *Paul Revere's Ride* (New York: Oxford University Press, 1994), 118.

[11] See Vincent Tinto, *Leaving College: Rethinking the Causes and Cures of Student Attrition* (Chicago: University of Chicago Press, 1993).

[12] Linda Shaw Finlay and Valerie Faith, "Illiteracy and Alienation in American Colleges: Is Paulo Freire's Pedagogy Relevant?" in *Freire for the Classroom: A Sourcebook for Liberatory Teaching*, ed. Ira Shor, (Portsmouth, New Hampshire: Boynton/Cook Publishers, Heinemann, 1987), 79-80.

[13]Gregory Colomb made this point in a faculty workshop he gave at Framingham State College on October 2, 1992.

[14]Paul Kameen, "Coming of Age in College Composition," *The Teaching of Writing: Eighty-fifth Yearbook of the National Society for the Study of Education* (Chicago: University of Chicago Press, 1986), 171.

[15]See Charles M. Sennott, "Framingham Mirrors a Complex Trend," *Boston Sunday Globe,* 20 July 1997.

[16]Barbara H. Solomon, ed., *American Families: 28 Short Stories,* (New York: A Mentor Book, 1989), 413.

[17]On the issue of whiteness in American college classrooms see Frances A. Maher and Mary Kay Thompson Tetreault, "Learning in the Dark: How Assumptions of Whiteness Shape Classroom Knowledge," *Harvard Educational Review* 67 (1997) : 321-349.

[18]A *chupa* is the ceremonial wedding canopy; a *ketuba* is the marriage contract; a *minyan* is the minimum of ten Jews necessary in order to conduct services.

[19]Jews were not considered mainstream, nor were they considered white, until the suburbanization of American Jews after World War II and a college education, thanks, primarily to the GI Bill, made possible this kind of upward—or at least outward—mobility away from the cities. See Karen Brodkin Sachs, "How Did Jews Become White Folks?" in *Race,* eds. Steven Gregory and Roger Sanjek (Piscataway, NJ: Rutgers University Press, 1994), 78-102.

[20]Winifred J. Wood, in "Double Desire: Overlapping Discourses in a Film Writing Course," *College English* 60 (1998) : 278-290, describes how she strives to get first-year Wellesley College students to understand the social implications of films, and is successful in moving them beyond personal writing to a professional

(public) voice. This leaves her wondering, though, how to get them to rediscover their valuable emotional responses as spectators.

[21]Since Claudia may have used her friend's real name, I've taken the precaution of changing the name used in her essay.

[22]A possible example of this can be found in Lad Tobin's account of a freshman student writing about his history as a shoplifter in "Car Wrecks, Baseball Caps, and Man-to-Man Defense: The Personal Narratives of Adolescent Males," *College English* 58 (1996) : 158-175. In that account the professor may be rewarding the student for good writing because the student came up with the insight that this crime was actually a redirection of the student's anger against his father. Without doubt, such insight can be taken to be a sign of growth in the student, not only as a writer but also as a person. One potential problem with encouraging such writing, however, is that students, wishing to secure the professor's approval, will engage in cursory self-diagnosis. For example, not all crimes have as their cause the way children were treated by parents; some may arise from impulses that must be explained in other ways, or simply cannot be explained. For an example of narrative writing that refuses to assign a reason for personal crimes see, for example, J. M. Coetzee's account, in *Boyhood: Scenes from Provincial Life* (New York: Viking, 1997), of maiming his brother.

[23]Jacob Neusner, *The Mishnah: A New Translation* (New Haven: Yale University Press, 1992), 616.